Lifelines for Money Misfortunes

Lifelines for Money Misfortunes

How to Overcome Life's Greatest Challenges

Stephen M. Pollan
Mark Levine

BICENTENNIAL
1807
WILEY
2007
BICENTENNIAL

John Wiley & Sons, Inc.

Published by John Wiley & Sons, Inc., Hoboken, New Jersey.
Published simultaneously in Canada.

Wiley Bicentennial Logo: Richard J. Pacifico

For general information on our other products and services or for technical
support, please contact our Customer Care Department within the United States at
(800) 762-2974, outside the United States at (317) 572-3993 or fax (317) 572-4002.

Wiley also publishes its books in a variety of electronic formats. Some content that
appears in print may not be available in electronic formats. For more information
about Wiley products, visit our Web site at www.wiley.com.

Library of Congress Cataloging-in-Publication Data:
Pollan, Stephen M.
    Lifelines for money misfortunes : how to overcome life's greatest challenges / by
Stephen M. Poll.
        p.   cm.
    Includes index.
    ISBN 978-0-470-13907-3 (cloth)
  1.   Finance, Personal. 2.   Responsibility. 3.   Crisis management. 4.   Problem
solving. 5.   Life skills.   I. Levine, Mark, 1958- II. Title.
    HG179.P5554345 2008
    332.024—dc22

Printed in the United States of Ame
10 9 8 7 6 5 4 3 2 1

Almost 25 years ago we started our writing partnership working together on a series of articles for New York magazine. We were guided in those efforts by one of the finest editors who has ever wielded a red pencil, Deborah Harkins. Debbie taught us many things, but the most important was to put the needs of the reader first. We hope she's still proud of our efforts.

Contents

Acknowledgments

This book couldn't have been written without the help of dozens of individuals.

The unsung heroes of this book are the clients and friends of the authors who shared the stories of the crises in their lives. They all have our deepest thanks.

Seven heroes whose names can be sung are those experts who shared their wisdom and insights with us: Gary Ambrose, Allen Bahn, Tom Ellet, Erik Kolbell, Linda Lubitz, Olivia Mellan, and David Newman.

Thanks to our editor, Debra Englander, who helped refine the concept and keep us on course.

Thanks to our agent, Stuart Krichevsky, who has always been the master of both palliative measures and revenue rehabilitation.

Special thanks to Brian Mahon, Stephanie Dahle, and Jacob Croke for all their support in the research and production of this book. They helped make a molehill out of a mountain.

Finally, thanks to our wives, Corky Pollan and Deirdre Martin Levine, for being our true Lifelines.

PART

I

THE SECRETS OF
PERSONAL CRISIS
MANAGEMENT

Alleviate the Pain and Learn the Essential Skill

O that my vexation were weighed, and all my calamity laid in the balances! For then it would be heavier than the sand of the sea; therefore my words have been rash. For the arrows of the Almighty are in me; my spirit drinks their poison; the terrors of God are arrayed against me.

—Job 6:2-5

If you're currently facing a financial or personal mishap you have my sympathy. I know you're angry, afraid, and anxious. But I'm not going to lie to you because I know you need the truth, even if it's painful, so here goes. You may not get another job right away, and when you do it might not be a better one. You may never meet someone else with whom you'll want to spend the rest of your life. Your ailing loved one's health may not improve. You may not be able to rebuild your home better than ever. It wasn't God's will that this happened. The pain you're feeling right now may never go away completely.

I'm sure you've heard much more optimistic words from your family and friends. Don't blame them for their white lies. They care about you. They see you're in pain, feel powerless to help you, and so instead offer words they think will provide comfort and hope. They don't realize platitudes don't help someone who is facing a personal or financial crisis. Having been through lots of crises myself, and more importantly, having helped others confront and overcome mishaps and disasters for more than 30 years, I know that what's most helpful is honest, pragmatic, step-by-step advice. You need a *Lifeline*—a plan to overcome the crisis—not a cliché.

I can't turn back the clock for you. No one can. There's no changing what has happened to you. And I can't make all the effects and impact of the catastrophe just go away. But what I *can* do is help you alleviate the pain you're feeling. I can give you that Lifeline, which can help you mitigate the effects of the disaster. In some cases, I can help you do things that will minimize the possibility of your having to face this same crisis again. Finally, I can work with you to develop an attitude and approach that will enable you to better deal with the inevitable calamities you'll confront during the rest of your life.

First things first, however. Turn to the table of contents and find the specific Lifeline that best matches the crisis you're facing. Read it and follow the instructions as quickly, and as closely, as possible. I promise that doing so will both ease your pain and get you on the road to recovery.

Once you've finished the specific chapter, and have gotten started on your Lifeline, come back to this first chapter and read the chapters in Part I from this point forward. If you do, I guarantee you'll be better prepared to confront and overcome the next disaster that comes your way.

Most people get a fair amount of fun out of their lives, but on balance life is suffering, and only the very young or the very foolish imagine otherwise.
George Orwell

If you're not currently facing a personal or financial crisis, don't feel like you're being neurotic reading a book about dealing with disaster. You're being proactive, dealing with the fears that strike everyone.

No one talks about it, yet we all lay awake some nights worrying, unable to still our racing minds, spinning out scenarios. What if your company is sold and you're fired by the new owners? What if your son smashes the car one night on the way home from football practice and is hurt? What if the mutual funds you're hoping will help pay for your daughter's college education don't bounce back? What if that mole your life partner just discovered is melanoma? What if your father has a coronary, leaving your mother alone and financially needy? These "dark nights of the soul" that strike us all from time to time are neither irrational nor excessive. Unproductive and distressing they may be, but they're not absurd.

You're not paranoid to sometimes lose sleep over potential mishaps or catastrophes. You're being realistic. To paraphrase the bumper sticker pundits: Stuff Happens. Accidents take place. Disasters strike. Crises occur. Mishaps affect our financial lives and catastrophes occur in our personal lives. People lose their jobs, often— today perhaps most often—through no fault of their own. Teenagers do get hurt, sometimes badly. Stock market downturns may not look long or serious from a historic perspective, but they can be disastrous if they hit when you're facing college bills or retirement. Serious illnesses do strike the previously healthy. Parents age, become frail, and eventually die. You needn't be a pessimist to believe that a human life is marked and measured by its crises as much, if not more so, than its triumphs. In fact, some schools of thought suggest that it's this kind of suffering that defines the human condition.

One of the tenets of Buddhism is that life is all about *dukkah*. That's a Sanskrit word that is most often translated as suffering, but can also mean affliction, anguish, anxiety, aversion, discomfort, dissatisfaction, frustration, misery, pain, sorrow, or stress. What Buddhism is really saying is that life, by its very nature, is all about impermanence and imperfection. Everything that has a beginning must also have an ending. And there's no such thing as perfection. Buddhists believe that all of our unhappiness comes from not accepting life's essential nature, and acting accordingly. Another Eastern philosophy, Taoism, says life is about balance between two poles, sometimes referred to as Yin and Yang. It suggests you cannot experience one extreme without also experiencing the other. In other words, to know true pleasure, you must also know true pain. To feel extreme joy, you must also feel extreme sorrow. In effect, it's the bad times we go through that enable us to appreciate the good times; grief is the price we pay for love.

I realize I've just reduced more than a thousand years of complex Eastern thought into a single inelegant and superficial paragraph. But I'm not a philosopher, and this isn't a book about philosophy. My name is Stephen M. Pollan and I'm a legal and financial consultant who has been offering advice on what I call "the business of living" for close to 30 years. Rather than offering up some fortune cookie philosophy, my goal is to teach you how to deal with the inevitable money and life mishaps you'll face in your life, and perhaps even how to avoid some potential catastrophes along the way. My plan is to do that, not just by offering step-by-step advice on specific emergencies, but by offering seven general rules you can apply to any mishap that comes your way.

- Accept the problem and own the solution.
- Unburden yourself.
- Diagnose the impact.
- Take your financial pulse.
- Start palliative measures.
- Launch revenue rehabilitation.
- Cultivate antibodies.

This is a book about what I believe is the most essential, yet totally untaught discipline in the business of living: personal crisis management. It's essential because, as I've already explained, our lives are filled with mishaps and calamities, ranging from petty personal annoyances to financial disasters and medical catastrophes. It's untaught largely because up until now, there's been no one to teach it.

Don't get me wrong: I'm not pompously claiming I possess some unique brilliance or skill. What I do have that's unique is wide-ranging consulting practice with an unusual client base with whom I have developed a very intimate relationship. I began my consulting practice after careers as a real estate developer, venture capitalist, and banker. Ironically, my private practice began in response to a catastrophe: I was diagnosed with tuberculosis, lost my banking job, and was disabled and unemployed for more than a year. When I began consulting, most of my clients were young people in their mid- to late twenties who were just starting to carve out careers and lives for themselves in New York City. As my practice grew and developed, I began to specialize—but not in the usual way. I didn't focus on real estate, career issues, business matters, family law, or any of the fields on which attorneys and advisors usually focus. I specialized in a demographic group: baby boomers.

My philosophy has always been that our personal, career, and financial lives are intrinsically linked. Your plans to start a business, for example, need to take into account your plans to start a family. Your search for a weekend home must be connected to your negotiations for an employment contract. This matched well with baby boomers' drive to integrate their lives, rather than mimic the sharp life divisions of their parents' lives.

> *As fire refines gold, so suffering refines virtue.*
>
> *Chinese proverb*

Because of my holistic approach and focus on a single demographic group, I've been able to find pragmatic tactics and attitudes that apply to every type of mishap. I've traveled with my clients on their journey from first jobs to looming retirement, from having children to burying parents, offering help and advice on whatever problems they face along the way. Sure, I've helped clients who've been fired, but I've also helped clients whose children became disabled in accidents. I've helped clients buy homes for themselves, and I've also helped clients pick and pay for homes for parents suffering from Alzheimer's. I've become an expert on personal crisis management, not by design, but by default. In effect, the tactics I've helped clients employ in specific cases have led me to the general strategies that can serve as a foundation for an overall approach to personal crisis management. Part I of this book covers those general strategies, while Part II offers the tactical, step-by-step Lifelines for dealing with thirty-three of the most common specific problems.

Besides drawing on the stories of many of my clients in the following pages, I've also drawn on a number of experts who've helped supplement my own experience and advice. What I've tried to do is offer truly pragmatic guidance. Much of what I suggest may be unconventional. Some of what I say may sound cynical. You may think some of my suggestions are manipulative. I offer no apologies. You see, my role is to be your advocate in these emergencies. I'll help you do whatever it takes—within legal, ethical, and moral limits—to deal with your crises.

The first thing you'll need to do is definitely unconventional: You need to work on your attitudes. Whatever the situation, you need to accept the problem, and take ownership of the solution.

Accept the Problem and Own the Solution

Misfortune is never mournful to the soul that accepts it; for such do always see that every cloud is an angel's face. Every man deems that he has precisely the trials and temptations which are the hardest of all others for him to bear; but they are so, simply because they are the very ones he most needs.

—Lydia M. Child

When faced with a crisis, the first thing many of us do is look for someone to blame. We might criticize ourselves any time we feel we've failed at a task or somehow come up short. "I should have realized that my job was in danger." "I never should have let Aiden drive in this weather." "I should have gone to the doctor the moment I noticed that mole." If another party or parties are involved, we might blame them. "I told Janet she had to quit smoking, but she never listened." "My supervisor is such a weasel, he sold me out." "That stockbroker only cares about his commissions—he shouldn't have had me constantly buying and selling." Sometimes, facing the most severe crises imaginable, we might even blame God. "How could God let my baby get hurt?"

Let's be honest. In some situations you may well have made a mistake. Maybe more than one. And it's possible, perhaps even likely, that in other cases someone else either screwed up, or screwed you over. Although in many cases a catastrophe is no one's fault, in some cases there clearly is a person or persons responsible. But so what? What do you get from assigning blame? Admittedly, understanding who, if anyone, is at fault can give you a leg up on making sure this doesn't happen again. If you didn't see the signs of an impending termination, you can take the lesson to heart and try to ensure you don't miss them again in the future. If your stockbroker is constantly encouraging you to buy and sell in order to maximize his commissions, you can switch your accounts to another broker. These are fine long-term responses to problems. But they do nothing in the short term to help cure the situation. They don't help you pay your bills if you've been fired and have nothing in the bank. They don't help you pay for your child's college education after the investments you'd hoped would cover the cost have gone belly up.

> *When is a crisis reached? When questions arise that can't be answered.*
> *Ryszard Kapuscinski*

Jan Farmer knows all about playing the blame game.[1] A professional violinist who had a full-time job performing with an orchestra in a major Northeastern city, he lost use of three fingers on his left hand in a freak accident during a recording session. The mishap left him permanently disabled, unable to play his instrument ever again. "I had all this time on my hands and what I ended up doing with it was spinning out scenarios. If only I had done x maybe it wouldn't have happened. If only they had done y it wouldn't have happened. I was caught up in trying to understand why and how this happened. As a result, I wound up complicating matters by trying to imagine how it would have turned out different if circumstances were different. My mind went into overdrive and I started twisting things in a hundred different ways. It was mostly nonsense, and it was definitely counterproductive. I wasted three years in this 'would-have, could-have, should-have' wilderness."

Assigning blame and conducting postmortems involve reliving the past in order to help in the future. But your problem is in the present, and that's where your head needs to be, at least until you've stopped the bleeding. Anger, fear, shame, and grief are understandable reactions. Expressing these emotions is healthy psychologically. But that doesn't mean you need to express them at the expense of doing anything else, particularly focusing on solutions. When it comes to overcoming crises these are all impotent, albeit psychologically necessary emotions: They don't help you cure your problems. What *will* help you is accepting the problem and taking ownership of the solution.

Acceptance

That's a lot harder than it sounds, because it involves approaching your specific situation, and perhaps your life in general, with a very objective and realistic world view. You must accept imperfection and impermanence, as well as accept there's no justice in the universe.

None of us is perfect, and we are all mortal. Unless you're seriously mentally ill, I'm sure you agree with those two statements. Yet few of us act in accord with them. Rather than just accepting our imperfection and the imperfection of others, we start analyzing rather than acting. Instead of taking steps to solve or mitigate our problem, we spend time and energy trying to figure out what went wrong and whose fault it was.

You may indeed have made a mistake. Other people may have made mistakes as well. That's because we are all human. You aren't perfect and you aren't all powerful. You can't control the universe. No matter how much you try to control a situation, some things will remain beyond your power. You can't control the actions of others, nor the world around you. No matter how much you may try to protect your children, they are still vulnerable. No matter how diligently you do your job, you can be fired. No matter how much you exercise and watch your diet, you could still get cancer. Fallibility and vulnerability come along with being human. We are all mortal.

I think it's particularly hard for American baby boomers to acknowledge their mortality. Two of the most pronounced traits in American culture are personal liberty and rugged individualism. We're brought up to believe that we have the right and the ability to do anything we set our minds to. After all, we conquered this continent and became the world's only superpower. FDR urged us to conquer Fascism and we did. We outlasted communism. JFK challenged us to put men on the moon in a decade and we did.

The baby boom generation was going to do even more. They were going to achieve great things in the world while also achieving great things spiritually and psychologically. They were going to be self-actualized as well as world winners. The largest generation in history, baby boomers changed everything they touched, simply due to their size. Boomers needed schools, so schools were built. Boomers needed jobs, so business expanded. Boomers needed homes, so real estate exploded. Boomers are starting to retire, so the Sunbelt is booming. I have no doubt Social Security and Medicare will be "fixed" as soon as boomers begin to depend on those programs. As the most "can-do" generation in the history of a "can-do" nation, American baby boomers have a very hard time acknowledging their own imperfection and impermanence.

We also have a very hard time acknowledging the universe isn't just. Bad things happen to good people and good things happen to bad people. The innocent and the weak suffer along with the guilty and the strong. We're a nation that, for all our diversity and multiculturalism, has an identifiable theology underpinning our society and culture. From the Puritans and Quakers who helped settle the original colonies, to the Mormons who settled Utah, and from the Abolitionists of the 1800s to the Evangelicals of today, religious belief has been a powerful force in defining American beliefs, culture, and character. Most of these religious influences have been theistic. *Theism* is the belief in God as creator of the universe, intervening in it and sustaining a personal relation to his creatures. Whatever our own religious and philosophical backgrounds, we've been raised in a culture that stresses that the supreme being is not only omniscient and omnipotent, but also a source of divine justice. As a result, we have a hard time accepting the lack of justice in the universe, since an all-powerful, all-seeing, activist divinity shouldn't let bad things happen.

I'm no more a theologian than I am a philosopher, so I'm not going to even try to enter into this question that has been debated for centuries. However, as an expert in personal crisis management, I know that to be able to deal most effectively with the inevitable crises in your life you need to somehow come to grips with this issue.

Suffering, once accepted, loses its edge, for the terror of it lessens, and what remains is generally far more manageable than we had imagined.

Lesley Hazelton

You can simply decide that the ways of God are beyond the ken of mortal men, and say it's a matter of faith. You can say there is no god and become an atheist. You can become a Buddhist and focus on your own role in the universe rather than that of any supreme being. You can decide that deism—the belief in a supreme creator who doesn't interfere in the universe or interact with humanity—makes more sense than theism. While deism hasn't been as powerful a force in our national life as theism, it does have a very American pedigree: Almost all the founding fathers of this country were actually deists. Alternatively you can try to come up with some kind of spiritual construct that works for you. Rabbi Harold Kushner, in his justifiably best-selling book *When Bad Things Happen to Good People*, came up with his own compromise: God has arranged the universe in a way that prevents even him from solving all its problems but that, because he is still caring and loving, he suffers along with the rest of us.

How you choose to deal with this issue is entirely up to you, but you need to get past blaming others or yourself or God as soon as you can. The more time you spend looking backward, the longer you'll be in pain and the more physical, financial, emotional, psychological, or spiritual damage you'll suffer. That's because the search for fault and blame locks you in place. It forces you to experience the initial shock and pain of the crisis over and over again. If you keep looking backward, every day will feel like the day you found out your employer was bankrupt, or the afternoon your saw your home flooded, or the evening you got the call your mother had died.

Instead of looking for blame and focusing on the past, you need to accept the catastrophe. It is what it is. There's no reset button in life. You are powerless to chance the past. You have every right to scream, to cry, or to go home and pull the covers over your head. But none of those actions, however justifiable, will change what has happened. The tears won't keep your mate from divorcing you, the screams won't bring back the money embezzled from your business, and the covers won't protect you from a banker who wants to foreclose on your home. When you lose your voice, run out of tears, or need to get up from bed to go to the bathroom, the crisis will still be there. Accept the problem as part of you and your life, and instead focus on taking ownership of the solution.

Ownership

Ownership is the flip side of acceptance. You may be powerless to change the past, but the way you deal with the present is completely and exclusively in your power. That doesn't mean you shouldn't reach out to others for help and support. As you'll see in the next chapter, that's a vital part of successfully weathering your mishap. It means you need to see yourself as the CEO of your recovery.

You, not your outplacement counselor or head hunter, are responsible for weathering a termination and finding another job. You, not your stockbroker, your daughter, or the college's financial aid office, are responsible for dealing with a market downturn that savages your college investment accounts. You, not your doctor, your clergyperson, or your mate, is responsible for facing and battling a cancer diagnosis. You are the one who needs to set the tone and goals, choose the strategies and direction, and make the important decisions. Far from a burden, this is actually a blessing.

That's what Alan Kramer learned three years ago when the 61-year-old divorced father of three was diagnosed with a brain tumor. "I didn't get a good prognosis," he recalls. "I don't know why, but the anger and bitterness quickly turned into something else. I decided I was going to act without reserve. I didn't hold anything back. I used every bit of my capabilities and intelligence. I drew on all my connections, and anyone and everyone else's connections, to get in to see the best doctors. I didn't care what anyone thought. I wasn't going to leave anything on the field. I swore that every decision would be mine. I can't prove it, but I think that attitude helped me recover as well as I did from the treatments and then surgery. I know that it gave me back a feeling of being in charge of my life."

Even though it doesn't involve any kind of physical action, taking ownership *will* actually start the recovery process. That's because by taking responsibility, you start psychologically reasserting control over yourself and your world. Feelings of helplessness will ease as soon as you mentally take charge. Once you stop thinking of yourself as a victim, you'll stop feeling like a victim. Once you start feeling better about yourself, you'll actually start feeling better physically. Physical pain won't vanish. Hardships

> *Let us be of good cheer however, remembering that the misfortunes hardest to bear are those which never come.*
>
> *James Russell Lowell*

will still have to be endured and sacrifices will still need to be made. But when you look at them as things you need to do in order to help yourself and your loved ones (as opposed to things that are being done *to* you or your family) they are far easier to bear. You'll begin living in the moment rather than dwelling on the past or dreaming of the future.

The future can be just as much a trap as the past. When facing a crisis many of us move from playing the blame game about what happened in the past, to writing the script for what we fear will happen in the future. We start spinning out worst-case scenarios.

You find a lump on your breast or testicle when you're taking a shower before work on a Monday morning. You fixate on it the rest of the morning and much of the afternoon, calling the doctor for an appointment when you come back to the office after lunch. From that moment until your appointment two weeks hence you have cancer—at least in your mind. You spin out all the scenarios, experience all the fears, and mentally have all the arguments and tear-filled conversations. You act as if the emergency exists, even though it doesn't. When you discover it's nothing more than a benign cyst, you will have spent two weeks in torment for no reason. If, unfortunately, your fears become real, you'll go through the same process all over again, this time in the real world rather than in your imagination. Those two weeks of preliminary disaster will do nothing positive for you. All they do is put you through a catastrophe that may not exist. Don't jump the gun. Don't put yourself through imaginary crises— you'll go through enough real ones. Own the solution and live in the present.

Owning the solution also allows you to frame your situation in a way that can provide some kind of benefit to you. The notion that there is opportunity within crisis has become a business cliché. Applying it to a personal or financial catastrophe risks sounding insensitive. However, I think that's a risk worth taking.

Good can come from the worst of tragedies—if we make that choice. That doesn't mean the terrible event becomes any less terrible. Nor does it mean that whatever happened suddenly shifts from being a disaster to a triumph. What it means is that we have within us the power to eventually take our pain and use it for a positive purpose.

Jerry D'Amato's company was floundering after his biggest customer went out of business. The cut in his revenue, coupled with his outstanding debt, made the company's survival doubtful. Realizing it was time to get out, Jerry began shopping the company. "I found a buyer and the lawyers negotiated a sale that would enable the company to stay in business and me to personally remain financially afloat," Jerry remembers. "Then, the day before the deal closed, we had a major fire in our largest facility. The place was a total loss. It was such bad timing that I actually laughed out loud; maybe that helped me keep from crying. I knew I had to do something right way. I called the potential buyer on the phone and said, 'Congratulations, the factory has been gutted.' He was still speechless when I explained that the deal was better now since the insurance company would be replacing all the old equipment. He'd be getting a completely new, modern facility at a bargain price."

> *The symbol in Chinese for crisis is made up of two ideographs: one means danger, the other means opportunity. This symbol is a reminder that we can choose to turn a crisis into an opportunity or into a negative experience.*
>
> *Virginia Satir*

Most people agree there's no greater pain than experiencing the loss of a child. But even this indescribable pain could be turned into something positive. The parents could, for example, subsequently dedicate themselves to work toward eradicating whatever it was that took their child from them. That won't bring their child back. And it won't remove their pain. But by taking ownership of the solution in this way, they can create some good out of an otherwise entirely negative experience. It provides meaning to an otherwise senseless situation.

Marilyn and Ernie Barnett lost their 16-year-old son six years ago. Robbie was struck by lightning while mowing the family lawn and died instantly. "One of the things we did after Robbie died was create a scholarship at the local college for a kid who wants to pursue the same thing Robbie was going to study," explains Marilyn. "It doesn't make Robbie's death worthwhile, but it makes it worth something."

There's no comparing a factory fire to the loss of a child. Yet if some good can potentially be squeezed from so devastating a death, certainly some good can be wrung from, let's say, being fired. Perhaps it's simply a personal change of heart, to spend more time and energy focused on your family and less on your job. That may not be on as grand or altruistic a scale as trying to cure childhood leukemia.

It's Only Money

Most of the mishaps over which we lose sleep have something to do with money—disasters like losing our job, or our investments taking a hit. Even those that aren't career or financial based often have a considerable money element to them—facing huge medical or home repair bills. The degree to which we fixate on money mishaps is ironic since, of all disasters, financial emergencies are the easiest from which to recover. Let me explain.

Money mishaps let you start over from scratch. There's no limit to how much money you can earn (or spend for that matter) in your lifetime. There is a limit to how much time you and your loved ones have to spend on the earth. When you or a loved one dies, or is disabled, or falls ill, you can't just start over again with a new loved one. Sure, you could remarry if your spouse dies, but that's a new relationship, not the old one starting over. Individuals are unique; money isn't. A dollar bill is a dollar bill. You could lose all your retirement savings when an investment goes bad in January, and yet entirely recoup the money if another investment booms the following June. And those new dollars are just the same as the old dollars. Granted, the older you are, the less time you have to recoup from a financial loss. But that just changes the equation and your risk analysis. So why do money problems cause us so much angst?

That's something Tom Martin asked himself almost every night for a year. He'd owned and managed a successful health club for more than 20 years when a series of problems hit. "First, a competitor opened nearby who received a huge tax break since he was building in an area that had been targeted for development," he explains. "Then, one of the major employers in town cut staff dramatically and I lost dozens of customers. Finally, my air-conditioning system failed at the start of the summer, and I had to install an expensive temporary system while paying for a new permanent unit. The business was in a death spiral. I don't think I got a good night's sleep for the year it took for me to finally sell and get out. At the same time, my closest friend in the world was watching his wife slowly die from cancer. Intellectually, I could see that my problem was nothing in comparison, but I still couldn't put things in perspective."

I think most of us would react the same way as Tom did. That's because most of us have an irrational relationship with money. The magic of money is that it has no intrinsic value, it is simply a means

(Continued)

of exchange. Without money we'd all be forced to barter, and as a result, would be severely limited in our choices. A cobbler wouldn't be able to trade his wares for milk unless the local farmer needed shoes for his family. Since money is a blank slate, we can project on it all our neuroses. For some, money is self-esteem or power; for others, money is love or control. We lose so much more sleep over money issues than we need to, not because we're afraid of losing money, but because we're afraid of losing esteem, power, love, or control. Money is just the totem for our deepest fears. To fully accept financial problems and take ownership of the solutions you'll need to internalize this fact. I'll do my part by making that point in every Lifeline in the second part of this book. But you need to do your part, too. Just keep telling yourself: It's only money.

But it's still something positive—and that's more than most of us ever take from a crisis.

Accepting your problem and taking ownership of the solution are things you can do on your own. But actually overcoming the disaster often means enlisting others. The next secret to Lifelines is unburdening yourself by reaching out for help.

CHAPTER 3

Unburden Yourself

You alone can do it, but you cannot do it alone.

—O. Hobart Mowrer

Just because you own the solution doesn't mean you have to shoulder the entire burden yourself. Yet many of us think we have to face up to crises on our own. Maybe we're embarrassed by what has happened and so we don't want to share the news with anyone else: "I can't believe I lost my job." Or it could be we think asking for help is a further sign of weakness: "I'm the one who picked those losing stocks, so it's up to me to pick some winners." Perhaps we're even fearful no one will be willing or able to help us if we ask: "They've got enough on their plate right now." All three rationalizations are wrong.

Embarrassment and shame over suffering a mishap is rarely justified and always useless. The crisis probably wasn't your fault, despite your feeling like it was. There's nothing you could have done to keep your supervisor from firing you and keeping her best friend when it came time to cut staff. And even if you did contribute to it, no one is perfect. Sure, maybe the speculative stocks you invested your retirement funds in weren't the wisest investment, but everyone makes mistakes. Besides, what does the embarrassment and shame do for you?

Actually, they just make things worse. By keeping crises private, you prolong and intensify the pain and fear you're feeling. Crises are like mushrooms: they flourish in dark, fetid environments. Expose the catastrophe to light and fresh air, and the healing process will begin.

Michael McDowell was in terrible shape after learning that his younger sister had been stricken with inoperable cancer. He and she were very close, and he felt the need to put on a brave front, not just for her, but to his wife as well. "I ended up shutting myself off from my spouse," Michael remembers. "I'd just say, 'I'm fine, I'm fine,' even though it was obvious I wasn't. Finally, she broke down and cried about my shutting her out. That led to my breaking down in response. I had felt like, as a guy, I was supposed to either crawl into a cave to deal with it, or just be macho and stoically stand up to it. I was being crazy. Why should I want to carry the load by myself when I didn't have to, and there were people around me who wanted to help?"

> I thought I alone suffered, but suffering is everywhere. When I went on the housetop I saw its fire in every home.
> *Shalok Shaikh Farid*

Walter Adams felt terrible shame when he lost his job as a marketing executive in the telecommunications industry. A victim of internal politics, Walter had been with the same company since graduating college, and after 23 years had risen from a junior sales position to becoming an executive vice president. He was paid handsomely enough for his wife to be a stay-at-home mom for their two children. "I saw myself as my job," he admits. "I literally had grown up in the company. Because of that, my whole social life was wrapped up in the company. When I was fired, all I wanted to do was curl up in the fetal position and hide. I was so embarrassed that I didn't call my wife right away. I didn't know what I'd tell her. I was afraid I could not support my family. Then, I didn't contact or call any of my business contacts for a month. And then when I did reach out, I began all the conversations with apologies, as if I'd done something wrong, even though I hadn't."

Self-Reliance can be Self-Defeating

Walter didn't realize that asking for help, whether material, emotional, or spiritual, isn't a sign of weakness. It's actually a sign of strength: a humble admission of your own humanity. Most people are, in fact, impressed when someone says, "I need your help," or admits, "I don't know how to do that," or asks, "What does that mean?" Admissions of dependence, fallibility, and ignorance of a topic are so rare they're ironically seen as indicating supreme self-confidence. Most of us have been sold a bill a goods about the importance of self-reliance. As little children we're praised for doing things by ourselves: "What a good girl: you stayed in here in the dark all by your-self and went to sleep." And then when we're elderly we view any lack of autonomy as a sign of impending death: "If I can't drive anymore I might as well kill myself."

Even our history books paint self-reliance as the most desirable trait. We're told stories of how the brave pioneers and settlers and immigrants and entrepreneurs are the ones who have made America great. Yet those pioneers relied on Native Americans and slaves to survive. The settlers relied on the communities of wagon trains and the railroad to conquer the frontier. The immigrants relied on rela-tives, or previous arrivals who formed welcoming ethnic enclaves, to ease into American life. And the great solo entrepreneurs usually weren't solo at all. Thomas Edison had a staff of inventors working for him at Menlo Park. Henry Ford couldn't have created the auto industry without Harvey Firestone and his tires. Bill Gates needed Paul Allen's help to launch and grow Microsoft.

Every life and every childhood is filled with frustrations; we cannot imagine it otherwise, for even the best mother cannot satisfy all her child's wishes and needs. It is not the suffering caused by frustration, however, that leads to emotional illness, but rather the fact that the child is forbidden by the parents to experience and articulate this suffering, the pain felt at being wounded.

Alice Miller

Not only are you deserving of help, but people are eager to provide it once you ask. When you ask someone for help, you not only humble yourself, you honor them. You demonstrate you think highly of them; you value their intelligence, effort, affection, or time. In fact, it's very difficult to turn someone down who has politely and honestly asked for help. It's the equivalent of kicking someone when they're down. Ask someone for help, particularly face to face, and they will invariably provide it, or if they truly do have more on their plate than they can handle, they will direct you to someone else who can help. When you don't ask for help because you're afraid no one will provide it, you actually guarantee your fear will come true: others cannot help you with a problem they know nothing about.

When Diane Lindsey learned that her older daughter Lily suffered from a form of autism, she was devastated emotionally. "What made matters worse was that Lily's school district was very resistant to providing the kind of services and environments she needed," Diane explains. "Every week I was fighting with her teacher, or the principal of her school about what they were supposed to do for Lily." Diane's oldest friend, Andrea, is an administrator in a nearby school district, yet Diane never reached out for help. "I knew Andrea was very busy, and besides, I didn't want to infringe on our friendship. Finally, things got so bad I realized I needed professional help and broke down and asked Andrea if she could recommend a special education lawyer. Instead of hesitating, Andrea said she'd been waiting for me to ask for help, and was actually a bit hurt I hadn't asked earlier. She told me exactly what I needed to do to get Lily's school to meet their obligations."

Asking for help isn't an abdication of your authority or responsibility. You still own the solution. You just don't have to be the architect of the solution—that might best be left up to a professional with experience in crafting strategies. And neither do you need to be the carpenter, plumber, or electrician of the solution. You are the hub of the wheel; the person who sets the goals and the agenda. It's not necessary for you to become an expert at any of the disciplines, crafts, or skills that will be employed on your behalf. All you need to do is be conversant with the situation. And that can come simply by asking questions such as: "What are my options?" "What are the pros and cons of doing it this way?" and "What would you do in my situation?"

Jody Balsam and her husband were devastated when they discovered their teenage daughter was engaging in dangerous and self-destructive behavior. "She was involved with drug dealing, alcohol abuse, and promiscuity," Jody confides. "It was like a giant rejection of our values and family, and of us as parents. We were getting caught up in all sorts of blame, of her and of each other. We thought about all the disciplinary techniques we'd ever tried or heard of, but we realized that, even though we were her parents, we were way out of our league. That's when we learned there are professionals who specialize in dealing with these kind of kids, who know the kind of radical short term responses that work, and who could help us develop a long-term solution."

Material Assistance and Emotional Support

There are two different types of help you'll likely need to confront and overcome your calamity: material assistance and emotional support.

Material support is actual nuts and bolts help to get things done. It could be the advice of a gerontologist in helping assess your aging parent's condition. It could be an attorney who can represent your teenage son who has been charged with DUI. Or it could be a carpenter who can install the temporary ramp you need to get in and out of your home while you're recovering from a severe injury.

When Naomi Maple learned her mother had been murdered by a disgruntled former employee of the office where she worked she was thrown into a world of which she knew nothing. "I don't think I could have made it through the process without a victim's advocate," Naomi notes. "She had the patience and expertise to help me through the whole criminal justice process. She listened to my questions and concerns, and recognized I was devastated and that this was a very confusing, often frustrating situation."

The animals are much more content with mere existence than we are; the plants are wholly so; and man is so according to how dull and insensitive he is. The animal's life consequently contains less suffering but also less pleasure than the human's, the direct reason being that on the one hand it is free from care and anxiety and the torments that attend them, but on the other is without hope and therefore has no share in that anticipation of a happy future which, together with the enchanting products of the imagination which accompany it, is the source of most of our greatest joys and pleasures. The animal lacks both anxiety and hope because its consciousness is restricted to what is clearly evident and thus to the present moment: the animal is the present incarnate.

Arthur Schopenhauer

Substantive help needn't always be skilled or specialized. Sometimes people can be assistants rather than mentors. Let me explain: Time is one of the most important assets any of us possess, and it's the only resource that's completely finite. There are only 60 minutes in every hour, 24 hours in every day, and seven days in every week. Help that allows you to spend your own time more productively is very valuable. The neighbor who brings a casserole over for your family's dinner while your partner is in the hospital is freeing you to spend more time at the hospital and less money at McDonald's. The sibling who watches your young children one afternoon is giving you time to go on an interview for a new job.

Ralph Cornish didn't know where to begin after his wife, Terry, died in a car accident. Ralph ran his own accounting practice, while Terry stayed at home taking care of the home and their two preteen kids. He was obviously emotionally distraught, but was also physically overwhelmed by the tasks of his daily life. "Me and the kids wouldn't have made it without my friends and neighbors," he stresses. "Neighbors brought meals over for us and picked the kids up from school. One friend even came over every weekend to clean the house and shop."

You'll need more than just material help. Emotional support is sometimes just as important as any physical assistance. Drawing on social capital—family, friends, and community—can provide a sense of solidarity for someone who feels alone. It can instill confidence in someone whose ego has taken a hit. It can provide reminders of all the positive elements of life that have not been damaged by the catastrophe. A burden shared is a burden lightened.

That's what Edward Kohl learned when his son was in a coma following a serious sports accident. "In the first few days my wife and I moved between paralysis and panic," Edward recalls. "The fear of what this could mean to our family was so overwhelming it really clouded our ability to think clearly. Our friends and family helped just by being there and being calm. It was like we could borrow their egos and get the strength to make reasonable, sound decisions."

Unfortunately, many of us simply don't have that much social capital on which to draw emotional support. In his landmark study, *Bowling Alone*, Robert D. Putnam described how Americans have become increasingly disconnected from each other. Time and money pressures, suburbanization and sprawl, electronic entertainment, and generational change have all contributed to this phenomenon. This makes it all the more important to open up to those who *are* in your social circle.

Ironically, asking others for help, whether material or emotional, could help increase your social capital. Many times people with whom you are just peripherally related or acquainted provide a surprising degree of support in an emergency. Maybe your outreach provides an opportunity for intimacy that never existed before. Perhaps they've experienced a similar mishap and so have an unusually large reserve of empathy. Or it could be that your changed circumstances provide greater clarity about the other person's qualities. Whatever the reason, you'll often find that asking friends, family and acquaintances for help actually increases rather than decreases your social capital.

After Michael McDowell crawled out of the cave he'd dug for himself in response to his beloved sister's life-threatening illness, he made some surprising discoveries. "Even though I'd hesitated to reach out to my wife, I knew that if I did, she'd be there for me," he says. "But what was amazing was the number of other people who, once I explained what was going on, rallied around me. There were people who I never considered close friends who went out of their way for me. One of the good things that came out of my sister's illness was that I found close friends I never knew I had."

Misfortunes leave wounds which bleed drop by drop even in sleep; thus little by little they train man by force and dispose him to wisdom in spite of himself. Man must learn to think of himself as a limited and dependent being; and only suffering teaches him this.

Simone Weil

Your Crisis Playbook

Having resolved to reach out for help, both material and emotional, your next step is to start what I call a *crisis playbook*.

Football is a very complex game involving the planned movements and actions of eleven individuals moving at very high speeds while opposed by eleven other individuals also moving at high speeds. So that the players on a team know what they're supposed to do in any given situation, the coaches diagram individual plays and formations. All the various plays and formations are then bound together into what's called a *playbook*. Players study their playbooks both before and during the season to make sure they fully understand their responsibilities and obligations.

Your emergency is no game, but it is undoubtedly complex. That's why I suggest all my clients get a journal or diary and physically write down everything they need to know. This could include checklists and contacts. There might be pro and con lists and random thoughts.

Words of Little Comfort

Not everyone to whom you reach out will offer words that comfort. Well-meaning people will often say things that offer little comfort, or may even spark anger. Sara Levy's husband, Alan, died on September 11, 2001, at the World Trade Center. He was 47 and she was 41. "One of the worst things people said to me was, 'You're young, you'll meet someone else,'" she recalls. "I know they were trying to offer hope but it didn't." "I hated when people would say things like, 'It was God's will,'" explains Edward Kohl. "It's no comfort to paint a portrait of a God who wills children to suffer severe head injuries." Tom Martin would get upset when people would tell him not to worry about his failing business because they knew things will work out. "They didn't know things would work out," he notes. "All they were doing was belittling my fears."

People with whom you are very close don't need to say anything in times of crisis—their support can be demonstrated nonverbally. People with whom you don't have that close a bond often don't know what to say, so fall back on trite aphorisms or clichéd affirmations. Try to cut these people some slack and remember that in emergencies, as in every other time, deeds mean more than words.

The form and content matter less than the fact that you are memorializing your plans, thoughts, and actions. Putting this information on paper in one place will keep you focused and organized. This is always good, but is essential during a crisis when the pressure is likely to lead to distractions and forgetfulness.

The first thing to do is write down, as concisely as possible, exactly what happened. No one other than you is going to ever read this, so don't feel the need to be eloquent or grammatical. The idea is to simply describe the situation.

Next, come up with a list of friends, family, acquaintances, coworkers, mentors, and contacts from whom you could draw emotional or material support. Once you feel your list is complete, jot down the telephone numbers or e-mail addresses of each person. Now, give them each a call or send them an e-mail, just to explain what happened. If you feel a moment's hesitation, go back and reread this chapter.

After you've opened up to everyone on your list, I'll bet you feel better. That's because you're no longer carrying all that weight yourself. It's also because you're now on the road to recovery. To continue down the road, just turn to the next chapter.

CHAPTER 4

Lighting the Darkness

Worry is not thought; complaining is not action.

—Mason Cooley

Things are always worse in the dark. At night we're often left only with our thoughts. And during a crisis those thoughts usually turn to the worst that can happen. In the dark, fears triumph over facts. To overcome whatever mishap you're facing you need to shine the light of factual analysis on your situation. It may not be able to free you completely of all your night time anxieties, but it can help minimize those fears and help you overcome your problem.

The best way to light the darkness is to, once again, focus on the present. When accepting the problem you needed to let go of the past. Now, when actively working your way through the emergency, you need to let go of the future. Just as our first response to a catastrophe is often to look backward for someone or something to blame, our second response is usually to worry about the long-term impact. Your father dies, leaving your mother alone, and your mind quickly focuses on whether she'll be able to take care of herself when she's in her dotage, even though she's 62, healthy, and active. You learn your homeowners insurance company is dropping you and everyone else in your state, and you focus on what could happen during the next hurricane season, even though it's six months away. You lose your job and you begin obsessing over how long it will take to find another job that pays as well, despite your having bills due at the end of this month.

That's what happened to Sandra d'Abruzzio. She had been lured from a position she'd held for almost 20 years to take a new job with a start-up high-tech company. After just six months on the new job she realized she'd made a mistake. "They had recruited me to be national marketing director," Sandra explains. "I had been a successful marketing person so this was the perfect step up for me. But after just a short while I realized they actually wanted me to do the job of a national sales manager, coaching and directing a field sales force—a job I'd had no experience doing. I did my best, but my first annual review was a disaster. Six months after that, I was let go. I was crushed. All I could think about was how the trajectory of my career had been destroyed. I spent the whole first month I was unemployed worrying about how I was going to get my marketing career back on track. I completely lost focus of the fact that I didn't have enough money to pay my bills for more than two months."

Part of the reason we look down the road so far is that, having been hit with bad news, we understandably turn pessimistic, and that leads to our spinning out worst-case scenarios of long-term permanent doom. I call it *writing the script*. Rather than focusing on what we need to do right now, we instead worry about what we might need to do down the road. Playing the blame game locked you in the past. Writing the script locks you into the future. Looking backward can eventually be a productive learning exercise, if it's done after the crisis has been handled. Looking forward can also be an important tool, as long as it's done after you've dealt with your current situation. You do that by first diagnosing its impact.

No one has the right to be sorry for himself for a misfortune that strikes everyone.

Marcus Tullius Cicero

Diagnose the Impact

The financial impact of a problem is often far less than we fear. Many times we conflate the emotional impact of a crisis—which may be enormous—with the financial impact—which may actually be minimal. By separating the two, you'll almost always find the impact is smaller than you anticipated. Making a list and coming up with firm numbers distills the crisis and chops it down into more manageable elements. Rather than being an enormous amorphous nightmare, it becomes a finite obstacle. And by memorializing your findings in your crisis playbook, you give it actual physical form.

Simply put, the financial impact of a crisis can be defined as the assets or income you have lost due to the event. It's the stream of income you lost when you were terminated. It's the cost of replacing your insurance policy when you've been dropped by your carrier. Financial impact is the value of how this is affecting you today, not how you thought it might affect you, or how you worry it might affect you in the future.

Diminished expectations—let's say, as the result of losing your job—don't factor into the financial impact of an event. The resulting change in your hopes and dreams is of psychological impact instead. The same is true of increased fears—let's say, of the effect on you of a natural disaster.

When Mitchell Lewis's father died, leaving his mother a 60-year-old widow, he had a hard time separating the financial from the emotional impact. "I know it sounds crazy, but I was trying to somehow put a number on the shift in my sense of obligation to my mother, now that my father was gone. It was only after talking to a therapist that I realized I was trying to do the impossible. All I needed to do was figure out how much time and money I'd need to spend to help her mourn and adjust her own life."

As I wrote earlier, financial issues are also easier and quicker to address than emotional issues. Dealing with them will give you back some sense of control over your life. Tackling the money element of a mishap will heal some of the ego bruising you've endured. The forward motion you achieve by dealing with the financial impact of a crisis will contribute to your feeling better emotionally. I believe our insides and outsides always match.

I'm not in any way trying to minimize the emotional, psychological, or perhaps even spiritual impact on you of a catastrophe. Those are all real and need your attention. In many of the Lifelines in the second part of this book I'll be writing about how clients of mine have dealt with these nonfinancial impacts. And I'll make a few general suggestions in the following pages. However, by their very nature these are unique wounds. Sure, most of us have to deal with the loss of parents, and there are similarities in the way people cope with those losses. But each is also a singular loss, remarkable in its emotional impact, requiring personalized treatment. I'm a legal, financial, and career advisor, not a therapist or clergyman. And I'm also not sitting directly across from you. I'll offer what emotional help I can, but you'll need to do most of the emotional work yourself, or with the one-on-one help of a therapeutic professional.

There is no true love save in suffering, and in this world we have to choose either love, which is suffering, or happiness . . . . Man is the more man— that is, the more divine—the greater his capacity for suffering, or rather, for anguish.

Miguel de Unamuno

Speaking of professionals, you many need to enlist one or more in determining the financial impact of this crisis. If there are medical issues involved, say you're temporarily disabled, you'll need a professional estimate from a physician as to how long you'll be unable to work. When legal questions will affect your analysis—say your landlord is trying to force your business out of its lease—obviously you'll need to speak to an attorney familiar with the issues. Financial emergencies, like receiving notice that your tax return is being audited by the IRS, call for enlisting a certified public accountant.

Get out your catastrophe playbook and write a description of the financial impact of what has happened.

Take Your Financial Pulse

Having determined the financial impact of a disaster your next step is to take your financial pulse. That means conducting a thorough inventory of all the resources you have available to deal with the situation. Record all this in your playbook.

Start by heading a page "fixed assets." On the left hand side of the page, list all of the large, valuable assets you own. This would include your home, your auto, any other real estate or motor vehicles. It should also include any valuable items or collections, like artwork, jewelry, or antiques, which are easily transferable. That means you could sell them quickly to some form of wholesaler, someone or some business who would resell them. While you may be able to sell some of your less valuable collections and possessions on your own at retail, say by auctioning them off on eBay, those shouldn't be included in your list. When your list is complete, come up with an estimate of value for each asset and write it next to the item's name. You can get quick and fairly accurate measures of value for real estate by contacting a broker or doing a quick search for comparable properties for sale online. Auto and other motor vehicle values can be found by consulting one of the standardized resale guides available online. Values for artwork, antiques, or jewelry can be based on insurance appraisals or conversations with resellers, such as galleries.

Turn to a fresh page and head it "cash and other valuables." Once again, on the left-hand side list the assets. Include bank accounts, IRAs and other retirement accounts, investment accounts, the cash value of any whole life or universal insurance policies, and the viatical value of death benefits.[1] Write down all your accounts receivables: monies you are owed by clients or customers for work already performed or products already delivered; or money you've lent to others. Now list any realistic short-term expectations as well. These might include early "inheritance" gifts from parents, loans from friends, or advances on salary. Rather than asking outright for these loans or gifts right now, just include a conservative estimate of what you think might be available. Note the values on the right side of the page, alongside the names of the items.

On a third page, create a list titled "institutional borrowing potential." Write down the names of each of your credit cards or lines of credit, including home equity. Alongside each, write down the maximum borrowing potential you have on each. There's often a difference between cash advance limits and credit limits on cards, so include both numbers, placing the smaller cash advance number inside parentheses.

Having now compiled lists of all your assets, it's time to turn to your liabilities. On a fresh page write "unextendable liabilities." Here you want to list any monthly or periodic obligations you have that cannot be reduced or extended through negotiation. These are the bills that, if unpaid, would eventually result in cessation of services, or repossession of property and would include rent charges, telephone and utility bills, insurance premiums, charge card debts, and auto and other lease payments.

The next page should be titled "extendable liabilities." These are the monthly or periodic bills that can be eliminated, reduced, or extended through discussions with the creditor. Some of these will be debts that the lender will gladly keep "current" as long as the interest is paid, such as credit-card bills, and mortgages. These lenders care more about earning interest than about prompt pay off of any balance. Other items listed here are payments due professionals, such as doctors and lawyers, or institutions such as hospitals. These creditors have already provided their service, so they can't take it back for nonpayment, and are often satisfied by good-faith efforts at meeting extended payment plans. Include here any estimated tax payments you need to make to the Internal Revenue Service and your state taxing authority. While these aren't actually extendable, you can postpone them with the understanding that you will be subject to fines and penalties for doing so. Finally, here's where you should list any debts you have to family or friends. They may not be happy about it, but they are the creditors likely to cut you the most slack in meeting your obligations. As before, don't make telephone calls to any of your creditors just yet. Simply list the amount you owe.

> *Perhaps catastrophe is the natural human environment, and even though we spend a good deal of energy trying to get away from it, we are programmed for survival amid catastrophe.*
> *Germaine Greer*

Taken together, the pages you've just completed are the equivalent of a balance sheet: a comparison of your assets to your liabilities, albeit in a form tailor-made for crisis management. The next step in taking our financial pulse is to compile the equivalent of an income statement.

Start on a fresh page headed "expected income." List all of the funds you can reasonably expect will be coming in on a regular basis. Obviously this would start with salary. If you've lost your job, include severance pay and unemployment benefits. List any payments you'll be receiving from disability insurance coverage or Social Security. If your investments yield a steady monthly income write that down as well. Finally, include any regular gifts you receive from parents or other relatives. As before, write the names on the left side of the page and the corresponding amounts on the right, and translate money you receive quarterly or annually into monthly amounts.

Turn to a fresh page and write "nondeferrable expenses" on the top. Now, start listing all your monthly expenses. My hope would be that you've kept enough records from the past few months so you can easily come up with a list and with estimates. If you haven't, do your best to draft an accurate list now. In the coming months you can return to the list and correct any over or underestimates and add any expenses you'd overlooked. Include the obvious, such as food, shelter, fuel, utilities, and interest payments on mortgages and credit card balances. But don't forget annual or irregular expenses like insurance premiums, subscriptions, entertainment costs, clothing purchases, retirement fund contributions, dues, and memberships. Focus on compiling as accurate a monthly expense list as you can.

We are not here to triumph by fighting, by stratagem, or by resistance,
Not to fight with beasts as men. We have fought the beast
And have conquered. We have only to conquer
Now, by suffering. This is the easier victory.

Thomas Sterns Eliot

It's now time for some honest analysis. Do you have enough money coming in right now to meet your current expenses? If you do, for how long will this last? When will you start running in the red? If you don't have enough to cover your current bills, how much will you fall short of breaking even? Your entire analysis is really about answering two questions: How much do you need? When do you need it?

Jacquie Stone's ceramic business had been borderline successful for its first five years. But then she landed a contract to provide bud vases to a high-end home products company. "I thought I'd died and gone to heaven," Jacquie laughingly relates. "My revenue tripled overnight. Doing wholesale work like this was so much more efficient than what I'd done before that I didn't think about any down side. I borrowed to expand the business to keep up with the new demand. Then, after only two years into our five-year contract, the home products company went out of business." Jacquie was able to do take her personal financial pulse. ("I barely had one," she jokes.) But to get a handle on the business's financial health she called in a local accountant. "We spent two afternoons going over the books," she explains. "At the end of those sessions I learned that I needed to raise $17,000 in operating capital in three months if I was going to keep the business afloat."

Start Palliative Measures

With your financial inventory and analysis completed it's time to start filling the gaps. That begins with palliative measures: defensive things you can do to stop the financial bleeding and to keep things from getting worse. As you engage in this process, don't think of it as a half measure to simply get you back to breaking even. Your goal should be to cut expenditures to the full extent possible. That will not only get you into the black as quick as possible, but it will also extend the time you have to fully recover.

Start by putting an end to any unnecessary purchases that you've planned but not completed. If you'd planned to have a new deck built this spring, call the contractor and put the project on hold. Are you still waiting for that giant flat-screen television you ordered to arrive? Cancel the purchase if you possibly can. If you're asked for a reason, or given any resistance, be totally frank. Explain you've had a financial emergency and simply can't afford to go through with the project or purchase. This is no time for false pride.

Turn to your list of extendable liabilities. Pull out our most recent bill and contact the creditor's customer service department. Say that you've had a temporary financial emergency and need their help. Explain that you would like to make interest-only payments for, let's say, six months to give you time to recover. The actual time period you choose should be slightly longer than you think you'll need since, however long you ask for the creditor will probably insist on a shorter period of time. With creditors like professionals, suggest paying them in equal portions over your chosen period of months, or perhaps offer a flat monthly payment which you can afford. Humility and honesty are your allies. These creditors would rather get something than nothing, or next to nothing, which is what they'd get if they turned the debt over to a collection agency. If you meet resistance on the telephone keep pushing the up button, asking to speak to the person's superior. Persistence will pay off.

> *Necessity may well be called the mother of invention—but calamity is the test of integrity.*
>
> *Samuel Richardson*

Next tackle your list of non deferrable expenses. Look at each item and figure out how you can reduce the cost. Buy hamburger rather than steak. Do laundry rather than sending everything to the dry cleaner. Cut your cable or satellite television package back to the bare minimum. Go to the library rather than Barnes & Noble or Amazon.com. Buy a travel mug and bring your own coffee in the car rather than stopping at Starbucks each morning. Increase your insurance deductibles and get rid of any coverage you don't need.

Instead of paying for coverage of valuable jewels, put them in a safe deposit box. Send the kids to public school. Cancel the lawn service and buy a mower.

One secret is to take no half measures. Don't look at the amount you spend at the health club each month and say, "I'll just cut out the towel service and stop hiring a personal trainer." Instead, cancel the membership altogether and buy a good pair of running or walking shoes. Make one large cut right away, rather than cutting little by little over a period of time. It's better to find later that you've cut more than you needed, than to discover you've got to tighten your belt even further. This is the best opportunity you will ever have to start your money life over. Cleaning up your finances is one good thing that can come from this mishap.

Another secret is to make spending as cognitive a process as possible. Take the credit cards out of your wallet and leave them at home. Pay cash or use a debit card as much as possible; that will force you to focus on amounts. You'll need to check how much you have in your pocket or how much is in your checking account. And then you'll need to physically hand the cash making note of what's left. Believe me, make spending money as painful as possible and you'll spend less.

Dr. Stephen Botha felt violated when he learned that his bookkeeper of over 10 years had embezzled over $25,000. "At first, what hurt the most was the feeling of betrayal," he says. "But then, when I realized how tight my cash situation was, the pain shifted." Botha hired a new accountant to help him overcome the disaster. "We went over all my spending, and when she saw how little attention I paid to it, she said it was no wonder I'd been embezzled. She suggested I give up my credit cards for two months and rely on cash instead. The difference was incredible. I spent a third less just by being aware of exactly how much was leaving my wallet."

While you'll be concentrating on financial efforts, there are some palliative measures you can take to reduce the emotional, psychological, and spiritual impact of an emergency.

Your social capital is perhaps the most important nonfinancial resource on which you'll draw to weather and overcome a disaster. That's why it's advisable you do everything you can to heal any rifts in that network. Now is not the time to stand on ceremony or hold a grudge. If you've wronged someone, now is the time to ask their forgiveness. Don't worry about it appearing to be conveniently timed. As long as it's an honest, heartfelt expression, when it's delivered won't dilute its message. In fact, coming on the heels of a personal disaster may even make it a more powerful message. People instinctively know that emotional truths tend to come to the surface in moments of trauma.

Everything in life that we really accept undergoes a change. So suffering must become Love. That is the mystery.
                    Katherine Mansfield

Now is not the time to stop taking care of yourself. Often we use crises to rationalize self-destructive behavior. "I need a drink to settle down." "A cigarette will calm my nerves." "I was so upset I ate a whole box of cookies." Sometimes we let disasters derail the normal pattern of our lives more than is really necessary. "I don't have time to go to the gym right now." "I'm just so drained that the last thing I want to do on a Sunday morning is to go to church." To get through whatever you're facing you need to be as much of a peak performer as you possibly can. It's now more important than ever to keep eating well, exercising, and avoiding harmful drug or alcohol use. Try to get out in the sunlight at least once a day. Keep up with your spiritual practices, whether that involves group worship or solitary meditation. If you're seeing a therapist don't stop now. If money is an issue, tell him or her. Therapists are the last professionals who, facing a client in economic and emotional crisis, will cut you loose.

Launch Revenue Rehabilitation

One of the best ways to speed your recovery from any money mishap is to realize there's a flip side to cutting expenses: increasing revenue. When faced with a crisis we instinctively look to cut back. I think there's a psychological element to this reflex: It's a subconscious way to punish ourselves for any role, real or imagined, we may have played in the event. It's the financial equivalent of self flagellation. Don't get me wrong. Cutting costs is essential in many cases, and is often the best way to right a financial ship that's taking on water. However, it's not all you can or should do to overcome your crisis.

Spend just as much time and effort rehabilitating your revenue stream as you do trimming your expenses. Look first to your current job. If overtime is available, take it. Ask your boss for a raise. Don't use your situation as the rationale for your request, however. One good argument is that your salary hasn't kept up with your market value.

The underlying messages are that you could find a better paying job elsewhere, and that your replacement would cost the company more money anyway. Another is that your responsibilities have grown beyond your previous job description; in effect that you're playing a different, more valuable role. Consider asking for a promotion or a

> *A great calamity ... is as old as the trilobites an hour after it has happened.*
> *Oliver Wendell Holmes, Sr.*

transfer if either would result in more income. The largest salary increases come from switching jobs, so put your career in motion as well. Update your résumé, activate your network, and contact head-hunters and employment agencies.

Don't limit your efforts at boosting your earned income to your primary job. Look for a second job. Consider taking on free lance assignments. Perhaps you can start a part time business, maybe turning a hobby into a money making venture. Just make sure these secondary work efforts don't adversely affect your primary job.

Shortly after Roberta Rourke's mother was diagnosed with Alzheimer's, she and her husband Ken realized they'd need to place her in a nursing home and help out financially. Roberta, a magazine editor, and Ken, a newspaper reporter, didn't have a very extravagant lifestyle to begin with. "When we did our financial inventory we had a hard time finding places where we could cut enough to make a real difference. That's why we both decided to start freelancing on the side. That way all we really had to invest was time. And having our bylines appear in other places actually helped our status at our primary jobs by raising our profiles. As long as we didn't write for competitors our employers thought it was a great idea."

Like Roberta and Ken, you may not be in this alone. Ask your spouse to work, if he or she has been staying home. Just make sure the added expenses don't cost you more than he or she brings in. If your spouse is already working he or she should take available overtime, ask for a raise, pursue promotions and transfers, and perhaps look for a new job. Your spouse can also pursue the same secondary job and part-time entrepreneurial efforts as you. There's also no reason why your children can't take after school or summer jobs, too. Whatever money they bring in can help them pay for their own entertainment or clothing. Besides, studies show that kids who work actually do better at school.

Look for ways you can boost your unearned income as well. You may be able to shift investments from a growth to an income strategy. Reverse mortgages can provide a stream of tax-free income. Can you rent out your vacation home or easily turn your finished basement into an apartment? What about taking in a roommate? Just make sure that anything you do is truly profitable, and that it doesn't inadvertently hurt your other income generating efforts.

There's are also some ways you can increase your emotional, psychological, and spiritual "revenue." If you haven't been taking care of yourself up to now, this is an excellent time to start. Adding a degree of discipline to your life will help you feel better. Unable to exert control over the world you can instead exert control over yourself. Go on a diet or launch an exercise program. Cultivate your spiritual side by going to church or learning to meditate. Efforts like these

> *We need not only a purpose in life to give meaning to our existence but also something to give meaning to our suffering. We need as much something to suffer for as something to live for.*
> *Eric Hoffer*

can help pull you out of a disaster. That being said, I know it's a heck of a lot to ask for you to do all this while confronting and overcoming an emergency. I encourage you to try to use this as a reason to start taking better care of yourself. However, if you can't, don't beat yourself up about it. Just try not to develop new bad habits.

One thing I do insist on is that you use this crisis as an opportunity to expand your social capital. I'm not suggesting you go out every night to make new friends—though that might not be a bad idea. What I am suggesting is that you tap into networks of people who are going through the same type of crisis you're experiencing. There are support groups for everyone today: people suffering from cancer, who are unemployed, who are caring for aging parents, and who are raising autistic children. There are bereavement groups and divorce groups. Service, religious, and philanthropic organizations often establish support groups for specific disasters that may strike a community. If the factory in town shuts its gates, odds are a local church will set up a support group for workers who've lost their jobs. When a hurricane or tornado hits a local service organization will establish a support network for those who are displaced.

David Kaplan was partially paralyzed in a car accident. "I joined a support group while at a rehab center and it made a huge difference,"

Your Crisis Balance Sheet

Fixed Assets

Home
Auto
Other real estate
Other motor vehicles
Artwork
Jewelry
Antiques
Collectibles

Cash and Other Valuables

Checking account
Savings account
Certificates of deposit
Money funds
Retirement accounts
Investment accounts
Life insurance cash value
Life insurance viatical value
Accounts receivable
Early inheritance
Gifts and loans
Advances on salary

Institutional Borrowing Potential

Credit card spending limits
(CC cash advance limits)
Business lines of credit
Personal lines of credit
Home equity line of credit

Unextendable Liabilities

Rent
Utilities
Telephone
Insurance premiums
Charge card balances
Lease payments

Extendable Liabilities

Credit card balances
Mortgage balance
Professional balances
Institutional balances
Estimated tax payments
Debts due family and friends

YOUR CRISIS INCOME STATEMENT

Expected Income—Monthly

Salary
Severance pay
Unemployment benefits
Insurance benefits
Social Security
Investment income
Regular gifts

Nondeferrable Expenses

Food
Clothing
Rent
Mortgage interest
Fuel
Utilities
Telephone
Credit card interest
Insurance premiums
Subscriptions
Entertainment
Retirement fund contributions
Dues
Memberships
Other

he says. "At first it was mostly that here was a group who knew exactly what I was feeling. I felt safe talking about my anger and fears. Then the group turned into a resource for me. These were people from whom I could get guidance on overcoming the new problems I was facing. And then eventually it became a place where I learned to be thankful for what I still had. I mean, there were people there in far worse shape than me. Instead of being bitter I became grateful that I still had a working arm and leg."

Crafting a Plan

Overcoming your crisis will probably require a combination of the efforts I've outlined. You may need to liquidate some assets, extend some liabilities, cut some expenses, and bring in some additional income. To deal with losing your job you might need to cut back on your spending and also tap into your retirement savings and max out your borrowing in order to keep your head above water while you're searching for a new job. If your spouse, who was the household's primary breadwinner, dies, you may need to borrow from your parents, sell your home, and go back to work. What matters most is that you come up with a recipe of efforts that works for you.

Once you've come up with a plan, record it in your playbook. Committing it to writing helps commit to it in the real world. It needn't be a polished document—this isn't something you're necessarily going to share with anyone else. I've found that a simple checklist works best. When drafting this checklist make sure to skip a line between each item. That allows you to reorder your tasks to meet changing circumstances or fresh insights.

There's no single right way to deal with a disaster. To afford the added cost of caring for an ailing parent, one child might find it more acceptable to craft a new more austere lifestyle, while her sibling might be more comfortable with borrowing against her home and using her own retirement savings. The only requirement is you play the hand you've been dealt the way you think best. Do that, and you will have triumphed over adversity.

CHAPTER 5

Cultivate Antibodies

Don't look forward to the day you stop suffering, because when it comes you'll know you're dead.

—Tennessee Williams

This isn't the only disaster you'll face in your life. You may even have to face this same emergency again. There are calamities that we are destined to revisit: the death of a parent being a prime example. Some, like the loss of a job, are likely to become repeated unwelcome visitors to our lives, due to the way society has evolved. And for many, if not most, of these crises, there's nothing we can do avoid them.

The secret to proactive crisis management isn't prevention, it's mitigation. You need to use the experience you've just gone through as a lesson in survival, not avoidance. Think of what you've just been through as a vaccine. It's a dose of the disease that can help make future bouts shorter and less serious. Your goal in looking back over what has happened is to cultivate antibodies to help you deal with the future attacks.

Certainly you need to determine what role, if any, your action or inaction played in the crisis. You also need to figure out whether others contributed to the disaster. But rather than use this as a reason to beat yourself up, or to criticize others, use it as a guide to future mitigation. Let's say you were fired. Instead of dwelling on your own, and your supervisor's behaviors, use what happened to position yourself better in your next job.

That's what Sandra d'Abruzzio did. Having been fired after she discovered she was expected to perform a role different than that which she was hired to fill, Sandra did her best to nail down the details at her next job. "When I finally received another job offer I made sure to negotiate an employment contract," she explains. "It wasn't an elaborate document by any means. But it did spell out my compensation and exactly what my job was to be, and also what my severance package would be if I was terminated. This doesn't mean I won't ever have to go through the same thing. But it does mean I'll be better prepared."

If neither you nor anyone else contributed to the disaster, you can cultivate antibodies by critiquing your response to the crisis. Did the plan you crafted work as well as you hoped? What will you do differently in the future if you face the same situation?

The easiest period in a crisis situation is actually the battle itself. The most difficult period is the period of indecision—whether to fight or run away. And the most dangerous period is the aftermath. It is then, with all his resources spent and his guard down, that an individual must watch out for dulled reactions and faulty judgment.

Richard M. Nixon

Roberta and Ken Rourke were able to find a nursing home for her mother diagnosed with Alzheimer's. And thanks in part to their both taking on freelance work, they were able to help with the bills. In hindsight, however, they've realized there were things they could have done to make the process more efficient. "Having gone through it, we now know how helpful it can be to have the help of gerontologists and lawyers who know how to navigate the system," Roberta explains. "When we have to deal with Ken's parents in the years to come, we'll hire professionals a lot earlier in the process."

Don't leave your team's efforts unexamined. How did each member perform? Was your insurance broker as responsive as you'd hoped? If not, either tell him he needs to do better in the future or line up a new broker. Did your good friend provide the kind of emotional support you expected? If not, you'll know you need to find another shoulder to lean on next time.

After firing the bookkeeper who had embezzled from him and getting his personal finances in order again, Dr. Stephen Botha reviewed not just his actions, but those of his accountant as well. "He was very helpful in helping me figure out how to overcome my cash shortage, but not when it came to setting up new business procedures. I realized I needed to find another accountant to make sure any future attempts to steal would be easier and quicker to spot."

Edward Kohl was surprised at some of the emotional support he received when his son was in a coma. "One close friend seemed not to be able to deal with the situation; he sort of withdrew. It's not that he wasn't there, it's just that he stayed in the background. At the same time, there was a colleague who was just incredible. I had never considered him a particularly close friend, but he was really supportive. There are some people who just seem to rise to the occasion and others who seem to shrink from it."

Finally, make a long-term assessment of how your finances could be better arranged to deal with future calamities.

The compensations of calamity are made apparent to the understanding also, after long intervals of time. A fever, a mutilation, a cruel disappointment, a loss of wealth, a loss of friends, seems at the moment unpaid loss, and unpayable. But the sure years reveal the deep remedial force that underlies all facts.

Ralph Waldo Emerson

Did you have sufficient cash on hand? For years I have been telling my clients they should have enough cash readily available in some form of money fund so they could pay their bills for three to six months. Funding this emergency reserve is, in my mind, more essential even than funding retirement accounts. That's because odds are you'll be facing one or more major financial hurdles well before you're facing retirement. Keep three months' worth in a money fund and put another three months' worth in something low risk and fairly liquid, like a short-term bond fund.

Was your insurance coverage adequate? The odds of being disabled are far greater than the odds of dying young, yet fewer people carry disability insurance than life insurance. Sure, disability coverage is expensive, but it can literally be a lifesaver. You can trim the costs by taking out a policy that pays benefits if you're unable to work at all, rather than if you're unable to perform your current job.

And you don't need to have a policy with benefits that are close to your current income. It's better to have some coverage and have to cut back your lifestyle somewhat, then to have no coverage and have to go on assistance. While you're examining your insurance coverage, take a close look at Federal Flood Insurance for your home. No homeowner's policy covers flood damage, and it's water rather than wind that's responsible for most catastrophic claims. The federal program provides essential protection for anyone whose home is at risk from flood damage. The same holds true for earthquake coverage in areas where that's the main concern.

Do you have adequate lines of credit in place? There's an old joke that says banks only want to lend money to people who don't need it. Take it from a former banker: It's true. When you're desperately in need of a line of credit—say your business lost its major customer—you won't be able to get it. That's why you should line up credit, both business and personal, when you're doing well. If your mortgage is paid off, take out a home equity line of credit. If you're holding credit cards with no annual fees but high interest rates, consider switching to credit cards with annual fees. They usually carry lower interest rates and generally will provide higher credit limits: just what you'd need in case of emergency.

As I've already explained, none of these efforts will prevent future catastrophes from striking. They'll simply make confronting and overcoming the inevitable challenges easier. When you think about it, that's really enough.

I'm 78 years old. During my eight decades I've buried both my parents and both my siblings. I've been fired, more than once, and I've been disabled and unable to work for eighteen months. For thirty years I've helped hundreds of people deal with the crises in

The Seven Steps in Personal Crisis Management

Accept the problem and own the solution.
Unburden yourself.
Diagnose the impact.
Take your financial pulse.
Start palliative measures.
Launch revenue rehabilitation.
Cultivate antibodies.

their lives, from the monumental to the mundane. If there's only one message you take away from this book, I hope it's this: Live in the moment rather than dwell on the past or dream of the future. Live your life as it is, not as it used to be or as you hope it will be. You are a human being, not a human becoming. The bumps in the road are the road.

PART II

LIFELINES FOR 33 OF LIFE'S MOST TRYING CATASTROPHES

A Quick Note

The advice I'm offering in each of the following entries isn't intended as comprehensive counsel. This is personal crisis management, not run-of-the-mill personal financial management. I encourage—no, I implore—you to get a more thorough grounding or more expansive counsel on these subjects after you've recovered from the immediate crisis. In addition, heed whatever wisdom is offered by your friends and family and any professionals you hire as a result of reading this book. They can focus on the specifics of your situation in a way I simply can't. The individual entries here are intended as specific adjuncts to the general advice I offer in Part I. If you've rushed ahead to this part of the book to address a pressing crisis, make sure to flesh out the advice by turning back to the first few chapters after finishing the relevant entry. Sprinkled throughout these entries you'll also find boxes offering advice that, while not directly relevant, could be very helpful.

Your Child'S College Fund
Has Come Up Short

Your son has just entered high school and it dawns on you: There's no way you can now start saving enough money to pay for his college education. Or maybe in the middle of your child's junior year in high school the college fund you've been assiduously building and investing takes a huge hit in a market collapse or interest rate climb. Or perhaps your daughter's SAT results are outstanding and suddenly she is talking Ivy League rather than State U.

Mike Bennett prided himself on his financial acumen. A human resources executive with a major media company, he felt he was on the right track. The cooperative apartment he and his wife stretched to purchase in the early 1980s had soared in value. He had been quite successful building a portfolio of individual stocks that consistently outperformed the market. Since he and his wife Kate both earned good salaries, they were able to afford to send their son Dylan to private schools, where he excelled academically. When the time came, they encouraged Dylan to aim high in targeting colleges, both firm in the belief that a degree from a prestigious university would give Dylan a leg up for the rest of his life.

Dylan set his sites on the Ivy League, and in an effort to maximize his college fund, Mike invested heavily in a number of stocks that he believed offered outstanding short-term potential. By and large, his choices performed the way he hoped. However, one company, a retail bakery chain, performed even better than anticipated. Mike took profits from many of the stocks in the college fund and diverted more of the total to the skyrocketing food stock. Then, at the end of Dylan's junior year in high school, the bubble burst. The bakery chain had overexpanded and institutional investors began dumping the stock. Other investors followed suit, and soon Dylan's college fund had lost more than 75 percent of its value. With little time to recoup and Dylan weighing Princeton, Columbia, and Cornell, Mike and Kate felt hopeless.

Accept the Problem and Own the Solution

It doesn't matter whether the shortfall is due to procrastination, poor timing, bad judgment, or increased expectations. You don't have sufficient funds available to meet an anticipated obligation, and there isn't enough time to make up the difference by staying on the same course. Sure, there's an added emotional element of guilt or shame at not being able to provide for your child to the degree you'd prefer. But few people today are able to pick up the whole tab for their child's college education. Tuition costs have climbed at a faster rate than almost any other major life expense. Four years at a top school can cost more than $175,000. The best thing you can do is concentrate on coming up with new alternative plans. Although you are not responsible for covering 100 percent of the cost of your child's college education, I believe crafting a plan to pay for that education is your responsibility. Take ownership of the solution by coming up with alternative plans to deal with the changed circumstances.

Unburden Yourself

The burden of paying for college needs to be shared in various ways by the student, the extended family, the university, and society at large.

You also don't need to become an expert in every alternative financing option. Due to the increasing need, there are dozens of loan, scholarship, and financial aid programs available today. In response, a new group of specialized professionals have sprung up. Educational consultants provide help in gaining admission to chosen schools but also in working out how to finance college.

All this means the team you need to put together to deal with this situation includes your child, you, your child's other parent (whether you are married or not), both sets of grandparents, possibly aunts and uncles, high school guidance counselors, college financial aid officers, your accountant, your bank, and perhaps an educational consultant. By the way, you can get recommendations for educational consultants from your accountant and attorney, or from the guidance office at your child's high school.

Diagnose the Impact

If your child has a particular school in mind, check with its admissions office for an estimate of the total yearly cost including tuition, room and board, books, and fees. If your child doesn't have a particular school in mind, get annual cost estimates from the top large public university and the top small public college in your state, and split the difference. Take that annual figure and multiply it by four to come up with a target fee. Then, calculate exactly how much is currently available in your college savings funds. The difference between the two numbers is the impact of this money mishap.

Take Your Financial Pulse

Do a thorough inventory of your assets. Are there any funds in other accounts you could divert to help make up for the shortfall in your child's college fund? I'd urge you not to invade tax-deferred retirement plans—the penalties would be severe—but give some thought to tapping any savings and investments earmarked for hopes rather than needs or for events further in the future. If you have money that you've been setting aside for a second home, it might better be spent now on tuition. Or if you have non–tax-deferred retirement savings, you could divert them to the tuition bills and still have time to put more away for your own future. This is as much a philosophical decision as a financial one, as I'll explain in a few paragraphs. My suggestion would be to conduct the inventory, but do nothing until you've looked at other outside options.

Start Palliative Measures

There are two types of palliative measures you need to undertake. The first involves protecting whatever you *do* have in your existing college fund. The second focuses on lowering, or at least moderating, expectations.

Do not, I repeat, do not take whatever is left in your college savings fund and invest it more aggressively to make up for past failures.

Doubling down in this manner will just make the situation worse. You need to do exactly the opposite. Your existing college fund may not be as much as you'd like, but it's better than nothing. In the short time you have available, you need to give up on growing this fund and instead concentrate on preservation. Prudently sell or dissolve any risky holdings in this account. If that means waiting a month or two, fine. But don't delay any longer than that. Invest the funds in short-term U.S. Treasury bonds, a secure money market fund, or certificates of deposit. Your goal is simply to outpace inflation. Having secured your current college fund in this manner, you have a rock-solid baseline for the rest of your efforts.

Next, sit down with your child and explain what has happened. This isn't a mea culpa; it's a planning session. Present the shortfall as a fact, not a possibility, but stress you're all going to work together to do the best you can. I know it's never easy breaking bad news to your children. I've had to do it myself a number of times. One solace is that this is an important life lesson. Part of growing up is learning to deal with adversity and respond to life as it is, not as we wish it could be. There are a number of options you and your child can consider. The first set of options involves a shift in expectations.

Is he or she dead set on a particular college? That exclusive private school may well be the first choice, but is it the only acceptable choice? What about a less expensive school?

Is junior college an option? Two years spent at a good junior college will only cost about $20,000, and it can provide for a smoother academic and lifestyle transition from high school to college. After two years, your child could transfer to a top-tier school.

Once those options have been put on the table, you should move on to discuss ways you could still expand the college fund.

Launch Revenue Rehabilitation

One option for additional college funds is future inheritance—not yours, your child's. If any of the grandparents have been setting aside money for your child, there's nothing wrong with suggesting that your child ask them to apply it to college costs now rather than pass it along when they die. This is their chance to ensure the money goes toward something valuable and worthwhile. Besides, if the gift is made now, they can receive thanks face to face, rather than through prayer. Similarly, if you have any siblings whose affluence and affection for your children could mean they'd be willing to help, now is the time to ask.

There are loan programs available to both you and your child. Loans provided by the colleges themselves, as financial aid, or subsidized by the states and the federal government, offer reasonable interest rates and payback plans, but qualifying is competitive. These loans are based on what is called *need*. This is a specific numeric assessment made by colleges and lending agencies. It is determined by subtracting the amount the lender believes you *should* have saved, based on your income, from the cost of the specific college. The remainder is your child's need. Any money the child saved on his or her own reduces that figure. The same is true for any scholarships he or she may have won.[1] In effect, your child's savings and scholarships save money for the school or lender, not you. Scholarships reduce the amount of financial aid your child will receive from the school, not the amount the school believes you and your child should be responsible for. Information on government loan programs will be available from local banks. You can find out about a college's own loan program by getting in touch with its financial aid office.

You and your child should be aware that as part of an aid package, the school may suggest a work study program. Usually, this requires the student to work in a somewhat menial job on campus—restocking books in the library or dishing out meals in the cafeteria—in exchange for a financial stipend that offsets costs.

If your own savings, contributions from extended family, and subsidized loans don't cover the full cost, there are also unsubsidized loans available to both students and parents. Although their interest rates and terms aren't as attractive as those of subsidized loans, they are still quite reasonable.

Once again, don't jump at any option or set of options until you've had a chance to explore and discuss all the alternatives. Odds are, you'll need to adopt a hybrid plan that draws on a number of these alternatives. Maybe your existing fund will cover a year's worth of costs. Perhaps Grandma can add a semester's worth of tuition to the pot. And maybe the school is willing to lend another year's worth of money at a subsidized rate. Then, by taking out an unsubsidized loan, your child could afford the remaining three semesters of costs. Or it could be your child is willing to attend a less-expensive school, or go to community college for two years and transfer. As a result, he or she might not need to take out an unsubsidized loan.

The bottom line is you have options and choices. If you and/or your child are willing to go into debt, almost no amount of tuition is beyond your reach.

Mike and Kate Bennett knew they faced some hard choices. They'd always told Dylan he shouldn't worry about college costs and had insisted that if he performed well enough academically, he could go to whatever school he'd like. Dylan had decided he wanted to go to Cornell University to study animal sciences, with the intention of going on to Cornell's Veterinary School after he graduated. Mike and Kate felt strongly that rather than lower Dylan's expectations and suggest he investigate less expensive schools, they'd do whatever they could to help him go where he wanted. If they couldn't cover the whole cost, they'd help him take out loans for the rest.

Mike took what remained in Dylan's college fund and invested it in government bonds due just prior to when his first semester's tuition came due. He estimated that the funds left would cover one year's costs. Kate contacted the financial aid office at Cornell and learned that, due to their income and assets, Dylan didn't qualify for financial aid. However the school offered some suggestions about unsubsidized loan programs. Kate determined they'd be able to take out loans for the three years of costs the college fund wouldn't cover. However, the payments would start immediately and would have a definite impact on their lifestyle. Mike and Kate analyzed their spending and came up with a list of *give-ups* that would help them cover the cost of the educational loans. They stopped paying for parking for their car and instead Mike woke up an hour earlier each day to search out a spot on the street. Kate stopped having a massage each month. They also scaled back their vacation plans dramatically, deciding they'd use their time off to both visit Dylan and relax at home.

Cultivate Antibodies

After you and your child have come up with, and set in motion, an alternative plan to pay for college, you can look back, learn some lessons, and apply them to the future. Obviously if you had made investments that were too volatile for a fund designated to address a short-term obligation, you should reconsider your financial strategy and advisor. However, the larger lesson I'd suggest you take from this is that it's probably a mistake to let children think you'll be able

There Is Another Option

College has never been for everyone. Even today, when a sheepskin is touted as a requirement for success in the twenty-first century economy, the lack of a diploma won't keep your child from climbing to the top in a number of fields.

Most obvious are the fine arts and other creative fields, such as fashion and cooking, where an apprenticeship or trade school may be a better entree for your child than a bachelor's degree.

Is your son interested in high tech? He doesn't need an M.I.T. degree. The list of those in the field who've succeeded without diplomas reads like a hall of fame. Does your daughter want to work on Wall Street? She doesn't have to graduate Wharton. Neither a recent chairman of Merrill Lynch, nor a recent chairman of UBS Paine Webber, graduated college. And both the Chicago and New York Stock Exchanges were headed by individuals without college degrees.

Maybe your child has shown an entrepreneurial spark since selling candy bars to finance a class trip. Why not use whatever money you've saved for her education to help launch a business instead? She'll never have more energy, and seed capital may provide a greater return on investment than tuition.

There's no reason to spend almost $200,000 on your son finding himself. There will never be a better time in your child's life to travel, volunteer, or just think about life than right after he or she graduates high school. This is the time to backpack through Europe, learn French by waiting tables in Paris, or read the Great Books while doing roofing in Oregon. Once he enters the real world, he'll be on the fast track to turning those real-life adventures into escapist fantasies.

By taking time off for an adventure and then attending a junior college, your son or daughter will spend less and have a life-altering experience to boot. Having a better idea of what he or she wants to do, as well as some notion of what it's like to work rather than just go to class, your suddenly mature child will probably spend more of his or her college time studying than you did.

to pay for their entire college education. Instead, sit down with your younger children now and promise you'll do as much as you can to help them, but that they'll need to bear some of the burden, too. If its appropriate, mention the kind of alternative strategies you've already explored and explain that you are here to help them to the extent possible, but also to help them help themselves.

You've Lost Your Job

You're called into your supervisor's office for an unplanned meeting and arrive to find her sitting alongside someone who says he's from human resources. Your boss, who rarely lets anyone get a word in edgewise, is suddenly struck mute. The human resources fellow, who you've never met before, calls you by your first name and has a phony smile plastered on his face. He speaks as if reading from a script, explaining that the company is terminating you due to lackluster performance, philosophical differences, a change in direction, or your choice in neckwear. He explains that if anyone asks they'll be told you were let go due to budgetary reasons. He casually notes that security is currently cleaning out your office. He says you'll receive a generous severance package of one week's pay for every year you were with the company, and brandishes the check. To get it, you have to sign a release and turn in your ID card.

David Gold compared the feeling of being told he was fired to being punched in the stomach. David had been working for the same advertising agency for almost 20 years, having started there right out of college. By the time he was terminated, he had moved up to become a senior vice president, heading up an important division. David left for his vacation with no sense his job was in danger. He'd received nothing but positive reviews and glowing reports. That made it doubly shocking when, on the day he returned, he was called into the president's office for a hastily arranged meeting. In a highly scripted three-minute presentation, he was told he was being let go. Two projects, which previously had been held up as successes, were now presented as failures and were sited as the rationale for his termination. Stunned, he barely responded. But when he was asked to sign a release he refused, saying he was too shocked to make any commitments at that moment. With that he stood up and left the room.

Accept the Problem and Own the Solution

Terminations have become ritualized behavior. Partly that's due to employers being burned for illegal behavior in the past. But mostly it's due to how often they're taking place. Being fired is now as much a part of the American workplace as bad coffee. Managers who used to dread letting people go are now inured to the act. Unfortunately, the same isn't true for the person being terminated. It still feels, as David Gold can attest, like being punched in the stomach.

The reason you were given for being fired probably has nothing to do with the reason you are actually let go. If you don't have an employment contract you're employment is *at will.* You needn't even be given a reason, though usually there's a rationalization such as *redundancy,* or *function no longer necessary.* If you're from a protected class of employee due to age, gender, race, or some other factor, your employer has come up with a rationalization that ensures it won't be legally liable. More Machiavellian managers may even have created enough of a paper trail to guarantee they can't be accused of anything.

It's not worth disputing these bogus claims. They'll never be voiced outside of the execution chamber. In order to further insulate themselves from legal action, the majority of companies won't provide any potentially harmful details of your termination if asked by future potential employers. All they'll say is you were terminated, not for cause, and that you were employed at the company from one date until another date. It's the workplace equivalent of supplying your name, rank and serial number. The disadvantage of all this employer spinning is you won't get the justification of being told the truth. The advantage is that *you* are free to spin the situation any way you would like.

It's also not worth debating the situation because it gains you nothing. There's no way to reverse a termination. Besides, debate just postpones the necessary acceptance of your newly unemployed status.

You've been fired. It's over. Now you need to focus on one thing and one thing only: getting as much from the SOBs who fired you as you possibly can. That's how you take ownership of the solution.

If you haven't yet signed a release form, don't. It's the best leverage you have for getting more from your former employer. When pushed—and you will be pushed—claim you're too distraught to think straight. Get the name and phone number of the executioner from human resources and say you will be back in touch tomorrow.

If you have signed the release form already, don't panic. In most states there's a legal requirement that gives you a certain amount of time to reconsider your having signed away any rights. After all, you were in no condition at that moment to make such a momentous decision. All it takes is a quick phone call to human resources to say you've changed your mind, followed by the statement that you'll be calling back tomorrow. Don't engage in a conversation. And don't worry about making them angry. What can they do to you? They've already wielded their ultimate weapon: they fired you. They took their best shot and you're still alive and breathing. From this moment on, you're the one with all the leverage.

Unburden Yourself

I know it might be embarrassing, but it's essential you call those closest to you personally and professionally. Tell your spouse immediately and let your children know what has happened in a manner and at a time appropriate for their ages. Yes, they will find it frightening, particularly if you are the sole or primary bread winner. But keeping them in the dark will make things worse in the long run. They will learn about this eventually. Efforts at concealment, even if your intent is to protect them, will be seen as signs you don't trust them. They'll also feel less helpless if they're allowed to be part of the solution, not just a victim of the problem. Other family and friends can supply emotional support, bucking up your ego which will naturally be a bit wounded. And letting them know what happened also lets you lay the groundwork for asking for material support you may need from them in the future. Make them a part of your team from day one and they will be less likely to feel used if you have to come to them later for more substantive help.

Activate your professional network as soon as possible. Fill them in on what has happened and say you'll be back in touch as soon as you've had a chance to take stock. It's really just priming the pump, but the sooner you do that the quicker you'll be able to act when it's needed. One person you certainly want to enlist is your patron or mentor within the company. Maybe it's the person who first hired you. It could be your boss's boss. Perhaps it's the head of the department or division from which you transferred. You're eventually going to ask this insider to become your advocate.

If you are in a management position I strongly urge you to contact an employment lawyer with experience in employment contracts and termination agreements. No, I'm not suggesting you sue for some form of discrimination, or even use the attorney as a way to scare the other side. Workplace discrimination cases are very difficult to prove and, win or lose, are always costly and time consuming. Sure, you want to get the most you can, but you also want this over as soon as possible.

You'll be using the attorney to review documents and agreements, not be your hired gun. When an attorney representing a terminated employee telephones, the call and all subsequent contacts are directed to the company's legal department or outside counsel. And take it from a lawyer, when two attorneys square off it becomes all about their egos, not the clients. You'll be doing your own negotiating with the human resources department. Document review will cost you between $125 to $300 an hour and should only take one or two hours. All the lawyer needs to know is that you were fired without cause (you didn't lie, cheat, steal, etc.); you don't need to spend any time laying out your grievances.

Diagnose the Impact

Superficially, the impact of this is simple to diagnose: You've lost a stream of income. But actually, you've regained partial control over the impact by negotiating your termination agreement.

The first area to consider is the amount of severance pay that's being offered and how it is to be paid out. Although there is no legal requirement to pay severance, it's an accepted practice. Companies that don't pay severance when someone is fired without cause will quickly earn a negative reputation and will find it impossible to hire any quality people. In theory, severance should be sufficient to carry you over until you get another job. The higher your position in an organization, the fewer comparable jobs exist. That means a job search will take longer. Similarly, if you've worked for a company for a long period of time, you've become an icon of the company; the more identified you are with an organization the more difficult it will be for an other organization to see you as a potential member of its own team. How much is enough? Simply put, there's never enough. Whatever has been offered, ask for more. Ironically, considering the circumstances, the argument that works best is that the initial offer is unfair. Before you make the direct appeal to human resources, explain what has happened to your in-house advocate, and ask him to put a word in for you. Human resources departments pride themselves on being fair and respond to political pressure. Get as much as you possibly can.

You may want to consider negotiating with the supervisor who hired you. He's unlikely to be wearing his guilt comfortably. Explain that you're calling to thank him for all he did for you over the years, letting that guilt bite just a bit deeper. Then say you have one more request, that he become an advocate for you with human resources. You're giving him a chance to get off the hook psychologically and emotionally, and you'd be amazed how many of even the hardest-boiled executives offer to help.

Payment could be made in a lump sum or over time. You can usually get more if it's paid out over time—in effect, the company keeps you on the books for an agreed period of time—but the problem is, you continue to be tied to the company. Your former employer can use its ongoing payments as leverage to enforce non-compete clauses. Most employers will also insist that the payout is mitigable. That means it can be reduced or eliminated if you receive income from a new employer. My suggestion is to push for a lump sum instead. It's not easy, but it is possible. Just make sure you add other types of compensation to the package.

Severance isn't the only thing you can ask for. You should get payment for any unused vacation or personal days. Prorated year-end bonuses should be included. Ask to keep your laptop computer and cell phone. Request outplacement counseling. See if you can keep using the company car for a period of time. Try to get your former employer to pick up the continued cost of insurance policies—health, disability, and life—until you're reemployed. You have the legal right through legislation called COBRA, to maintain your employer provided health insurance coverage for 18 months, albeit with you now picking up the tab.

Have your attorney carefully study any provisions in the agreement that could limit your future employment. These are called *restrictive covenants* and are efforts by your former employer to keep you from passing along inside knowledge and information to competitors. The law looks very unkindly on broadly restrictive covenants so if you raise a stink your former employer is likely to back down.

Take Your Financial Pulse

Once the termination agreement has been finalized, it's time to take your financial pulse. How many weeks or months of income will the severance provide? How much unemployment insurance are you entitled to, and for how long? What other liquid assets are available? It's not yet time to invade tax deferred retirement savings, but if you've any "rainy day" money set aside now is the time to turn it into an umbrella. Can you get a loan or an advance on inheritance from parents? Add up all the revenue you can come up with and figure out how many months living that can cover at your current lifestyle.

Start Palliative Measures

If you've never done it before, now is the time to do a complete analysis of your expenses, line by line.

Focus first on cutting automatic monthly expenses. For example, can you trim your telephone service? How about opting for a cheaper cable television package? Can you mow the lawn rather than hire a gardener? Can you shift from the pricey gym to a membership at the local YMCA? Are you paying more for homeowners and auto insurance than is necessary? Can you launder clothes at home rather than use the dry cleaner?

Then, turn to your purchasing. You don't have to live on rice and beans, but you also shouldn't be living on filet mignon. Rather than following an austerity approach, try to make spending a cognitive act. Use cash and debit cards rather than using credit cards; that will make spending less reflexive. Try to buy just the things you need, rather than the things you want. Make this a family effort. And show appreciation for the efforts of everyone. Your daughter's willingness to go to day camp rather than sleep-away camp during the summer is a big deal for her, so treat it with the respect it deserves.

I think it's best to make major reductions and lifestyle changes right away, rather than making minor cut backs immediately and then trimming more later if your finances don't improve. You're not going to be able to get a sense for how long your job search will take until you've been actively searching for a month or more. It is hard to go back to the well for more lifestyle cuts after you've realized you'll be out of work longer than you initially expected—this actually creates a second crisis. It's best if everyone takes the full lifestyle hit now, when the blow of the termination is still fresh.

Launch Revenue Rehabilitation

It's not enough to just cut back on expenses. You'll need to do whatever you can to increase your revenue as well. If your spouse hasn't been working outside the house, now might be a good time for him or her to reenter the work force.

It's always more difficult to find a job when you're unemployed than when you're working. It's also tough to be a good interviewee when you're worried about paying your cab fare. That's why I suggest you look for what I call a *stepping-stone job.* This is a job you take to simply bring in money in the short term. It needn't have any connection to your previous career, or offer opportunity for growth. The two things you should care about in a stepping-stone job are income and the freedom to continue to pursue other opportunities. I don't mean physical freedom. Your requiring an interviewer to meet you in the evening after work is actually a plus, making you more, not less, attractive. It's mental freedom I'm talking about. You don't want to have to devote a great deal of intellectual energy to this position; it's a job not a career. Show up on time. Do your work. Cash your check. That's it. If interviewers question you about why you want a job that seems beneath your experience, say you're thinking of changing careers or want to learn a new industry.

This explanation may actually come true. Do your best to look on this job search as an opportunity. You'll never have a better chance to change careers or move to a new location and start fresh. You'd be surprised how often stepping-stone jobs become the avenue for a transition into a new career or industry.

David Gold knew his termination would have a considerable impact financially. His wife was a stay-at-home mom taking care of the couple's two preschool-age children. They had just purchased a home and, as a result, were already stretched fairly thin. The first person David called with the bad news was his wife, even though he thought she'd be terrified. He was right. That's part of the reason the second call he made was to an attorney: David knew he'd need to get as much from his former employer as possible. Bypassing the president who had fired him, David contacted the chairman, who'd recruited David out of college. David explained that he was so closely identified with the agency he'd probably have a great deal of trouble finding another position. The chairman, who'd had no role in the termination, commiserated with David and said he'd do what he could. Meanwhile, David and his attorney came up with a response to the agency's initial severance offer. When David contacted human resources, he found them willing to accede to all his requests. With that complete, David and his wife conducted a complete financial inventory and came up with areas they could cut back and a few people they could approach for emergency help if necessary.

Cultivate Antibodies

I have to be completely honest with you. In the past five to seven years, a great deal of my practice has centered on employment issues since so many of my clients have had to deal with terminations. In all that time, I haven't yet seen a single client who was fired find a new job with a salary equal to his or her previous position. Today, the only people who are getting increases in new positions are those who have been recruited while still employed.

Warning Signs

Don't be caught by surprise again. There are always warning signs of impending termination if you know where to look. In most cases, if you spot any of these you won't have enough time to land a new job before you're axed. However, you'll still have some time to get your finances in order and be more aggressive at your execution.

If you're given a mixed performance review, the seeds for firing you in six months are starting to be planted. If you're given an outright negative review, your termination is planned for the next three months. If any responsibilities or powers are taken from you, or if your presence is no longer required in a standing meeting, the handwriting is on the wall. If you're asked to provide a written description of your job, they're figuring out how to write the advertisement for your replacement. If you're asked to compile a list of all the projects you're working on, along with a status report on each, they're preparing the briefing for your replacement. If people stop talking when you enter a room or walk by, you'll be gone by the end of the week.

I've come to realize that everyone who is employed is just waiting to be fired. The best way to insulate yourself from this crisis happening again in the future is to leave a job on your own accord. Think of it like an investment in the stock market. The only way to know when a stock has reached its highest point and it is most advantageous to sell, is to wait until the price starts to go down. The only way to truly know when your job is in jeopardy is to wait until you're fired. I tell my clients they should start *job fishing*, rather than job hunting. That means constantly having a baited line in the market to see what offers come along. The time to leave a job is when things are going well, not when they've started to go sour. The best way to keep from getting fired again in the future is to quit.

3

You're Insurance Company Has Dropped You

Three weeks after receiving a check from your insurance agent for the fender bender you had in a mall parking lot, a form letter arrives stating that your coverage is being dropped in two months. Or maybe a letter just arrives out of the blue saying your homeowners insurance company has decided to stop providing coverage in your state and your policy will expire in 30 days.

Wendy Lieberman hadn't made a single claim on her condominium owner's insurance policy in the 22 years she'd been living in a Florida retirement community. That's why she was shocked when she received notice that her coverage would be dropped in three months. Although her community had suffered some damage in the past three hurricane seasons, and she had made a claim on her auto policy due to damage from a fallen tree, her apartment had been undamaged. When she contacted the insurer, she was told her claims history had no bearing on the decision. The company had decided not to write any more property insurance in the entire state of Florida.

Accept the Problem and Own the Solution

Why it happened doesn't matter. Insurers today are dropping customers who've never made claims and who aren't big risks, simply because they've decided to randomly reduce their exposure. That's why I've told clients never to hesitate to file claims—you may as well get something for all those premiums you've paid before you're dropped.

Homeowners and auto insurance carriers can effectively drop you for no reason at all, so there's no point in trying to get a reversal. Just make sure they've provided as long a grace period as called for in your contract. Barring that, you have to accept it and own the solution, which is to find a new insurer.

Unburden Yourself

The heavy lifting here should be done, not by you, but by an insurance broker. If you don't have a broker already, now is the time to find one. Brokers differ from agents in that they don't represent a single company, and instead are free to place their clients with any company. That means it's likely they have experience dealing with the same situation you're in now. Ask your accountant, attorney, or a real estate agent you trust for recommendations.

Diagnose the Impact

It's obviously not good to be without insurance coverage. However, the situation is most dangerous if the home or auto that was covered is actually owned by a lender or leaser. If you don't have insurance coverage your mortgage, auto loan, or lease will be in default. That means time is of the essence.

Take Your Financial Pulse

It's almost certain your cost for similar insurance will now be higher than before. Find out from the broker what the cost of similar coverage will be, and then after you've picked your jaw up off the floor, start considering ways of cutting the cost.

Start Palliative Measures

There are a number of ways you can try to cut your premiums when buying a new policy. Make sure you're not paying for unnecessary coverage. For example, if you would never even try to replace the diamond engagement ring that has been in your family for generations, don't cover it. If something is truly irreplaceable, either due to sentimental value or because it's one of a kind, there's no point in it being insured. If you don't use it often, put it in a safe deposit box.

Take larger co-payments and increase your deductibles. The more risk you assume on your own, the less your out of pocket costs will be. Be open to buying coverage from insurers that aren't "A" rated. Work closely with the broker, making sure to ask why certain coverage or insurers are being suggested. In some situations, you simply need to make the best of a bad situation and get whatever coverage you can.

Launch Revenue Rehabilitation

If you've been carrying anyone else on your coverage, this is an opportunity to ask that person to contribute more to the cost. Let's say your daughter is listed on your auto insurance policy. Circumstances have changed, so there's nothing wrong with now asking her to contribute what she can to help offset the increased cost of coverage.

Once Wendy Lieberman learned she wasn't the only person who'd property insurance coverage would soon be canceled, she contacted some of her neighbors, asking what they planned to do. A retired insurance executive who lived in her building suggested she get in touch with a local broker he knew. Wendy called the broker, who then explained that there were a number of options. A couple of smaller insurers were still open to writing policies of the type Wendy needed. However the cost would be much higher for

Emergency Health Insurance

If you're ever facing a gap in your health insurance coverage, the most affordable option may be a combination of a High Deductible Health Plan (HDHP) and a Health Savings Account (HSA).

HDHPs are inexpensive health plans that offer coverage only after you've already paid several thousands of dollars in medical bills. They provide catastrophic coverage only.

HSAs are tax-free savings plans, sold by banks, credit unions, and other institutions. You fund the savings plan with your own money, and as long as you spend it only on medical bills, it remains tax free. The money can accumulate from year to year. Currently, an individual can contribute $2,850 annually, while a family can contribute a total of $5,650.

the same coverage. Wendy went over her finances with her daughter and realized she had sufficient assets to accept more of the risk from storm damage. She took a policy that provided less coverage for a slightly higher premium than she was paying previously.

Cultivate Antibodies

There's nothing you can do to prevent this from happening again in the future. All you can do is prepare yourself to better deal with it if it happens again. I'd suggest the best way to do that is to have your insurance broker do a yearly search for both less expensive and more expansive coverage. In effect, ask for all your options every year.

You're Temporarily Disabled

W hile trying to install new Christmas lights on your roof, you are hit with a sudden wind that causes you to lose your balance. You fall off the ladder onto the ground, breaking one arm and dislocating your shoulder. Or maybe you're diagnosed with coronary artery disease requiring you to undergo bypass surgery. In either case, you'll be temporarily unable to work as you usually do. In the case of the fall, you'll be able to do some work, just not all you were doing before the injury. In the case of the surgery, you'll be completely unable to work for about three months.

A successful freelance photographer, Jay Mitchell was on the sidelines shooting a college football game when he experienced severe chest pains and shortness of breath. Luckily, one of the training staff for the home team was standing nearby and overheard Jay complaining to one of the other photographers. Jay was hustled into the medical facility at the stadium, and after a brief exam, was put in the ambulance on call at the game and rushed to the closest hospital. He had suffered a large heart attack that caused considerable muscle damage. Jay's cardiologist said he didn't need bypass surgery, but would need to spend at least six weeks recovering, during which time he needed to avoid exertion, heavy lifting, and any activity that could lead to fatigue. Jay realized he would be out of work for at least six weeks.

Accept the Problem and Own the Solution

The damage has been done. Nothing you do or say will turn back the clock. Try to get past any anger you may have and instead focus on gratitude. Things truly could have been a great deal worse. You could be reading the entry on permanent disabilities right now. And while you're probably going through a great deal of physical pain and discomfort, your financial situation is better than if you were fired from your job. Your problem will last for a period of time you can easily estimate. If you lost your job, there's no telling how long you'd be out of work. Owning the solution means working to minimize any financial pain and sacrificing you and your dependents will suffer while out of work.

Unburden Yourself

You'll probably need medical professionals to help you recover from your disability. And since you'll temporarily be less able, you may need to hire some physical assistants, such as practical nurses, health aides, pick-up and delivery services, and house cleaners. Friends and family could also help fill any of these gaps. But the most important potential members of your team may be ones you'll never see outside a wood-paneled office.

Most individuals who suffer from a temporary disability will need to enlist some outside legal help to obtain all the benefits they may be due. That's because it can be a complicated bureaucratic process, and you'll have your hands full dealing with making any necessary changes in your day-to-day life.

If your injury or illness was caused by the action or inaction of someone else, you may have grounds for legal action. The actual legal process is beyond the scope of this book. The best counsel I can offer is to find a good personal injury attorney and listen to the attorney's advice. Instead of choosing a lawyer based on advertising, contact the attorney who handled your real estate transactions and wills and ask for a recommendation. If you don't have an attorney of your own, ask close friends or family members who do have an attorney to ask their professional for a recommendation.

If your disability is somehow work related, speak with the workers compensation contact in your company. Workers compensation qualifications and benefits differ from state to state. There are attorneys who specialize in handling workers compensation claims, so if you feel your rights aren't being adequately addressed, consider enlisting help. If your disability will result in your being unable to do almost any work for a year or more, you may also qualify for federal Social Security Disability benefits. This is another complex, bureaucratic procedure that has spawned yet another legal specialty. Once again, when hiring a workers compensation or Social Security Disability attorney, don't choose based on advertising. Ask your regular attorney for a suggestion.

If you have employer-provided disability coverage, the benefits coordinator at your company should be able to steer you to a claims person at the insurer. If you've been carrying your own disability coverage, get in touch with your insurance broker, who can be your advocate in making a claim.

Diagnose the Impact

The financial impact of a temporary disability depends on whether you are totally or partially disabled, and on how long your disability is likely to last.

If you are a totally disabled, you'll lose your regular income. If you are partially disabled, you may be able to do something less physically demanding. Let's say you were a field salesperson and broke both your legs. You may be able to do telephone sales prospecting until you're recovered and can resume traveling. That means you may just lose some of your income due to performing less valuable work or working fewer hours.

This total or partial reduction in your income will be multiplied by the amount of time you expect to be disabled. Ask your doctor for a conservative estimate as early in your treatment as possible. Then, ask for updated estimates of your recovery date during your rehabilitation. The staff who are actually physically working with you will be better judges of that than the professionals who will be reading reports instead.

Take Your Financial Pulse

Your stream of income and your expenses will change when you're temporarily disabled. How much, if anything, will you now be receiving in salary? Will that be supplemented by workers compensation or disability benefits? How will your expenses be reduced by the change in your employment status? On one hand, your travel costs may drop substantially. The same goes for your food bill, now that you'll be having lunch at home every day. On the other hand, some of your expenses may be higher. Odds are, medical expenses will now be more. If you're home all day, you may spend more on telephone calls and utilities. Your inability to do certain tasks may mean you need to hire help around the house.

Start Palliative Measures

Since your disability is temporary, consider suspending and deferring expenses, rather than making outright cuts. That could save you from having to pay initial fees that go along with restarting, or keep you from having to reapply perhaps under less auspicious circumstances. Most health clubs, for instance, allow you to suspend membership for a number of months. Many creditors will grant temporary relief quite readily. Some will let you skip one or two months outright due to medical emergency. Others will provide drastically reduced monthly payment plans. Professionals are likely to simply suspend your bill until you've recovered. Institutions, such as private schools and hospitals are also very flexible when they know the problem is temporary.

Launch Revenue Rehabilitation

Since you're unable to work in the short term, you'll need to look to others to help boost your income. Now is the time for your spouse or children to boost their contributions to the household revenue stream. Now is also the time to approach family and friends for help. Just as creditors will be more amenable because your situation is so clearly temporary, so will potential lenders. This is one time when asking family and friends for less than you might need makes sense. The initial approach will be easier, and coming back and asking for more can be blamed on your lingering illness. Loans like these will be perceived as medical rather than financial help.

Jay Mitchell was grateful to be alive, but he knew he faced a number of financial hurdles. Since he was self-employed, Jay had no paid vacations or sick days he could draw on. He had investigated taking out disability insurance back when he first went into business for himself, but he simply could not afford the premiums. Even though he suffered his heart attack while working, an attorney friend made some calls and told him he wasn't covered by workers compensation. There was also no one else who was legally liable, unless he wanted to sue the owner of the neighborhood diner where he ate three or four times a week. Jay had two wedding jobs already booked for the time when he'd be out of work. He'd have a couple of photographer friends cover the assignments for him, and they'd kick back 10 percent of the fees, but that was the extent of the income he'd be bringing in. Jay was owed almost $5,000 for work he'd already done, so he contacted his agent and pushed him to collect the money as soon as possible. He went over his expenses carefully, and figured he'd be able to cut back some, but not enough to cover all his bills. Jay called his bank and asked for some relief. The bank said they'd let Jay pay interest only for the next two months on his mortgage loan, and skip the next month's payment on his business line of credit. Jay has some retirement savings he could tap into if necessary, but decided that would remain his last resort. Instead, he decided he would take out cash advances on his credit cards, and use the money he had set aside for a vacation to help keep him afloat for the next six weeks.

Don't Panic

Think twice before making any drastic changes in your life or lifestyle. Many people react as if their temporary disability was actually permanent. I was diagnosed with tuberculosis in the 1980s. At first, my family was relieved, since we'd originally feared I had advanced lung cancer. But then, as the specter of eighteen months without being able to work took shape, I began to panic. I had disability insurance, but it wasn't nearly enough to pay our bills. I was a contract employee at the time so I'd have no job to go back to when I recovered. I started thinking about all the drastic changes the family would need to make, including selling real estate. It was my wife who calmed me down. The most important thing she said to me was, let's not get rid of anything we might not be able to replace later. We didn't. Instead, we cut back in small ways. I made deals with creditors. My wife went to work. I borrowed money from family and friends. I started doing consulting work and teaching part time when my health improved. Eventually, those halting efforts at going back to work became my fourth career, which I'm still practicing today.

Cultivate Antibodies

Obviously, do whatever the medical professionals tell you to maintain your regained health. Once you do recover, make sure to investigate disability insurance if you didn't already have that protection in place. If the costs seem prohibitive, consider what is called *annually renewable disability insurance.* It's a type of policy offered by a handful of companies that has escalating rather than level premiums. The policies are a bargain when you're young, but become more expensive as you grow older and become more likely to be disabled.

5

You're Permanently Disabled

The last thing you remember is that you were driving home from work just like you had every day for the past 11 years. The next thing you know, you're waking up strapped to a hospital bed, with tubes connecting you to high-tech equipment. You suddenly realize you can't move your legs. Or you're sitting in the ophthalmologist's office, listening to him explain there's nothing more that can be done, and soon you'll be totally and irreversibly blind.

At first Janet O'Neil thought the hoarseness was just voice strain. After all, she had been performing nightly at a Manhattan nightclub for three months. But when her usual methods didn't help, she visited her primary care doctor. He thought he saw some polyps but sent her along to an ear, nose, and throat specialist to make sure. The ENT did a more thorough exam and told her there was a small tumor in her larynx right by her vocal chords. He took a biopsy, and less than a week later called with the bad news that it was cancer. Things moved so quickly from that point on that Janet didn't have much time to think about what it all meant. She learned the tumor was small, appeared not to have spread, and could be treated with just chemotherapy and radiotherapy. She probably wouldn't lose the ability to speak, but her singing career was over.

Accept the Problem and Own the Solution

You may have had no control over what happened to you, but you have total control over how you frame it. You are still alive and in the world. You can choose to view yourself as someone who is less now than you were before, or you can look at yourself as someone who is different now than you were before. That's a profound distinction. Viewing your new life as different will lead you on a course of discovery. It will send you on a search for what you have gained rather than lost. That may sound hopelessly romantic and idealized, especially coming from someone who isn't permanently disabled. But that is exactly what I have been told by clients who are permanently disabled. One described to me how her disability has made her a better, less self-centered human being because she has become an advocate and spokesperson for others with her condition. Another called his disability a gift, since it led to his becoming the primary caregiver for his son. None came to this appreciation overnight, yet each did in one way or another. They all explained that acceptance let them take ownership of who they had become.

Unburden Yourself

Until you are fully adjusted to your abilities and capabilities, take advantage of every opportunity for assistance. Support groups, social workers, occupational therapy, home aides, assistance animals, and supportive technologies all have their places and roles. You won't know what works best for you unless you explore the options. In addition, don't hesitate to take advantage of government or charitable programs. As a member of society who has paid taxes and donated to charity in the past, you have contributed to the creation of these resource pools. You are entitled to make a withdrawal if you need it. You wouldn't feel guilty getting insurance benefits after having paid premiums, would you? Well, this is no different.

Don't hesitate to explain your needs to family and friends, either. Some will feel compelled to offer to do everything and anything for you. This isn't an insult. It's a reaction to *their* feeling weak and unable to fix things, not to their thinking *you* are weak and unable to do things. Others will hesitate to offer even the most minor assistance—help they may have offered before your disability—for fear of giving insult. Ask these people for help and they'll gladly give it.

Diagnose the Impact

You need to become as much of an expert on your physical condition as any doctor. Get multiple opinions. Research treatment options. Ask about experimental programs and research trials. Investigate alternative therapies. Become an informed skeptic. Accept no information on face value. Instead, ask for evidence and examples, whether you're speaking to your physician or responding to an e-mail from an online support group. The more knowledge you have about your abilities and limitations, the better.

Next, apply that knowledge to your working situation. Will you be able to continue doing the same work, even though you're now disabled? There are many occupations that you might be able to continue in, even if disabled, thanks to technology. For example, even if you're paralyzed from the waist down, you'd still be able to work as an accountant. You'd just need a wheelchair and a handicapped-accessible workplace. Will your condition require you to shift your work? If you're paralyzed from the waist down, you might not be able to continue working as a large animal veterinarian, caring for farm animals in the field, but you could work as a companion animal veterinarian, working with pets in an office. In some cases, your condition might require a complete shift in occupation. A carpenter who's paralyzed from the waist down will need to look for different work, say as a shop foreman or a construction manager.

Take Your Financial Pulse

Translate what you've learned about the impact of your condition to your financial life. First, look at your income. If you'll need to shift what you do, how will that affect your earnings? If you're not able to do the same work, what other types of work could you do, and what would your income be? Then consider how your condition will affect your expenses. Although some of your costs may drop—no more spending on eyewear and contact lenses if you're blind—you'll probably have a series of new bills. If you'll need assistance to continue your work as before, how much will that cost and who will pay for it? Who will pay for any training? Will your home need to be remodeled? Will you need a wheelchair, a car equipped with hand controls? Try to quantify your need for assistance. Will you need in-home assistance? How about at work? How much will it cost to hire this help? Who will be paying for it?

Start Palliative Measures

The way that you approach cutting costs in response to a permanent disability depends on the degree to which you'll be able to maintain your income. If, on the one hand, you'll be able to continue your previous work, or work in a slightly different type of position, you should approach your expense trimming the same way as in any other catastrophe. Look at your current spending and figure out areas where you can slow down, cut back, or eliminate outflows. If, on the other hand, you'll need to completely change your work, you should take a more radical approach.

When a permanent disability requires starting over in a new career, it should be accompanied by starting over financially as well. Trying to shoehorn your old personal finances into your new life is apt to lead to frustration and bitterness. That's because your expenses will now be higher, while your income will be lower. It makes more sense economically and emotionally to completely alter your financial life to fit your new circumstances. Take a fresh look at every element of your financial life through the prism of what you'll now be earning and spending. Consider selling your home and buying something less expensive, or renting. Start with a zero-based budget and spend on an austerity basis, adding in only those things you can afford.

Launch Revenue Rehabilitation

Start your revenue rehabilitation by looking for every source of new income you can find. Do you have disability insurance that will help compensate for lost earned income? Do you quality for any short-term or long-term assistance, through Social Security, workers' compensation, or any other government programs? Are there any charitable grants available? If you have any future expectations, perhaps from parents, ask for it now, when you really need it. Pursue litigation with the intent of getting a settlement you can turn into a stream of income. Investments and savings should be redirected from growth to income instruments. Don't hesitate to tap into retirement or college savings funds. Desperate times call for desperate measures. Make sure your family is on board with your efforts, and ask them to contribute as well.

Janet O'Neil vacillated between feeling blessed and cursed. Blessed that she was still alive, that she had a husband who loved her, and that she had good health insurance to cover her treatment. Cursed in that her cancer had chosen to attack the one part of her body crucial to her career; a career for which she had sacrificed a great deal and in which she had struggled mightily for years to succeed. Janet did have some disability insurance, which would help her and Tim deal with the time she was in treatment. However, it wasn't *own occupation* coverage, meaning it would stop paying benefits as soon as she was able to go back and do any type of work. She and Tim had to start their financial lives over from scratch. They had an inner-city apartment because she had needed to be close to clubs and theaters, where she did most of her performing. Tim did a reverse commute out to a suburban corporate park where he worked as CFO of a business services firm. They decided to put their apartment up for sale and look for an exurban home that would be more affordable. The move would result in a less-expensive lifestyle across the board. Janet cashed in her retirement savings and Tim borrowed money from his parents so they could afford for her to go back to college to get certification as a music teacher.

Cultivate Antibodies

In this situation you're not looking to cultivate antibodies to better weather a future crisis— it's unlikely you'll experience a second permanent disability. Instead, your goal should be to look ahead. Focus on what you still have rather than what you've lost. Think about what opportunities this new life affords you, not what you can no longer afford. I've always found that the people who are most grateful for what they have are those who had previously lost the most.

Your Spouse Is Having an Affair

After coming home from a business trip, your spouse is distant and irritable. Finally, after a sharp exchange over an apparently meaningless matter, she breaks down and confesses she is having an affair with a coworker. Or after months of hang-up phone calls, strange behavior, and distance, it dawns on you that your spouse may be having an affair. You secretly follow her when she's supposed to be meeting a friend for lunch and you discover she's rendezvousing with a neighbor for a tryst. Later than day you confront her, and she confesses the affair has been going on for months.

Beth Cohen thought she'd surprise her husband Adam by showing up at the international trade show he was attending in Chicago. The Cohens had both worked in the consumer electronics industry before they were married and they'd attended the show together until they'd had children. Adam had said he'd wished Beth could come along, but understood she wanted to stay home with the kids. It was a spur of the moment whim that led Beth to ask her mother to stay with the kids and book a flight to surprise Adam at the hotel. It *was* quite a surprise, because when she arrived and told the desk clerk she was Mrs. Adam Cohen, he explained there was already someone with that name registered and staying with Mr. Cohen in Room 1649.

Accept the Problem and Own the Solution

Acceptance doesn't mean forgiveness. It means *both* parties agreeing this is a problem that threatens the very fabric of the relationship, and also agreeing work needs to be done. If there isn't this kind of acceptance by both parties, you'll need to move toward dissolving the relationship.

Unburden Yourself

If you and your spouse agree to try to heal your relationship, you'll need to enlist the help of a marriage counselor. Ask any other therapeutic professional or clergyperson with whom you've had experience for recommendations. Alternatively, ask your primary care physician. The key is to solicit suggestions from people who you know will keep the matter private. That's why you shouldn't discuss this with friends and family unless you're prepared for it to become a general topic of discussion.

One professional you shouldn't enlist just yet is an attorney. Attorneys typically serve as advocates in adversarial proceedings. Their training and experience lead them to fight for one side and against the other. This is especially true of matrimonial lawyers. When advocates like this are brought into a conflict, there's almost no way for it to be resolved amicably. If you hire a lawyer at this point, you're almost guaranteeing you'll separate and divorce. That still might happen, but if you wait if gives you a chance to heal the relationship.

Diagnose the Impact

Infidelity has no financial impact, other than whatever the adulterous spouse spends on the affair. However, it has extraordinary emotional impact, shattering the bond of trust between two people. You and your spouse will need to decide whether it is worth working to restore this trust. That should be done with the help of an experienced marriage counselor.

Take Your Financial Pulse

There is nothing wrong, or threatening, for you to have a thorough grasp and understanding of your individual and joint financial holdings. This is especially true for spouses who may have played only a minor role in managing the family's finances up until now. Whatever else happens to your marriage from now on, use this crisis as an opportunity to take a more active role in money management.

Start Palliative Measures and Launch Revenue Rehabilitation

This lifeline is a rarity in a book that focuses on the financial ramifications of crises, in that I'd urge you to take no steps beyond taking your financial pulse. One of the first things a matrimonial attorney would advise is to begin surreptitiously setting aside funds of your own, keeping it from becoming *communal property*, which later may be divided equally. This may be savvy advice for those who are definitely going to divorce. However, I don't think it's appropriate if you haven't yet reached that decision. It's a natural impulse to want to respond to one breach of trust with another. But it's wrong. If you feel compelled to do this, I'd suggest you've already decided to divorce. In that case, don't waste the time and money involved in counseling: Just turn to the Lifeline on getting divorced.

Beth resisted the urge to create a scene by storming up to Adam's hotel room. Instead, she left a phone message for him saying she was flying back home. When Adam returned two days later he found the kids away at Beth's mother. Adam begged for forgiveness. After hours of tears and anger they agreed to start marriage counseling to see if they could salvage their marriage. Despite her mother's urgings, Beth hesitated contacting a matrimonial attorney. She did, however, call up their financial advisor and took notes about all their financial holdings so she knew exactly how much they had and where it was.

Cultivate Antibodies

While you can't go back and undo the damage done to your relationship, you can do the hard therapeutic work necessary to figure out why this happened, and make sure this doesn't happen again. Many marriages have survived a single indiscretion. Few have survived serial adultery.

You're Diagnosed with an Incurable Disease

You'd been worried about the tremor in your hand and the stiffness in your arm for a few months. It was only when you realized you could no longer keep your family from noticing it that you decided to speak with a doctor, who confirmed your fear: you have Parkinson's Disease. Or perhaps the weakness in your leg progressed to the point where you were having trouble walking. That led to a doctor's visit and a subsequent battery of tests revealing that you're suffering from ALS.

The moment 48-year-old Cheryl Green got the news, she knew her whole world would be changing. An exercise fanatic, Cheryl visited her family physician to treat a nagging cough. She thought it was some kind of respiratory infection, at least until the doctor started asking her a number of other questions, making particular note of the pain she'd been feeling in her hip while jogging. A series of tests revealed Cheryl had stage-four lung cancer that had metastasized to her bones. She had smoked for perhaps five years, but that was during and just after college—almost 30 years ago. There was, however, a history of cancer in her family. A high school administrator, married to a college professor, with a 14-year-old son and a 17-year-old daughter, Cheryl knew she'd just been given a death sentence.

Accept the Problem and Own the Solution

Whatever the specific diagnosis and subsequent prognosis, there are few more life-altering experiences than being told you suffer from an incurable disease. Many people never accept their own mortality. Being forced to face it squarely isn't easy, but it's something you must come to grips with if you're going to move forward.

One client of mine who has been diagnosed with an incurable, degenerative disease has told me that he had to grieve for the life he'd thought he would live, but soon he made an unexpected discovery. He realized that he now had the power to replace the life he'd "lost" with a new one, entirely of his own creation. We are all going to die. Yet few of us know when or how. He believes knowing approximately when he'll die, and from what, has actually been a gift, allowing him to live in a way he never could before. His way of owning the solution is to prepare himself and his loved ones and to live every remaining moment to it's fullest.

Another client of mine, dealing with inoperable breast cancer, has said her way of accepting the situation was to stop seeing what cancer had taken from her, and instead, focus on what cancer had given her. A very driven corporate executive who previously had little time for others, she's become a prime force in a number of organizations working toward a cure and providing care for those with few financial resources. Cancer has given her a way to serve others and society, which she never would have otherwise experienced. She's said that her way of owning the solution is to keep becoming a better person.

Unburden Yourself

Obviously, you'll be enlisting the help of a number of medical and care providers. While it's admirable to want to do as much as you can yourself, it's sensible to try to leverage your time and energy. When you have limited resources, it's best to spend them where they provide the most good emotionally, psychologically, and financially. If going to the supermarket or spending two hours in the park with your kids will both leave you drained for the rest of the day, opt for the latter and get some help with the former.

Lean on your existing professionals for help in making changes and arrangements, and don't hesitate to bring new people on board if you need more expertise. For instance, not every financial planner is well versed in the techniques you may need. I'd strongly suggest you enlist the help of a social worker experienced in health care programs in your area. There should be someone like that affiliated with a hospital nearby. Most important of all, get the names of attorneys who specialize in what's called Medicaid planning and Social Security Disability qualification.

Enlist the help of family and friends as well. Ask for what you need, and if you don't get it, ask someone else. Don't waste time worrying about the hurt feelings of those who'd like to make this all about them, rather than you.

You may not want to make knowledge of your condition public immediately. Your employer may not be as supportive as you'd like, or need. If you fear that's the case, speak with your attorney about your legal rights on the job and what you can do to protect them.

This is one of those crises in which drawing on support groups is extremely valuable. No matter how well meaning and supportive your family and friends are, they cannot fully understand what you're feeling and experiencing. In addition to drawing on the group's support, provide some of your own. Sometimes the best way to gain strength is to offer it to others.

Diagnose the Impact

There are a number of factors you'll need to weigh in diagnosing the financial impact of your condition. The place to begin, clearly, is with your medical prognosis. You need to ask your physicians and caregivers to give you a sense of how long you have to live and how your condition will progress. The time frame you're given should be taken as nothing more than a rough estimate. For instance, if you're given a median figure, it means that half the people with the condition actually live longer. If you're given an average, it's nothing more than a mathematical calculation, which is dramatically influenced if a small number either live much longer than the rest, or die much sooner than the rest. The inexactitude goes for suggestions as to how you will progress. What you need to do is get an educated guess, use that as the basis for your plan, and then continue to ask for expert estimates as time passes, so you can tweak your plan to match your progress.

How will your condition affect your ability to work? For the moment, forget about whether you want to, or whether your employer will be supportive. Instead, just focus on your physical ability to continue doing what you normally do to earn a living. If you are still able to work, plot your ongoing ability to work against the estimates you've been give about the progress of your condition. How long will you be able to work full time or part time; at the office or at home?

Next, consider your personal obligations. I don't mean outstanding credit card debt or loan balances—you'll list those when you conduct a financial inventory. I mean moral and ethical obligations; everything from caring for your aging mother to making sure your pets have a good home. Recognizing that you may not be able to do everything, develop two lists: one of the minimum things you feel you need to do—leave your spouse financially solvent—the other of what you'd like to be able to do—make sure your aging father is always taken care of.

Take Your Financial Pulse

Conduct a traditional financial inventory, listing your fixed assets, cash, institutional borrowing potential, unextendable liabilities, extendable liabilities, expected income, and nondeferrable expenses. Your diagnosis doesn't change the numbers themselves. What it does change is your plan. All your previous financial decisions were based on the assumption that you'd live a lifespan similar to the rest of your family, and that you'd continue earning an income until you reached an age when you decided to either retire or scale back your working life. If you were prudent you probably took some measures, like buying life and disability insurance, in case that didn't happen. Well, now you need to start over and factor your new physical status into the equation.

Rather than calculating the gap between your assets and income and your liabilities and expenses, start by looking at how your medical expenses will change. Get some information from your physician and your support groups. Do a thorough study of your medical and disability insurance benefits, with the help of your broker and customer service reps from your insurers. Pay careful attention to gaps and limits to your benefits, both annually and over your lifetime. Add a section to your crisis playbook that lists these gaps and limitations.

Add another section to your playbook titled convertible assets. This consists of assets you can either turn into income streams, borrow against, or sell to boost your cash. Next to each asset, list either its current cash value or a technique for turning it into cash. For example, if your home is worth $250,000 and you have a mortgage balance of $150,000, list $100,000 cash. Go over your personal property closely. Do you have a collection of books, DVDs, or CDs? Write down the names and numbers of local sellers of used books and recordings. Check to see if there's an eBay brokerage business in your area. This is a shop that takes property on consignment and sells it on eBay for you, either for a flat fee or for a percentage of the selling price. Sure, you might be able to post a sale of your set of Cuisinart cookware yourself. But is that how you want to spend your time and energy right now?

Finally, list the life insurance benefits your survivor will receive upon your death. Go back and eliminate the cash value of any life policies from your earlier listings. Take the viatical value of your life policy and list it in parenthesis next to the benefit value.

With all this information in place, compare the cash value of all your assets and income to your expenses, and then to the personal obligations you listed earlier. Do you have enough money and insurance benefits to pay your current and future bills for the rest of your life? Do you have enough money left over to meet the obligations you need to cover? Finally, do you have enough money remaining to meet the obligations you'd like to cover? If the answer to all of these questions is yes, you can approach your condition from the emotional, psychological, and spiritual perspectives. But if the answer to any of these is no, then you'll need to take some financial actions.

Start Palliative Measures

There are two general ways you can look to trim expenses in your situation. First, you can reduce what you spend. Some trimming will be relatively painless, since most of us spend more than we really need to. However, I wouldn't cut back without some serious thought and deliberation. How do you want to spend the time you have left? What do you want your remaining life to be like? My suggestion would be to be liberal about cutting your spending on *things,* but very conservative about cutting spending on *experiences.* For example, you might want to cut back your spending on clothing and get rid of your expensive vehicle, but not cut back on going out to dinner or traveling. One client of mine in this situation put it this way: He said he wanted to keep having experiences that merited being documented by photographs, but he didn't want to buy a camera and pay for the prints. If someone else wanted to take pictures and foot the bill, that was something else. He said it was the experience that was the most valuable.

Speaking of having someone else foot the bill, that's the second way you can trim expenses. Medicaid is a federal program designed to help those in financial need pay for health care costs. By understanding how the system calculates eligibility, individuals can artificially impoverish themselves so the government will pick up the costs. This is called Medicaid planning. It's a controversial process. Some feel it's wrong to take advantage of the system in this way. Others feel that what matters is living up to the letter, not the spirit, of the law, and that until the government provides a better health care system for its citizens, you've every right to get as much as you can from it. My feeling has always been that it's my responsibility as an advisor to tell my clients and readers about every tool that's available to them—as long as it's legal. I leave the moral and ethical judgments up to them, and you.

Do not. I repeat, do not, tell your creditors about your prognosis. Rather than leading them to ease up, the news will lead them to press you for full repayment now. Tell them you've got a temporary disability and ask for one or two months of help. If you've no dependents or heirs, feel free to die in debt. Believe me, as a former banker and venture capitalist, I can tell you they've built enough profit into their lending to cover your dying in debt.

Launch Revenue Rehabilitation

I would not suggest you look to increase your earned income, even if you believe you'll be able to continue to work for some time. Unless your job truly is the thing you love most in the world, I wouldn't suggest you dedicate more time to it right now. And that's what is required if you want to get another job or a raise at your current job. Instead, I'd look for outside sources of income and to increase your unearned income.

There's nothing wrong with asking your spouse and children to help pick up the slack by bringing in more income. The fact is, they will be responsible for themselves to a greater degree once you are dead. Frankly, this gives them a head start on a road they're likely to travel eventually. If you're expecting any inheritance from your parents or other relatives, have a talk with them now. If it will be too difficult for them, either emotionally or financially, to provide you with that inheritance now, ask them to instead assume some of your future obligations. For example, if your father has set aside money for you in his estate, ask him to change his will so those funds go directly to your daughter's college fund, taking the place of funds you now won't be able to provide. If you were to receive one-third interest in the family business, along with your two siblings, ask them to agree to provide the cash value of your one third to your spouse instead.

Speak with an attorney who specializes in Social Security Disability. She will be able to help you apply for and obtain all the federal and state government benefits for which you could possibly qualify.

Sit down with a savvy financial planner and ask her to go over your savings and investments with an eye toward turning them into income and cash. Be direct and honest about your prognosis. There's no point in holding onto growth stocks when your time frame is only five years. It's okay to delay selling if it's a question of weeks, but don't delay for two months or more simply to sell at a better time. Unless there's a historic bump, it won't make enough of a difference.

Designate one friend or family member to be in charge of selling off your personal property now. Pass along the info you gathered about resellers or eBay brokers. Give this assignment to someone with a desire to help that outweighs her financial ability. They'll do a great job for you.

Once all these efforts are underway, you need to do some prioritizing. If you have dependents, my advice is that your first priority should be having enough money to pay your bills. Second, you should do whatever you can to ensure your dependents won't be in debt. Third, you should focus on fulfilling any obligations you feel are needs, say paying for your aging parent's nursing home bills. Fourth, you should look to maximize the enjoyment you get from life in the time your have remaining. Then, and only then, would I look to set aside funds for obligations you'd like to fulfill, such as providing an inheritance for your children. My heartfelt suggestion would be that you instead look to incorporate your children into that fourth category. Do things for them and with them now: Take them with you on that trip you've always wanted to take. After all, I'm the guy who wrote the international best seller *Die Broke*. I think that when we die, our last check should be written to the undertaker—and it should bounce.

Cheryl Green and her husband spent more than a few days crying and praying. But they soon decided they had a limited amount of time and they'd rather spend it doing things that would make them all feel better. Her doctors believed she had about a year. Cheryl explained to the principal and superintendent that she'd be leaving at the end of the school year. Her husband arranged to take a sabbatical from the university. Using their knowledge of education, the Greens arranged it so that their children could accompany them on an extended exchange in Europe, something Cheryl had always wanted to do. The Greens spent most of Cheryl's retirement savings, which they'd cash in. Upon their return, both their children picked up their lives, as did Cheryl's husband. Cheryl spent her last few months in a hospice not far from her home.

Cultivate Antibodies

You're not going to go through this experience twice. At least not as far as we know. The antibodies you're looking to cultivate are actually in the bodies of your family and friends. Through your actions, you can be an example for them about how to live a life that really matters. Not that they will be facing this same crisis in their lives—God forbid. But the way you face your situation will be an unforgettable lesson for them, not about how to die, but about how to live.

You've Lost Your Major Client or Customer

Over breakfast one Monday, a headline in the morning paper catches your eye. A spokesperson for your major customer has announced the company is closing all its local operations completely and immediately. Or maybe you're sitting at your desk downloading e-mail when a message comes from your biggest client titled "urgent." You instantly open it and find she has decided to stop using you and instead has hired someone else, or will be doing her purchasing elsewhere.

Miranda Stanhope's cleaning business had grown significantly in the seven years it had been operating. It began with Miranda and one friend cleaning homes and apartments. Their reliability set them apart from most of the other cleaning businesses in their small city, and their client base grew. Eventually, Miranda expanded to take on business customers as well. In her fourth year of operations she landed the contract to clean the offices of the major employer in town: a company that manufactured a major subassembly for vending machines. This soon became her major client, representing 20 percent of her revenue. That's why it was so distressing when she heard the company was hiring another firm.

Accept the Problem and Own the Solution

In this money mishap, acceptance doesn't mean surrender, it means submission. Let me explain. Depending on why you've lost your major client or customer, it may be possible to rehabilitate your relationship and keep its business. To do so, however, you'll need to accept the rationale for the client or customer shifting its business, whether it's valid or not, and submissively ask it to reconsider.

Part of owning the solution is to take responsibility for what has happened, whether or not you're actually responsible. Another part is to aggressively look for new clients or customers to take the place of the recently departed. You might want to look to a larger blend of smaller clients. And the final element of the solution is to examine your business and, if necessary, restructure it to meet what might be a long-term decrease in revenue. This is a great time to review your business plan, examining every aspect.

Unburden Yourself

This is one situation where you may need to bear the entire burden yourself. Even if the problem with your customer was, for example, that your salesperson insulted her, you will need to be the one who apologizes and tries to come up with new revenue. It might be that your suppliers' price increases were responsible for your having to up your fees, leading a major client to bolt. You can't look to the suppliers for help. Long term you may need to terminate the salesperson or seek out cheaper suppliers. But for now it's all on your shoulders.

The only exception might be enlisting others to help in your intelligence gathering. Let's say a client announces he's leaving, but doesn't give you a reason. You could have a mutual acquaintance, perhaps another professional, subtly probe for information. An accountant who's fired by a client could ask his stockbroker friend who shared the same client to simply say that he "was surprised to hear" of the change. That could elicit information the client might be too embarrassed to pass along directly.

Diagnose the Impact

Losing a revenue stream like this is similar to when an employee is terminated. The only way to fully diagnose the impact is to do a thorough calculation of your revenue and expenses and determine how much time you have to find replacement revenue. Ask your accountant to do a pro forma profit and loss statement and cash flow analysis.

Start by preparing a list of all your monthly business expenses, including your own salary. Project out to the end of the next fiscal quarter, and prorate quarterly expenses, such as taxes and insurance over the months until they are due. Don't look for cuts, just an accurate assessment of what the business normally spends. Include your monthly debt service. Make sure to account for the loss of your customer or client, which may actually lower some of these numbers.

Next, list all your accounts receivable, noting how much is due, and just as importantly, when it's due. Estimate your regular monthly revenue, subtracting the amount you received from the now departed client or customer.

Use these two lists to project how long you can potentially continue to meet your current monthly expenses with your now reduced revenue stream. This is the length of time you have to rehabilitate the customer, find new revenue, cut costs, or restructure your business. It's your window of opportunity.

Take Your Financial Pulse

Just because your business can cover its current expenses, doesn't mean it's healthy. As long as an individual or family can break even, they're okay, since their goal is to provide food, clothing, and shelter for themselves and their dependents. Any extra is a bonus. A business, by contrast, exists to make money. If all it's doing is breaking even, it's actually beginning a downward spiral because costs invariably increase, while revenues may not. The loss of your client or customer should be proof enough of that truism.

Ask your accountant for an up-to-date profit and loss statement and balance sheet. Compare the current assets to current liabilities, as listed on your profit and loss statement. This is called your *current ratio*. A healthy business will have twice as many current assets as current liabilities; a ratio of 2:1. This allows the business to respond to any problems or opportunities that develop. Of course, if yours is a very stable business and this recent loss of a client or customer is truly an aberration, you might be able to get by with a current ratio of 1.5:1 instead. Alternatively, if you're in a very erratic industry, a 3:1 ratio might be healthier.

The idea behind the exercise is to make sure that this is a business actually worth saving. I've always been amazed at the number of entrepreneurs who never closely examine their business finances.

They run their operations like an extension of their personal life. If they can pay their bills, they think they're doing okay. I've had dozens of entrepreneurs come to me for advice who were shocked to discover they weren't even breaking even, despite having stayed in business for years.

The loss of this client or customer is a golden opportunity to reexamine your business. I suggest you ask yourself, "If I had a choice, would I go into this business again?" Well, you do have a choice now. If the answer is no, dissolve or sell the business and either find a job or start a different business. If the answer is yes, pull up your sleeves and get to work rescuing it.

Start Palliative Measures

Go back to the list of monthly expenses you prepared earlier. Examine the items and highlight any optional expenses that could easily be cut, such as equipment replacement or luxury items. Now isn't the time to set up a wireless network throughout your office just to keep up with the technology, or to continue to provide free snacks for all your employees.

Don't automatically highlight publicity and advertising costs as potential cost savings. Unless you're truly in dire straights, this may actually be the time to boost rather than trim your marketing efforts. Put off any changes to this part of your budget until after you've had a chance to explore opportunities for revenue rehabilitation.

Be careful when it comes to trimming payroll costs as well. It may seem counterintuitive, but it's better to terminate one employee than to cut the salaries of a number of employees. Trim the salary of six staffers and you'll have six people looking to leave. Fire one staffer instead and you'll have five grateful employees, at least for a little while. Rather than cutting salary, see if you can cut back on benefit costs. Don't drop an important benefit entirely, unless you can't help it. For example, instead of dropping health coverage, see if you can save money by shifting to a plan with larger co-payments or higher deductibles. Explore HMOs and Health Savings Accounts as potential cost-saving options. Present it as asking your employees to become partners in saving the business.

Contact your vendors and suppliers. Tell each what has happened and ask for temporary price rollbacks, better terms, or both. Indicate, subtly if possible but directly if need be, that what just happened to you could soon happen to them if there's no change. Do the same with your professionals.

Speak with your creditors and landlord. Explain you're working on repairing the damage and don't anticipate any long-term difficulty, but you could use any help they're able to provide in the short term. A month or two of interest-only payments, or the promise of two free months rent now to be made up for in six months time, could be a big help.

Launch Revenue Rehabilitation

During your window of opportunity, you need to purse a two-pronged approach to revenue rehabilitation. You need to try to get your client or customer back. Simultaneously, you need to expand your marketing and sales efforts to find sources of revenue that could compensate for what you've lost.

Find out why your client or customer has left. If it is going out of business, or it no longer needs your service, obviously there's nothing you can do to get it back. In those cases, just focus on finding new revenue.

It's possible that the client or customer left because of something you did or failed to do. Maybe the company was angered by something that occurred or it felt you made a costly error. In those cases, you need to become a supplicant. Forget about whether their assessment is right. What matters is perception, not reality. Personally express your sorrow for what has happened, apologize, and ask for the opportunity to make up for what has happened. Offer a discount as a way to demonstrate your gratitude for pointing out this problem and helping you repair it. Take over the account yourself, if someone else had been servicing it.

Maybe the client or customer left because a competitor enticed it away by offering more for the same money, or the same for less money. In that case, you need to examine the economics of the relationship. If you can match this new arrangement and at least break even, then offer to meet your competitor's price. Explain your change of heart by saying that you were able to find a new cost savings. Getting the revenue stream back in place, even if it's just at a break-even level, will give you time to cultivate new customers or clients.

When you first started this business you pulled out all the marketing stops. Desperate to attract customers, you tried everything and anything until you'd built up a solid revenue stream. You need to recapture that same sense of urgency you felt in the early days. But now, you can back that enthusiastic desperation with a far better knowledge of what works. Now is the time to increase, not decrease, your marketing expenditures. To pay for these expanded efforts, consider investing more of your own money into the business, or taking on friendly investors, like family members.

When Miranda Stanhope learned the client who represented 20 percent of the revenues for her cleaning business had hired someone else, she was in shock. But with her business's future in the balance, she knew she had to take action. She did a financial analysis that told her she had about three months to address the issue, and that her business was indeed healthy—as long as she found a replacement for that lost revenue. Miranda contacted the operations manager who had originally hired her firm and learned the reason they lost the contract was that a franchise operation from out of town had underbid her. Miranda knew this account gave her the prestige she needed to land other commercial business, so she set out to win it back. She met the franchises' low bid, even though it meant she'd only break even on the account, and won back the contract. At the same time, she launched a new campaign to land more commercial accounts. Nine months after losing the contract she'd regained it and landed an additional three new commercial accounts, responsible for more revenue than the company who'd temporarily dumped her.

Cultivate Antibodies

Take a highly personal role in your redoubled marketing efforts. Don't rely on others to sell your services or products. Get back on the road or on the phone. Having been in business for awhile, you've probably delegated some of the client or customer contact to subordinates. Now is the time to reassert your being the face of the business. Touch base with every existing customer. Personally ask if they're satisfied with your products and services. Go on prospecting calls with your salespeople. Attend trade shows and fairs yourself.

This hands-on effort is very important. No one can sell you better than you. It can also help forestall your losing another client or customer down the road. It's possible that over the years you've lost some of your sense of how the business is doing. Don't feel bad—it's

Apologizing to a Client or Customer

The strategy and tactics you employ for apologizing to a client or customer depends on whether the client perceives the fault was with you, or with someone who works for you. If you're thought to be at fault, be contrite, honest, and apologetic, but move on to a solution to the situation as quickly as possible. If your staff is to blame, do whatever you can, within reason, to show it was an individual's error, not something for which you or the company should be blamed. Accept responsibility, however. It's okay to have these kind of dialogs over the telephone, since that might make the customer feel less uncomfortable. Words cost you nothing other than pride. The more effusive you are in your verbal apologies the less costly this might be. Offer to make reasonable material amends or alterations if an apology won't suffice.

natural and common in most companies for the owner to lose touch as the business ages and grows. However, this may be why you were surprised by the loss of the important client or customer. There were almost certainly signs of trouble that you just didn't pick up.

Get back into more frequent contact with your clients or customers. This won't guarantee you'll never lose one again. But it should guarantee it won't come as a surprise.

Your Business Lease Isn't Renewed

After 10 years in the same location, renewing your lease had become a routine process, involving a short and friendly negotiation with your landlord that resulted in an acceptable rent increase. That's why you were shocked when your landlord telephones nine months before your lease was up for renewal to let you know you have to find a new location. He says he has agreed to sell the building to a company who wants your office space for its own operations.

Jason Betz had been running a successful hobby shop business from a strip mall location for more than 10 years. He had built up a diverse and loyal customer base by catering to his customer's unique interests. As a result, his regulars stopped by weekly, often just to browse or chat. He'd never had a problem with his landlord before, and had been prepared to negotiate an affordable rent increase when his lease was due for renewal again in late October. Jason was stunned when the landlord stopped by in late February to tell him he'd have to move in the fall. The anchor tenant, an upscale market chain, decided it needed more space and threatened to leave unless it could take over the adjacent two storefronts, one of which was Jason's.

Accept the Problem and Own the Solution

If your landlord was simply looking for a rent increase he would have asked you for one, or solicited another possible tenant and used it as leverage to negotiate. He's not renewing your lease because he's receiving something from this future tenant that you can't possibly provide. That's why you need to accept the inevitability of your business needing to move and instead focus on owning the solution. The answer isn't simply finding another location. You need to reexamine the entire issue of your business's location.

Unburden Yourself

Although you're an expert on your own business, this may be a situation where some outside expertise could come in handy. Your experience is with operating your business in its current type of location, let's say a suburban strip mall. You're probably not familiar with either the economics of say, a location with less traffic that relies on customers making a definite trip to your destination, or the potential of Internet or mail-order sales. Consider hiring a business consultant with real estate experience to help you analyze your options. Ask contacts at your trade association for recommendations of consultants with experience in your industry. Speak with your accountant, attorney, and banker and ask for suggestions of consultants with knowledge of your local market.

Diagnose the Impact

How important was your location to your business? Did you rely on foot or vehicle traffic for most of your customers? Or did most of your customers make a special trip to your location? If the latter is the case, you may not need as visible or expensive a location. While you might have needed traffic in the early days of your business, now that you're established it may not be as important. Does it make sense to expand your virtual location? Could Internet sales offer an opportunity to make up for a location with less traffic?

Have you been paying market rate for your location? If not, can you afford what a similar location will cost? If you have been paying market rate, are there other locations available for the same price? If you'd need to spend more for a similar location, would the additional rent expense make your business less viable?

While traumatic and disruptive, a shift in location could provide the opportunity for you to expand your business or shift to a potentially more profitable business model.

Take Your Financial Pulse

Do a thorough analysis of your current finances, paying particular attention to any expenses you can defer until after your move. Once you have an idea of what your new rent costs will be, rerun all your numbers and see if there are any areas you'll need to adjust. If you're shifting your business model, take the time to draft new business and marketing plans now, before the move, so you have schedules and checklists.

Start Palliative Measures

Your palliative measures should first focus on getting as much time as you possibly can from your current landlord. Six months is the minimum you should accept; a year would be ideal.

Once you know how long you still have in your current location, begin proactively contacting your lenders, suppliers, and vendors to let them know you'll be changing locations. Present it as a positive development. Say the new location will increase your profitability in the long term, but let them know you may need some forbearance during the transition period.

Next, launch an aggressive publicity campaign letting your current customers know about the upcoming move. Explain that it's designed to improve the great service they've already come to expect from you. Point out new services you'll be offering in the future location. Explain the advantages—to them—of the new site. Prepare maps that clearly show the new site and hand them out to customers. Publicize the move so extensively that no one, not even a casual customer, will be surprised by it.

Launch Revenue Rehabilitation

To boost your revenue upon reopening, you'll need to make it more than just another day. Turn it into a special event. That means more than just balloons and streamers. Provide white-glove service tailored to the needs of your customers or clients. Offer refreshments, small gifts, or a voucher for a free tank of gas. Show personalized attention to everyone who walks in the door. Mail out coupons that are redeemable on site. Send e-mails provided special discount codes for online purchases. Have unadvertised in-store specials to make the visit worthwhile. Offer special discounts or free shipping to every client who uses the new Web site or places a phone or fax order. And continue the promotions for at least a week; a month if you can afford it. The way to rehabilitate your revenue is to ensure every existing customer or client feels compelled to show up at the new location in the first week or month, and having done so, feels it was worth the effort.

Knowing he'd need to uproot his hobby shop business just prior to the Christmas season, Jason Betz seriously considered closing for good. He spoke with an old friend from his industry association about his options, and then paid his accountant to do a thorough analysis of the dollars and cents. Jason thought of becoming a completely mail-order/Internet business, but after some investigation realized he'd be competing against much larger businesses and wouldn't be able to offer what had become his strong suit: personalized customer service. Instead, Jason decided to become a destination merchant. Very few of his customers were serendipitous walk-ins. Most made a special trip to his shop. That meant he might be able to be just

Commercial Lease Hazards

It may have been some time since you last signed a commercial lease, so here are some things to watch out for. First, make sure the lease has renewal options that stretch out for as long as your loans. If you are incorporated, the lease should be signed by the corporation, not you. This will insulate you from personal liability. Don't take the landlord's word for anything. The only binding promises are those expressly spelled out in the lease agreement. Make sure the square footage calculations actually represent "carpetable" space. Some landlords try to pass along costs for the space under or even outside the walls. Pay close attention to any pass-along costs for lobby or common areas, air conditioning, heating, taxes, and insurance. It's not unheard of for landlords to try to recoup more than 100 percent of these costs. Try to get a lease that is assignable. That will let you sell the business or pass it on to your heirs. A lease that allows the space to be used for "any legal purpose" gives you the flexibility to change your business if need be. Any rights the landlord has to cancel must be specifically spelled out, and compensation should be provided. Increases and, as you now know, renewals, also need to be clearly outlined in the document. Finally, have the document examined by an attorney before you sign it.

as successful with a less expensive, more isolated location. After six weeks of searching with a real estate broker, Jason found a small former warehouse facility in an industrial area. He got the landlord to pick up the cost of renovation. Jason had a general contractor draw up interior plans that would turn the space into as much a clubhouse as a retail shop, fitting what he thought would most meet his customers' wants and needs. As soon as the plans were sketched out, Jason began getting feedback from his customers. He expanded what had been a very institutional marketing campaign to promote this reopening. By the time the shift took place, his customers were actually excited. The extensive opening-week promotions helped him have as good a Christmas as he'd ever had.

Cultivate Antibodies

The only way to guarantee this could never happen to you again is to own, rather than rent your location. If you have the financial resources to consider a purchase, you should. Barring that, however, all you can do is get a long-term lease with previously agreed rent escalations, with as long a notice of nonrenewal as you can negotiate.

You Receive a Bad Performance Review

In anticipation of your annual performance review at work, you've prepared a polished pitch for a salary increase, based on what you perceive to have been the stellar job you've done in boosting the company's bottom line. But you never get a chance to deliver your spiel. Rather than being complemented on your work, your superior outlines a series of ways in which your performance hasn't measured up to what she expected. You feel endangered rather than emboldened.

Terry Dante had always dreamed of a career in publishing. She was overjoyed when, fresh out of college, she landed a job as an editorial assistant for a well-known publishing company. After two years on the job, she felt as if she was well on her way. Then she was promoted to be the assistant to a very successful but mercurial senior editor. After six months, she received the first negative review of her career. Although she didn't think she had nothing to learn, Terry felt most of the criticism was personal, rather than professional. She was stunned and stung by the critique and said little during or afterward. Later that day, Terry spoke with her former superior, who had shifted to another company. Her mentor confided that regardless of what Terry did from now on, her days with her new boss were numbered.

Accept the Problem and Own the Solution

No matter what your superior or the company's human resource department says, getting a bad performance review is the equivalent of being put on notice that you'll soon be fired. It doesn't matter what you do from here on. You could become the top performer in your department, sell more than anyone else in the company, or get honored by your industry: you've still been branded, and that can never be removed in this organization.[1] That doesn't mean you shouldn't address the situation; appearing to act on the review's findings will provide you with more time to find a new job. The way you own the solution is to take charge of your work life by finding a new position.

It's essential that you don't defend yourself or contradict the reviewer, regardless of how off base the criticisms might be. Disagreeing and arguing will only make things worse. In addition to whatever else you're being charged with, the reviewer will now add "argumentative," and "doesn't accept criticism well" to the list. Instead, thank her for the criticism. Stress how important this job is to you and how you hold your superior and the company in high regard. Say that you know this a problem for the company that only you have the power to fix, and that you're eager to make things right.

If you've already reflexively defended yourself against the attacks, stop back in to see the attacker. Apologize for your earlier defense and say you were shocked and upset at the time and so acted without thinking. Now that you've had a chance to sort things out you can see that this is actually a great opportunity for you. Explain that you understand it's her perception of your performance that matters. Stress that you're looking at this as a wake-up call to ensure your future with the company.

Unburden Yourself

There's no need to broadcast the bad news, but you do need to share it with your spouse and/or one or two close and savvy friends. Emotional support is important in times of stress, and besides, you'll probably need to hear a few good words about yourself right about now. Friends who are savvy about the workplace will be able to help you figure out ways to show how hard you're trying to turn things around—while you're looking for another job.

If you believe this negative review is the result of discrimination based on your gender, age, race, religion, nationality, sexual orientation, or physical status, it might make sense to speak with an attorney who specializes in employment matters. The attorney will be able to quickly analyze your situation to tell if there's a chance of success-ful legal action. Perhaps more importantly, the lawyer will be able to offer suggestions as to how you can position yourself better to demonstrate an unjust termination, when that happens in the future. Only go down this path if you, *and* someone else whose judg-ment you trust, believe there's definite discrimination. And even then, realize this is better seen as leverage for increasing a severance package than grounds for fighting and winning a legal action.

Diagnose the Impact

How long do you have until your next scheduled review? That's how long you have to find another job. You were given a negative review to begin a paper trail in preparation for your termination. Unless you do something to justify being fired for cause—theft, assault, extended absences, or lateness—you're safe until the next review, when they have a chance to formally say you haven't improved sufficiently.

Take Your Financial Pulse

How much money do you have in your emergency fund? Whatever the answer, it's not enough. Do you have any major expenses com-ing due between now and when you anticipate you'll be terminated? Investigate whether you might be able to defer or trim them. Com-pile a list of all your sources of available funds, including credit cards and family members. Put together a similar list of all your expenses, with contact information for every creditor. The idea is to do as much preparation for a possible termination as you can now, when you're not under immediate duress.

Start Palliative Measures

Do whatever you can to extend the amount of time you could live off your emergency funds. Trim your expenses to the extent you can and bank the savings. Consider making any illiquid assets more readily available. If you have equity in your home, apply for a home equity line of credit now. Pay down your credit card balances and stop using the cards right now. Don't make any large purchases that aren't absolutely necessary.

Simultaneously, renew your vows at work. Prepare a memo that outlines your understanding of the criticisms you received at the review, and then describes exactly what you'll be doing to address each. In the memo, suggest short interim review periods or benchmarks so both you and the company can judge your progress. Present this memo at a formal meeting with your supervisor. While there, reiterate your gratitude and your determination to help the company solve this problem. Don't be surprised if your request for interim reviews is denied; this doesn't fit the script your superior has already prepared. But use the denial as an opportunity to ask your supervisor for personal, informal interim reviews. Such meetings will be tough to refuse and will go a long way to ensure you're safe until the next formal review. They'll also provide you with an early warning system if your boss decides to speed up the process for some reason. Remember, your goal is to delay what's an inevitable termination for as long as possible so you have more time to conduct a job search.

Launch Revenue Rehabilitation

With termination in the near future likely, you need to start looking for another job as actively as possible. Rather than looking for better jobs, look for similar jobs. Expand the criteria of jobs for which you apply. Broaden your networking to include people and industries you previously thought weren't perfect matches. Approach head hunters and employment agencies.

I'd suggest altering your philosophy toward job searching a bit. Make your first goal just getting an interview, regardless of whether you think the job is right for you. And at those interviews, don't focus on whether you want the job. Instead, concentrate on getting an offer. Only then, when you have an offer, should you begin thinking about whether the job is right for you.

You see, many times interviewers fall in love with certain job candidates. A great job candidate is more attractive than even the most skilled and efficient employee. That's because a job candidate is all potential. She has never made a mistake, never let a supervisor down. The interviewer sees a candidate as being able to do everything and anything. Faced with being able to land a potential messiah, sometimes interviewers will increase the salary they're willing to pay, offer to change job titles, maybe even rewrite the job description.

By opening yourself up to a greater range of potential offers, you increase the chances of getting a new job sooner. And remember, that's the goal. You want to land that new job before you lose this one, because someone who is employed is always a more attractive candidate than someone who is unemployed.

With her next review scheduled for six months later, Terry Dante kicked her job search into high gear. She began going to more publishing events after hours to expand her networking chances. She also started answering ads for other editorial assistant positions, rather than holding out for junior editor slots. Terry, who had been planning to move to a more expensive apartment, decided to stick it out in the apartment she shared with two other women. She also canceled a planned vacation to Paris with her college roommate. At the same time, Terry did her best to placate her difficult boss. She asked for interim informal reviews, which soon became nothing more than the editor responding "fine" to memos Terry e-mailed. At an interview for an editorial assistant's position with a small but well-regarded firm that paid the same salary as she was currently earning, Terry hit it off with the publisher who was doing the interviewing. She left the interview with an offer for an immediate assistant's position, and the promise that she'd be first in line for the next junior editor position that came open.

Cultivate Antibodies

It's impossible to ensure you'll never again get a negative performance review. However, you can make sure you'll never have to launch a hurried job search again. How? By being on a constant job search. I call this job fishing, rather than job hunting. You should always have a baited hook in the job water, looking to get bites. And whenever you get an interview, go on it, regardless of your initial feeling, and try to get an offer. Today, the only people not destined to be terminated are the self-employed. The secret is to beat your employer to the punch and leave for another job before you can be fired.

You're Wrongfully Accused of Bad Behavior at Work

Sitting at your desk one afternoon, absorbed in your work, you hear a knock and glance up to see your supervisor standing in your office doorway. She comes in, and without sitting down, tells you she has noticed that you have been coming in late with some regularity. She suggests that in the future you do your best to come in on time, turns, and leaves. Or you get a call to come in to see human resources. When you arrive, the HR person doesn't ask you to sit and instead leans back in his chair. He says he has received a complaint from another employee that you may be guilty of harassment. He says he is in the process of investigating the matter. He adds that he will get back to you and says you can go back to your desk.

Matthew Stein was always an outgoing, emotional manager. He prided himself on creating and leading project teams with the same kind of inspirational style as the coach of an athletic team. His successes led to his being given charge of a team tasked with creating an entirely new communications strategy and package of materials for a major financial services firm. The work was arduous and frustrating, requiring long hours, lots of creativity, and the ability to deal with multiple, sometimes conflicting constituencies. Throughout the project, Matthew sensed the lead graphic artist was somewhat uncomfortable with Matthew's leadership style. There wasn't time to make a change, and the woman's work was excellent, so Matthew decided to just let it go. After three grueling months, the team succeeded. At the celebratory dinner, Matthew was all hugs, kisses, and high fives with everyone, including the graphic artist. It was a week later that he was called in by his superior and told someone had accused him of *inappropriate touching*.

Accept the Problem and Own the Solution

No one ever said work was fair. People are often rewarded for their political skill rather than the quality of their work. Sycophants can rise up the ladder while truth tellers remain stalled. And sometimes you can be wrongfully accused of bad behavior. In these kind of crises, you face a difficult choice. You could deny the accusation and fight to restore your reputation, or you can absorb the criticism, mitigate the impact of the charge, and redouble your efforts to find another job.

I would love to be able to tell you how to wage a successful battle against wrongful charges in the workplace. It would be a thrilling and epic fight, one that might become a real inspiration to others. However, it would also be a pyrrhic victory. I pride myself on offering pragmatic advice and counsel, and in the workplace that means pointing out that discretion is always the better part of valor.[1]

I believe you need to accept that you have been wrongfully accused and, rather than directly fighting against it, you need to mitigate the damage in ways that imply your innocence. The way you take ownership of this solution is to get this matter behind you as quickly as possible and do what you can to move on, both inside and outside the company.

Unburden Yourself

Since you are being wrongfully accused, there's no reason to conceal this situation from family and friends. Tell them what has happened. Explain why it's unjust, and accept their sympathy and support. This will help you deal with not being able to pursue public vindication in the workplace. What matters is that your friends and family know you're innocent.

Diagnose the Impact

The impact of a wrongful accusation on your career is probably negligible. However, the impact of this accusation on your current job is profound. Companies are like small towns. Innuendo, gossip, and rumors spread fast and are indelible. In this workplace, you will forever be branded by the charge. People tend to believe that where there's smoke, there's fire, and that even if you didn't do what you were accused of, you must have done something. No one likes to accept that someone who is totally innocent can be accused—until, of course, it happens to them. The only way you can fully clear your name is to find another job.

Take Your Financial Pulse

Anyone who isn't independently wealthy needs to be financially prepared for a period of unemployment. That means having an emergency fund of enough money to pay anywhere from three to six months of your bills. This shouldn't be kept in a checking account. A savings or investment vehicle that will allow you to have reasonable access to the funds in an emergency is better. If you don't have an emergency fund when you're wrongfully accused, start one. If you do have one, start building it up by cutting back where you can.

If this charge leads to a formal negative review, then your job status will move from endangered to "one foot out the door." In that case, you'll need to cut back and save more, and find another job as soon as possible. It's almost certain that you'll be terminated the next time you're up for review.

Start Palliative Measures

The most important immediate palliative measures you can take are political rather than financial. Once you've recovered from the shock of the initial charge, ask for a one-on-one meeting with your superior.

Remember, you can't directly fight the charge without making yourself seem argumentative and disruptive. Your superior isn't really concerned with truth. He is concerned with making the problem go away. The key, therefore, is for you to solve the problem, and at the same time to deny the accusation without really denying it; to argue the point without starting an argument. That's not as difficult as it sounds.

Let's say you believe the accusation is based on a mistaken perception: A subordinate misunderstood a critique and viewed it as harassment. Apologize to your superior for doing something that created a false perception. Say you will apologize directly to anyone the superior suggests for doing anything that could lead to a wrong perception. Tell your superior this will never happen again. Stress you will be working on your behavior to ensure in the future no one would ever be able to get that same perception. Follow up with a written memo reiterating all your points. By not arguing the point you are, in fact, arguing the point. You are pleading guilty to the lesser charge of not acting in as clear a manner as you should.

Let's say the accusation is based on behavior being taken out of context: perhaps you've been coming in 30 minutes late because you've had to drive your spouse to and from chemotherapy treatments before work, and have been compensating by staying 30 minutes late. Once again, you need to apologize, not for the act itself, but for not making clear the context. Say the behavior was due to personal issues beyond your control. Apologize for not bringing the issue to your superior's attention. Explain that you thought you could handle the matter without it becoming a work issue, but obviously you failed. Finally, say the situation has since resolved itself so it won't be a problem in the future. Don't offer any explanation of the personal matter.

An uncaring, distant superior will hear only the apology and the promise it won't happen again. He'll still put you on the endangered list, but you should be safe until you're up for review. A caring superior will instinctively take the bait and ask about the personal issue. From that point on, the dialog becomes about your problem rather than the accusation. Again, you're not safe, but you've bought yourself enough time to make a proactive move of your own choosing.

Launch Revenue Rehabilitation

Financially, your revenue rehabilitation involves finding another job. In the short term, however, you need to engage in some political rehabilitation. Your overt response to the accusation is to not engage with the specific charge, but to admit to a mistake that allowed your actions to be misperceived. This works great with your superior. To rehabilitate yourself to the wider company, you need to launch a more covert effort.

Confide in one or two workplace peers with whom you're close. Have these conversations outside the workplace, reinforcing the personal aspect of your relationship. Tell them what has happened, explain that you don't think it worthwhile to openly fight the charges, but stress your innocence. Say you hope, if anyone in the office asks about what is going on, they'll support you in any way they can. In effect, what you're doing is launching a subtle public relations campaign. Soon enough, word of what actually happened will spread throughout the company's gossip network. This won't be enough to entirely remove the stain on your reputation, but it will at least get your case on the record. Whispers will stop being about what "you did" and instead be about the conflicting stories.

When Matthew Stein heard he was being accused of inappropriate touching, he immediately figured the source of the charge was the graphic artist didn't like his leadership style. After taking some time to gather his thoughts, Matthew returned to his superior's office for a frank conversation. He apologized to his boss for doing anything that could be misinterpreted. Matthew promised it would never happen again and that he would apologize to everyone on the team. Later that afternoon, Matthew called the team together and issued the same apology. The next day, over lunch with two other project leaders with whom he was close, he explained what had happened and why. Of course, by the end of the week, Matthew's side of the story had spread throughout the company. Matthew also revised his résumé to include this latest triumph and began actively looking for another job. Four months later he had another position.

Cultivate Antibodies

No one is ever immune to false accusations. That said, you can minimize the odds of this happening again by refraining from any behavior that could be misconstrued. How do you do that? By being 100 percent business while you're at work. Don't trade gossip at the coffee pot. Don't go to lunch with a crowd of your peers. Don't go to happy hour after work to blow off steam. Make sure the word *job* is a verb, not a noun, in your vocabulary. It's what you do, not part of who you are. Do your job well. Follow the rules. Keep your nose clean. Be civil to everyone. Bring your lunch and eat at your desk or alone out in the fresh air. Show up on time. And most important of all, constantly be on the look out for your next job.

12

You Can't Make Your Loan Payments

Late one Saturday afternoon you're sitting in the yard relaxing with the family. Suddenly, you hear one of the kids cry out. Your heart stops until you turn and see that both kids are okay. But then your eye catches sight of the dog who is slowly hobbling toward you, holding one of its rear legs up in the air. That evening you have to lay out $3,000 for emergency orthopedic surgery for the dog. Or perhaps the emergency strikes further away. That's what happened to Darren Kelly.

Darren had always been close to his uncle Liam. Liam was a colorful character who'd immigrated to the United States on his own at age 23 after World War II, and had then arranged to bring his younger brother, Darren's father, over as well. Liam never married and lived an adventurous life, working as a chef in restaurants, on cruise liners, and finally on off-shore oil rigs. He made good money and liked to spend it. At 70, he finally retired and bought a small home in the Florida Keys, where he spent his days drinking, fishing, and chasing younger women. Darren tried to see him at least once a year, usually on his own. Darren's wife had decided years ago that it wasn't a good idea for their children to spend too much time with Great Uncle Liam. When Darren got a call from one of Liam's neighbors that his uncle had died of a massive coronary, he was stunned. Part of him thought the man would live forever. That shock turned to anger when he learned that Liam had literally spent his last penny. The hospital wouldn't release Liam's body until the bills had been paid, and the local funeral home wouldn't pick the body up for cremation unless someone paid the bill in advance. Having just maxed out his credit cards on their summer vacation, and having only enough in his checking account to cover the next two months of bills, Darren knew he was facing a financial emergency.

Accept the Problem and Own the Solution

There are times when emergency expenses hit and you've no choice but to throw your budget out the window and deal with the pressing issue. Berating yourself for not having sufficient emergency funds or for having maxed out your credit won't help. Scolding someone else for having contributed to the emergency won't make matters any better. Besides, odds are you and they have more pressing issues to deal with at the moment.

When you're facing not being able to meet all your monthly bills you need to take ownership of the solution. That means prioritizing all your expenses, paying those you must, and deferring those you can. The bills you'll have the most success deferring are the payments on secured loans, such as your mortgage and auto loan. That's because the last thing these lenders want is to take the asset from you. Foreclosure sales never yield anything close to an asset's real value. The lender isn't in the home or car selling business; it's in the lending business. However much initial reluctance they show, they'll be willing to work with you.

Unburden Yourself

Don't hide the situation from your family. They can help you by doing their share to cut expenses and bring in extra money. Besides, money mishaps are a part of life. Letting your children see how important it is to have savings, and how you're taking charge of the problem are excellent lessons for their own lives. Obviously, don't scare them into thinking you're all going to starve or be homeless. But also, don't pretend there's nothing wrong.

Diagnose the Impact

Determine exactly how much the emergency will cost. Make sure to include ancillary costs, such as fuel and lodging if you'll need to travel, or prescriptions and rehabilitation if it's a medical mishap.

Take Your Financial Pulse

Do a complete financial analysis. Draft a list of all your monthly expenses. Look back in your checkbook for any less regular bills, such as insurance and taxes, prorate them monthly, and then add those to your list as well. Go over the list and note those bills that cannot be deferred at all, since they'd result in immediate problems. These might include things like health insurance and commutation costs. Then, go over the list and see which expenses you can reduce, such as food, entertainment, and fuel. Put an asterisk next to these. Finally, go over the list for expenses that can be deferred at least temporarily, such as credit card payments, and mortgage and auto loan payments. Put an X next to these items.

See how the total that you're spending for the emergency compares to the total of those expenses you've marked with an X. If the cost of the emergency is larger than the total of these deferrable bills, look to the expenses items with asterisks for places you can cut back. If the cost of the emergency is less than the total of the deferrable bills, see if you can cover the gap by paying interest only on your secured loans, such as your mortgage and auto loans.

Start Palliative Measures

Now is not the time to spend on any luxuries or on anything you don't really need. Cut back your variable expenses to the extent possible. Then, turn to your secured loan payments. The secret here is to be proactive and to understand your creditors' needs. It's better to offer an explanation of why you won't be making a full payment this month than it is to offer an excuse for why you missed a payment.

As I've noted, secured lenders don't want to take back your home or car. They want you to pay back your loan. More specifically, they want you to pay the interest on your loan. That is how they make money. If you give them a warning in advance, they'll have information they can note on your file, making it easier for them to be lenient.

Call the customer service number for the lender. Wend your way through the automated phone system so you can get to an actual human being, preferably from customer service rather than collections. Ask for the person's name and write it down, along with the date and time of your call. Tell the customer service representative that you've had an unexpected emergency expense. You can go into some detail if you'd like. They won't really care about your explanation, but it could lend credence to the rest of your statements. Say you understand they may need to assess late fees, but that you would appreciate any forbearance they could show. Most often, you'll be able to get more time from the first person with whom you speak. If they say they're unable to let you slide, ask to speak with their superior. Keep pushing the up button in this manner until you find someone with the power to give you additional time. Offer to make an interest-only payment if you must.

Follow up every conversation with a letter, noting the date and time of your call and the name of the person with whom you spoke. Spell out exactly what was discussed and how you plan to proceed. Keep a copy for yourself and send the original to the creditor's customer service department. This will be one other thing for them to add to your file and serves to document that you indeed initiated the conversation.

If you're unable to get enough of a reduction in your monthly bills from negotiating with your secured creditors, begin contacting unsecured creditors, such as your credit cards. Make the same pitch to them, suggesting the interest-only option right away rather than seeing if you can get complete forbearance for a little while. Even telephone and utility companies will try to work out a deal with you, since they don't want to cut off your service unless they absolutely must.

Bear in mind that most lenders won't start to actually bother you until your account is more than one month late. Then, you probably have another two months before they become aggressive about the debt. It's likely that if you make regular partial payments until your finances recover, they won't put your account in for collection.

Launch Revenue Rehabilitation

Do whatever you can to bring in additional funds to help catch up financially. If you can take a second part-time job, do it. Encourage a nonworking spouse to look for a job. See if there are any assets you could quickly sell for a cash infusion. If you're owed money, push to collect it, offering to accept less than the total in return for immediate repayment. If you can borrow from family to help you through the crisis, give it consideration—but only as long as you think your relative will be a more understanding creditor than your banker.

Darren used his debit card to pay for the $400 airfare to get down to the Florida Keys. He was able to stay in his uncle's house, but it cost him $2,000 to clear up the hospital bills and another $800 to the funeral home for collection of the body and immediate cremation. He telephoned a local Realtor to put Liam's house up for sale. Having done what he could to take care of his uncle's affairs in the short term, Darren flew back home to take care of his own new problems. On the flight, Darren crunched some numbers. He calculated that if he could get one month's forbearance from his mortgage lender, and then pay interest only for another two months, he'd be able to weather the crisis. As soon as he got home, he contacted the customer service department at the bank that held his mortgage. He got through to a human being, explained the situation, and suggested his solution. The customer service rep took down the information and asked him to hold while she checked with her supervisor. She got back on the line and told Darren the bank would be willing to

The Rolling Emergency Fund

I think the best financial plan for potential disasters is to set up what I call a *rolling emergency fund*. Start by determining the total of your monthly bills. Make sure to include a monthly amount for debt service on your outstanding credit card balances as well as a monthly amount for quarterly or other periodic bills, such as taxes and insurance. Open a money market account with check-writing privileges and build up the balance until you have enough to cover one month's bills. Then, continue saving until you have a second month's worth of expenses set aside. Transfer these funds into a certificate of deposit with 30 days maturity. Arrange for automatic rollover whenever it comes due. Next, build up more savings in the money market. When you've set aside enough for another month's worth of expenses, transfer those funds to another certificate of deposit, this time with a maturity of 60 days. Once again, set it up for automatic roll over when due. Follow the same pattern until you've enough to buy a third certificate deposit in the amount of your monthly bills. This time, purchase one with a 90 day maturity. At that point you'll have enough months to cover your bills for four months, and you'll have the money earning the maximum interest and not coming due until you'll need it. Once established, do your best not to touch this rolling emergency fund unless you experience an actual financial emergency.

let him make interest-only payments for three months. Darren did a quick calculation, then agreed. He followed up with a letter that afternoon.

Cultivate Antibodies

There will be times in life when you face unplanned financial emergencies—that's the truth underlying this entire book. You can't avoid them, you can only mitigate their impact. The best way to do that is to make sure you're prudently protected with insurance, and you've an emergency fund that will cover your bills for anywhere from three to six months. I know that's not an easy thing to accomplish. Insurance is expensive, and saving is difficult. However, until you have these kind of safety nets in place you'll always be vulnerable to money mishaps.

Your Parent Dies

You are wakened in the middle of the night by the telephone. You pick it up and through the sobs you can make out that it's your mother calling. You're stunned when she blurts out that your father has died. Or you return home from work to find a message on your answering machine from the director of your mother's nursing home, asking you to call as soon as possible. From the tone of her voice, you can tell she's calling to let you know your mother has finally died.

Neil Greenblatt received the call late on a Thursday afternoon. It was from a friend and neighbor of his 83-year-old mother. Neil's mother had died from a sudden stroke. Neil's father had died 15 years earlier, and his mother had been living alone in a retirement community ever since. Neil hung up the phone, took a deep breath, and told his wife, who had been sitting on the edge of the bed watching while Neil was on the phone. After hugging him and promising to "hold down the fort," she suggested he get down to his mother's as soon as he could. Neil went downstairs to his computer and booked a flight for the next afternoon.

Accept the Problem and Own the Solution

The death of a parent is something almost everyone will have to face at least twice. Add the inevitable deaths of stepparents, in-laws, and favorite aunts or uncles, and it's obvious this is the most common grieving experience. That said, each situation is unique. Some parents die young and leave spouses behind. Others die after prolonged illnesses or long declines, years later than their spouses.

Acceptance usually comes easier the older the parent is when he or she dies. If he or she was ill or enfeebled, death is often seen as a relief rather than a trauma. In addition, an extended lifetime gives ample opportunity for love to be expressed in words and deeds. There's also lots of time for issues to be resolved, for slights and disagreements to be forgiven, if not forgotten. In these situations, when there's usually no surviving spouse, owning the solution is mostly a financial process for grieving children.

Acceptance can be much more difficult if the parent dies at a young age. First, there's the shock. While intellectually we assume our parents will predecease us, we only begin to emotionally and psychologically prepare for that to happen after we've begun to sense our own mortality and see our parents begin to decline. The death of a young parent is a rude and premature introduction to the impermanence of life. Then there's the specter of the surviving spouse. She isn't just a figure of sympathy. Unspoken but certainly felt is the child's fear that the surviving spouse could now become an emotional or financial burden. That perfectly natural fear invariably leads to guilt feelings. Finally, there's the possibility, maybe even likelihood, that there were unresolved issues between a parent that dies unexpectedly young and children. Relationships between parents and children aren't static. They ebb and flow continuously over the years. Mark Twain once said, "When I was a boy of 14, my father was so ignorant I could hardly stand to have the old man around. But when I got to be 21, I was astonished at how much the old man had learned in seven years."[1] An early death means there was less time to expose, work out, and overcome the inevitable petty and major issues that arise between parents and children. That's why owning the solution to the problem of an early parental death, particularly when there's a surviving spouse, is more emotional than financial.

Unburden Yourself

You needn't face your grief, nor any financial responsibility brought on by your parent's death, alone. Now is the time to lean on friends and family members. You may also find it helpful to involve your parent's friends as well. Besides providing material and physical assistance, their speaking of the bonds they shared with your parent could be very consoling.

If your other parent is alive, it's essential you let him or her choose how much of the financial, legal, and organizational burden to assume. Older people need to retain control over their lives as much as possible. This is particularly true when something has happened that makes them feel helpless and out of control. Although this was your parent who died, it was their spouse. They are the principal mourner. They are the primary beneficiary. And they should be the primary decision maker, whether or not they have been named beneficiary.

Your deceased parent can no longer be affected by what happens. Your living parent will be profoundly affected. While ceremonies and activities will center on the deceased, remember they are, or at least should be, designed to help the living. If your mother wants to have a bagpiper play at your father's funeral, even though you know the old guy loathed bagpipe music, support her choice. I don't think he'll mind. In fact, he'll probably appreciate that you're doing what you can to comfort his spouse. Offer to help your surviving parent. Provide counsel and suggestions, and take on tasks if you're asked. But don't usurp your surviving parent.

If you've no surviving parents you still don't need to assume the entire financial, legal, and organizational burden. Ironically, if your deceased parent was well organized, you can let her assume some of the burden by following her written and spoken wishes. If there's a will, hire an attorney to file it with the court. You don't need to use the same lawyer who drafted the will, though that's often done for simplicity's sake. Filing a will for probate is a simple procedure, and the fee should be based on what's common for the locality, not on the size of the estate. Once the will is filed, you'll receive testamentary letters naming the executor in the will; that's probably you. Leave as much of the decision making as you can to your deceased parent. I'm not suggesting channeling her spirit, though if that works for you that's fine. I'm only saying you should follow the will to the letter and dispose of assets in the manner stipulated.

If your parent left no instructions, the executor has the right to dispose of assets as he sees fit. However, if there are other parties involved, such as your parent's siblings, and your brothers and sisters, I'd suggest bringing everyone together and trying to work things out internally. If that's not possible, you shouldn't assume the role of Solomon. Instead, bring in an attorney, preferably your parent's rather than your own, to help resolve matters.

Diagnose the Impact

The emotional impact of the death of a parent is always profound. If it comes unexpectedly when your parent is young, and you've had a good relationship with your mom or dad, it can result in a deep sense of insecurity. Even though you may have been a fully emancipated adult for years, parents provide a certain emotional ballast to our lives. They are the safety net underlying our world; the people we feel will be there for us no matter what happens. When parents die, you feel alone in a way you never have before. If the death of a parent comes when the parent is older, it's an introspective rather than unsettling experience. It leads to reflection about the entire arc of her life, and indirectly about the arc of your own life. It often feels more like a moment of observation and commemoration, rather than of mourning.

The financial impact of your parent's death depends on the extent and disposition of the estate. If your parent is survived by a spouse, the estate will simply pass to her. If your parent's spouse has already died and the assets in the estate are worth less than its liabilities, debts will be paid and the estate will be dissolved. If the assets are worth more than its liabilities beneficiaries are due their inheritance.

It's important to note that any debts accrued by your deceased parent, which were not held jointly with anyone else, are the responsibility of the estate, not the surviving spouse. That means that if your mother had her own credit cards and died owing $3,000, it is her estate, not you or your father, who is responsible. But since the estate's assets have now passed on to someone else who isn't responsible for the debt, the creditor actually can only claim partial rights. The upshot of all this is that credit card companies in this situation will simply write off the money they're owed. That doesn't mean they won't try to collect it from survivors. However, if you just keep responding that the card holder is deceased, the credit card company will eventually give up.

Take the Estate's Financial Pulse

Depending on the applicable state law, unless the will states differently, a surviving spouse might automatically have all assets automatically pass to her, or the spouse might get one half and any children the other half. If you believe your surviving parent may have financial difficulties, turn to Lifeline #18: Your Parents Need Financial Help.

Disposition of the estate falls to the executor. Assuming it's you, your first step is to take the estate's financial pulse. Get yourself a fresh legal pad, a box of pencils, and a pencil sharpener; you're going to be compiling lots of lists in the next few weeks.

The first order of business is to take care of your parent's remains. Did she have funeral plans either preplanned or prepaid? If plans have already been made, and there's enough money to cover the cost, follow them to the letter. If the funeral has been prepaid, simply contact the funeral director and hand over control. If your parent didn't make any plans, you'll have to take charge. A couple of things to consider: Funeral expenses are not an indication of how much someone is loved; and most of the exorbitant expenses surrounding funerals revolve around preservation and presentation of the corpse. The least costly processes are immediate cremation or direct burial. Personally, I feel either of these, followed at a later date by a memorial service, is a wonderful tribute to a beloved parent. As the executor, the decision is yours. Put the interests of the estate above those of individual survivors. That being said, try to be diplomatic and not cause a family rift if you can help it. When you speak with the funeral director make sure to order twice as many death certificates as you initially believe you'll need.

If your parent had a safe deposit box and you or someone else is a signatory to it, empty it as soon as possible. I'm not suggesting there are ill gotten gains inside. It's just that boxes are sealed upon the death of an owner, and there may be important papers and documents inside. For example, it's not uncommon for people to put the deeds to cemetery plots and copies of their will inside safe deposit boxes. There may also be valuable jewelry that your parent didn't want to insure.

Go through your parent's home with a fine-tooth comb looking for important papers, as well as any valuables that might have been secreted away. Everyone has a story about a relative who had diamond earrings sewn into the hem of drapes, or who stored $30,000 in cash inside their old toolbox. Hopefully, you'll at least find some files of important papers.

Take out your legal pad and head one page "assets." Start listing every asset you can think of. Next to each asset, list its value (if obvious), location, and if there's anyone who your parent said should receive it. When you list financial holdings, make sure to include account numbers and the addresses and telephone numbers of the financial institutions. If any of these accounts are jointly held, the survivor is now the owner, not the estate. Contact any such individuals and give them whatever paperwork and checks you've found. Similarly, if any of these are tax-deferred retirement accounts, contact the beneficiaries and give them the paperwork, along with a death certificate. If they deposit the funds into their own retirement accounts, they won't need to pay taxes on the money.

Turn to a fresh page on the legal pad and head it "liabilities." List every debt or bill you can think of. Go through your parent's checkbook to see what checks they've been writing regularly. Look for any unpaid bills and open any mail that has accumulated. Fill out a forwarding form at the local post office so all subsequent mail will be sent to your home address. If your parent had an e-mail account, go online and arrange for all mail to be forwarded to your own account.

Look for evidence of any life insurance policies. If you discover a policy, contact the agent, broker, or insurer. Explain that the policy holder has died and you are the executor, and ask to be led through the filing procedure. Contact every financial institution holding assets of your parent. Explain what has happened and ask to be walked through the proper procedure for transferring control of the accounts.

Start Palliative Measures

Stop any regular services that are no longer necessary. If your parent owned her own home, make sure to continue services necessary for the upkeep of the property. Cancel memberships and subscriptions and see if the estate is due any refunds. Destroy all your parent's credit cards. When bills arrive, bear in mind what I said earlier about the estate, not the survivors, being liable. My suggestion would be to respond to every initial mailing by simply marking the bill "DECEASED" and sending it back, along with a copy of the death certificate. If nothing else, this will give you some additional time to get your paperwork together and to have funds set up for you to easily pay bills out of the estate rather than your own pocket. When pressed for payment by anyone, explain that the estate will pay its debts once the funds are in the executor's control. Repeat that like a mantra to any further protestations.

There's a philosophical element to deciding how to handle the estate's bills. You will need to come up with your own answer, but

I think that if the money is there, and if the bill is for something that was actually used or purchased by the deceased, then it should be paid. Just because your parent died, there's no reason why his doctor, for example, shouldn't receive payment for his services.

Launch Revenue Rehabilitation

Rather than looking to boost the estate's revenue, your goal should be to pay off the estate's liabilities and disperse the remaining assets as quickly as possible. The sooner the assets are in the hands of the beneficiaries rather than the estate, the better.

Neil Greenblatt chuckled to himself soon after arriving at his mother's apartment. Thanks to what he used to call her morbid obsessiveness, he knew where all her important papers were located. The first thing he did was find her two checkbooks. He was a joint holder of both accounts, so he could use them to pay any immediate bills. Then he found her will and a copy of her prepaid funeral arrangements. He called the funeral home, and the funeral director explained that he'd contact the hospital. Neil's mother was to be flown up to her former hometown, where she would immediately be interred next to her husband. There would be private graveside service for family only. Neil then collected the unpaid bills and all the files and packed them in his briefcase. He made two copies of the key to his mother's apartment, leaving one with her neighbor and another with a bonded caretaking service recommended by the community. He went online and arranged for all his mother's e-mail to be forwarded to his own account. He got the keys to his mother's car, filled it with gas, and used it to drive back to the airport. On the way to catch his return flight, he stopped at the post office and filled out a forwarding form so all mail would be sent to his house. Once he settled in his seat on the plane, he took out his mother's files and began compiling lists of all her assets.

Cultivate Antibodies

You can't prevent the death of other parents. But you can mitigate the emotional, financial, legal, and organizational problems their deaths could cause. Encourage your parents to prepare wills, if they haven't already. Suggest they dispose of some valuables and possessions now, while they are alive. Not only will the recipient get use of them sooner, but your parent will be able to receive thanks and get the pleasure derived from seeing the recipient enjoy the gift. Ask your parents about their wishes for their funerals. Advise them to preplan or even prepay for what they would like. If you're going to be the executor of their estate, ask them to go over their finances with you, at least to the extent of showing you where their files are, and where their money is.

More important than all of this material planning is making sure that you've emotionally prepared for their death. How do you do that? Actually it's quite simple: Love them. Show and tell them how you feel about them, as often as you can, and for as long as they are able to understand you. *Love* is a verb, not a noun; it requires action for it to be complete. Speak with them as much as you can. Ask them to share their memories. The stories they tell, far more than any money they leave, are their most valuable legacy. I've found that my parents are still alive in their continued presence as memories in the lives of their children, grand children, and great grandchildren.

14

You Need to Send Your Child to Private School

Y ou land a new job that forces you and your family to relocate from a major city to a more rural area. You learn that the local schools don't measure up to what your 12-year-old daughter is used to. Since you and your spouse want your daughter to eventually attend an elite university, you begin looking for a private school, even though you can't afford it. Or you learn that your four-year-old son's apparently slow development is due to his suffering from a form of autism. When you speak with representatives from the local school district, they encourage mainstreaming and insist that he really doesn't need the degree of attention his psychologist recommends. You realize he's not going to get the schooling he needs in the public schools and so start looking for a private school, even though you can't afford it.

Jim and Andrea Noonan knew their daughter Amy had special needs. From an early age, she had shown signs of developmental problems. When she was four, she went through a battery of tests that revealed she had a bipolar disorder as well as Asperger's Syndrome. The Noonans were lucky enough to live near a major medical school that had excellent programs for children like Amy. When it was time for her to enter the school system, specialists from the medical school prepared exhaustive assessments of her needs. The affluent suburban community in which the Noonans lived prided itself on its special ed program, and so it was very responsive to Amy's needs. Shortly after Amy finished the second grade, Jim received a promotion requiring the family to move from their Northeastern suburb to a mid-sized Midwestern city. When the time came to meet with the new school district to discuss Amy's needs, the Noonans were shocked. The principal of the school dismissed Amy's earlier assessments out of hand and took pride in the low number of students at his school classified as special ed. When the Noonans started going over all the support Amy had received in her previous school, they were told that simply couldn't be provided in her new school, and besides, it wasn't necessary.

Accept the Problem and Own the Solution

Before you accept this problem, you need to determine whether it actually is a problem. Assuming private school will be a financial burden for your family, make sure you are doing this for the right reason. What is the right reason? Well, I believe it's that your child won't receive the level of care and attention he needs from the public school. I chose my words very carefully. This should be about what your child *needs*, not what he *wants*. And it should certainly not be about what *you* want.

There are a great many excellent private schools that provide their students with a rich educational experience. But there are just as many public schools that do the same. And in fact, I'd suggest that being part of a more diverse community of students is of educational benefit as well. Although you may bemoan the quality of the teachers at your local public schools, be aware they need far more training and credentials than the teachers at private schools. A bright, motivated student can succeed in any environment. And a bright but unmotivated student can fail in any environment. If your child is a high achiever, he will continue on that path no matter how different or less advantaged the public schools. In addition, he may actually have an advantage when applying to elite universities, since those institutions are actively looking for students from less advantaged regions to ensure a diverse student body.

There is no doubt that students who attend some private secondary schools have an easier time securing admission to some elite universities. Headmasters at these prep schools cultivate connections with admissions officers at top-tier private colleges. In addition, since most of the parents who send their children to these private schools are affluent, they can become a great fundraising source for the private colleges. This self-supporting elitist network is just a fact of life. The question is, to what degree should you sacrifice in order to buy your child a ticket into this network?

If it's a matter of your not buying a new Mercedes, or forgoing European vacations for a few years, I'll accept your decision to send your child to private school for its more enriched environment or its better connections at elite colleges. But I assume that since you feel you can't afford private school, the sacrifices required would be far more substantial. They might include working longer hours and cutting back on the family's lifestyle. They could involve diverting all the family's savings and investments to paying the prep school tuition, or putting the family into substantial debt. I don't think those kind of sacrifices make sense unless your child absolutely needs private school.

Generally, that need arises because of some form of learning or behavioral disability. Public schools may be required by law to provide for special ed students, but that doesn't mean they actually provide all that's required. And they very rarely provide more than the bare minimum they must to meet state and federal regulations. Special education is very expensive for school districts, and they are loath to allocate so much of their limited budget to a small number of students. Many will go out of their way to minimize spending, whether that means fighting assessments or just dragging their feet and throwing up bureaucratic barriers. If your child needs special help that it appears only a private school can offer, then it's worth owning the solution of sacrificing to pay the tuition.

Unburden Yourself

Although this may require sacrifice on your part, you may not need to carry this burden alone. In fact, I'd urge you to bring in some professional help in the form of a special-education attorney. This is a specialty that is growing in response to the increasing number of children who are being diagnosed with conditions requiring special education. Although public education would hate to admit it, when it comes to negotiating with the parents of students with special needs, they are in an adversarial position. And whenever you are facing an adversarial negotiation, it pays to have a knowledge-able and skilled advocate representing you. You can get the names of special education attorneys from either your family lawyer or from advocacy organizations. Expect to pay anywhere from $150 to $300 an hour for their services, depending on where you are located. This is one situation where hiring the right lawyer will be well worth the money.

Another advocate for your side can be a mental health professional who has treated your child previously. A mental health professional with experience in special education issues will know exactly how assessments should be written so as not to open to debate. This type of assessment isn't an exact science. There's a great deal of subjective analysis that takes place. That's why subtly and artfully worded reports can make the difference between your child getting what he needs or your having to fight tooth and nail for it.

Finally, don't hesitate to enlist a spy for your team. Classroom teachers, particularly those who have gone into special education, are often more child-focused than school administrators. A caring teacher who knows your child, and who also knows the way a school works, could be a source of very helpful inside information. He could let you know exactly what buttons to push, and how to push them.

Diagnose the Impact

Research the three private schools within driving distance from your home, which would be best for your child. Gather all the information you can about the schools. Calculate how much tuition will cost, and what other fees and expenses would be involved in sending your child to each. Don't forget to include travel costs. The decision as to which would be best will involve balancing the quality of the school, the cost of attending, and the time required to travel back and forth each day. Translate the cost of each school into a monthly figure.

Take Your Financial Pulse

Since this is an entirely new expense, you'll have to look for the money to meet it by cutting back elsewhere. Compile a comprehensive list of all your monthly spending. Next to the name and amount of each item, jot down how much you think you might be able to save by cutting back. Don't forget to include things like retirement fund and college savings investments. I'd suggest you, in fact, start with that last item. Rather than set aside money for your child's future possible higher education, invest it in his or her current primary and secondary education. The impact of superior early education for someone with special needs will be more profound than the impact of going to an elite college. If there isn't sufficient money in the college fund to pay for private school now, see if you could come up with the funds through lifestyle changes. Before you make any cut-backs, investigate other palliative measures and opportunities for revenue rehabilitation.

Start Palliative Measures

One of the problems facing all schools is that few parents of their students choose to become involved. This is doubly true for private schools, since the majority of their students are from affluent families whose members are more likely to write a check than volunteer time. It's possible you may be able to negotiate a tuition reduction by promising to provide volunteer work for the school. In addition, if you're from a minority group, you may be able to negotiate some form of scholarship, since even private schools are under pressure to have a diverse student population.

Launch Revenue Rehabilitation

Palliative measures, while worth trying, aren't likely to yield enough to make private school affordable. Revenue rehabilitation, however, offers a couple of excellent opportunities.

If your parents or your spouse's parents are planning to leave any money in their estate for your child, it makes sense to approach them now and ask for it to be used to help pay for private school tuition. This is a chance for the money to make a huge difference in your child's life. Besides, this gives your parents and in-laws a chance to both see the good their gift will do *and* receive thanks for their generosity in person.

Unlikely as it may sound, your public school system might be the best place to turn for money to pay for your child's private school tuition. Public schools are required by state and federal law to meet the needs of all the children in their district. Once your child's needs have been assessed by a professional, the school must develop a plan to address those needs. Some school districts take this obligation very seriously and do indeed provide whatever is necessary. Other districts, however, do all they can to minimize this spending. That's because the cost per child for special ed students is far higher than for mainstream students. Public schools sometimes try to intimidate parents into accepting whatever the school is willing to provide. One very successful strategy is for parents to hire a special education lawyer to represent them in negotiations with the public school district. Knowing they are dealing with someone they can't intimidate and who knows the regulations as well as if not better than they do, school officials often shift from aggressive to obsequious. Meeting your child's needs may actually cost the district more than it would to simply pay for your child's tuition at a private school. That's often the goal of special education attorneys. They will push the district to provide all your child needs, then explain that alternatively, for less money, the district can pick up the tuition and travel costs for your child to attend a private school already designed to meet his needs. Often the district agrees. If not, it's forced to provide the necessary services.

Reeling from the dismissive treatment they'd received from the school in their new community, the Noonans got in touch with a contact they'd cultivated at a national special ed advocacy organization. He recommended a special education attorney located in their new city. The attorney wasn't surprised by the Noonans' experience, noting that she had dealt with the district on a number of occasions and it had always been recalcitrant. He told the Noonans not to worry, and suggested they get in touch with a number of private schools in the immediate area. When the Noonans said they couldn't afford the tuition, the attorney told them not to worry about that yet. At the Noonans' next meeting with the school principal, this time with their attorney present, the difference was dramatic. The attorney took charge, pointing out what the district was required to provide, but suggesting that if it preferred, it could simply pick up the cost of Amy's attending a nearby private academy. The principal and the school district's attorney readily agreed.

Cultivate Antibodies

If there is any preventative measure you could take from this experience, I suppose it's this: If you have special needs children, the quality and philosophy of an area's public school district is perhaps the single most important factor in choosing where to live. If you are asked to move to an area for work, and have a special needs child, make sure to fully investigate the schools before accepting, and if you find them wanting, ask for additional compensation to pay for your child's education in a private school.

15

You're Getting a Divorce

When you married right after college, you thought it would last forever. But after only a few years, you both realize you want different things so you decide to divorce. Or after almost 20 years of a turbulent marriage, which you've both endured in an effort to provide a stable home for your children, you decide to split now that the kids are in their teens.

Robert Sayre and his wife, Elena, met while Robert was studying for his MBA in Europe. Elena was a member of the French foreign service at the time. They decided to marry and move to New York City. Robert became an investment banker and Elena got a job at the United Nations. Despite both being very career driven, they found the time to have two children and make a family life for themselves and their daughters on Manhattan's Upper East Side and in a weekend home in Connecticut. As the years progressed, they became more and more focused on their individual careers. Both traveled for business a great deal and spent many evenings at business-related events. Eventually, the only time their lives really intersected were when they shared time with their children. Elena eventually confessed to an infidelity, which prompted Robert to confess to one of his own. The Sayres decided it would be best if they divorced.

Accept the Problem and Own the Solution

Preserving a problematic marriage in an effort to protect children simply doesn't make sense anymore. With about 50 percent of all marriages ending in divorce, it's simply not the stigma it once was.

In fact, in some communities, blended families are becoming the norm rather than the exception. Everyone, including parents, therapists, clergy, and teachers, have a better understanding of how to make sure kids don't see themselves as being responsible for the dissolution of their parents' marriage.

Since you're reading this chapter, I assume you've tried but have been unable to salvage your marriage. You now need to accept divorce as a strictly economic problem. Of course there will be all sorts of emotional issues involved, but the more you can separate them from the practical matters of money and visitation, the easier this problem will be to solve. Money, since it is a neutral medium of exchange, has the magical ability to absorb all our conscious and subconscious feelings. But any effort to use money as an emotional tool, let's say to punish a spouse for infidelity, will backfire. Couples tend to polarize, particularly when they're divorcing. If you use money as a way to hurt your spouse because you feel hurt by the break-up of your marriage, your spouse will invariably respond in kind. That's when divorces become acrimonious and kids truly are hurt by the process and its aftermath. I believe the secret is to accept your need to separate the emotional from the financial elements of this problem and to own the solution of reaching an economically fair solution.

Unburden Yourself

The tendency to use money as an emotional weapon is one reason divorces get nasty. The other reason is that lawyers get involved. Lawyers are advocates. They tend to see all situations as adversarial—contests in which someone wins and someone else loses. With emotions already running high, lawyers tend to fan the flames so they ignite into an all-out war in which the big winners are, surprise, the lawyers.

Rather than buy into this adversarial process, I'd suggest you and your spouse both unburden yourselves by jointly hiring a mediator. A mediator works for both parties and, using the state guidelines, tries to find a fair and logical solution to issues like the division of assets, support, and visitation. Think twice about asking your attorney for the name of a divorce mediator. He may try to talk you both into hiring lawyers. Instead, speak with your marital or family therapist or a clergyperson.

Diagnose the Impact

There's no way around it: The financial impact of a divorce will be dramatic. In most states, marital assets are considered community property and must be split equally. Child support is awarded based on the need and availability of money and lasts until the child is emancipated. Spousal support is also based on need and availability, taking into account the employment potential of each spouse. If a spouse receiving support remarries, he or she loses the support. Generally, each spouse must change their lifestyle dramatically, since after the divorce they'll have only about half as much income to live on as they had when married.

Take Your Financial Pulse

I've become a firm believer in using divorce as an opportunity to start your financial lives over. Rather than looking to figure out ways to somehow maintain the same home, the same spending patterns and the same lifestyle, I suggest my clients sell all jointly held assets, split the proceeds, and each begin fresh. I think the pressure of trying to maintain children in the same home they lived in before the divorce contributes to continued acrimony between the ex-spouses and often plants false seeds of potential reconciliation in the children. If it just seems like Daddy moved out, there's the possibility of Daddy moving back in. If everyone moves out, it's clear things have changed permanently.

Take your financial pulse by calculating your income from all sources, including child or spousal support. Then determine what, if any, savings and investments you have. List sources of borrowing, including credit cards and family and friends. Next, begin listing your expenses. Don't start with the amount you paid previously when married. Instead, begin simply by listing all the things on which you'll need to spend money each month. Don't forget to include periodic expenses such as insurance, taxes, and investments in retirement plans.

Once your list is complete, begin filling in the numbers, starting with those items over which you have the least control. For instance, if you're paying for your own health insurance, odds are that's an area where you've very little control over what you need to spend. Your real estate expense is probably in that category, too. There's likely a range in cost for the type of property you need, under which you couldn't fall. Let's say you need a two-bedroom apartment for you and your daughter. You want it to be close to your daughter's school and to allow you to get to and from work as well. The more limited your options, the less control you'll have over what you need to spend. The idea of this exercise is to figure out how much you can afford to spend on each item, rather than how much you want to spend. It will force you to live within your means and to prioritize your spending; two essential elements to surviving the financial consequences of a divorce.

Start Palliative Measures

Once your budget is established, you can begin to look for ways to save money on each item. You might find that your needs have changed now that you're single. For example, it could make more sense to have a membership at a fitness center you can attend early in the morning before work, rather than at a golf club you could only use on the weekends, since that's when you'll be with your children. Don't obsess over your former spouse's spending. As long as she is meeting obligations to your children, then her spending is no more your business than your spending is hers.

Launch Revenue Rehabilitation

Having trimmed your spending and established a workable budget and affordable lifestyle, turn to efforts to increase your revenue. The most effective is, obviously, to find a better paying job. But don't overlook opportunities to make money through part-time freelancing or other self-employment efforts. Getting further education or training might be a great long-term strategy. Just make sure you can afford both the costs of the training and the impact on your income. Don't pressure your ex-spouse about getting a job if she hasn't; she is more impacted by a lack of income than you are. Besides, any efforts to exert influence could backfire.

Even though Robert and Elena Sayre were both very successful, and their split was amicable, there was a great deal of financial stress. They hired a mediator who helped them craft a fair agreement. Robert paid child support and a small stipend for spousal support. They sold their large condo on the Upper East Side and their weekend home in Connecticut and split the proceeds. Robert bought a smaller apartment in Brooklyn, which was close to his office, and Elena and the girls moved to a much smaller apartment on the Upper West Side. For the first time since they were married, both Robert and Elena started to pay attention to their spending. They're happier emotionally and both believe things are better for the girls, now that they're no longer subject to their parent's constant bickering.

Cultivate Antibodies

Despite having been happily married for many years, I don't think it's my place to offer advice on maintaining a happy marriage. Let me instead focus on how to avoid the financial problem of divorce. Two words: *prenuptial agreement*. Most Americans have a reflexive negative reaction to the idea of prenuptial agreements. The sense is that they're unfair documents pushed by rich domineering men on poorer, usually younger women. Interestingly enough, in other countries there's no such prejudice. In Canada, for example, they're quite common.

I've always advocated prenuptial agreements for second or third marriages in which one or both spouses have children from previous marriages. In that instance, they're an excellent way to protect the rights of children to inherit assets that were built up by their parents, rather than seeing those assets transfer to a subsequent spouse. Similarly, I've pushed for prenuptial agreements when one or both parties are involved in family businesses. It seems unfair for a divorced spouse to acquire interest in a business run by their ex-spouse's family. There are ways of making these documents quite fair. For instance, they can contain sunset clauses so they expire, say, upon the birth of a child or after a certain number of years of marriage. Or, in the case of the family business, an insurance policy can be purchased by the business on the life of the spouse, naming the non–family-member spouse as beneficiary. That way, the spouse receives some value for his or her "share" in the business without any issues of ownership arising.

As the years have passed and I've seen more and more of my clients go through divorces, I've come to believe that there's nothing wrong with prenuptial agreements in any and every case. I look at them now as being similar to the termination agreements I negotiate for my clients with their new employers. The existence of such an agreement doesn't plant the seeds for future dismissal. Neither will a prenuptial agreement plant the seeds for a future divorce. This is an instance where it's important to have an advocate, so it's necessary that each party to a prenuptial agreement have his or her own attorney. In addition, it's vital that signing such an agreement not be a precondition for getting married.

You're Facing Large, Uncovered Medical Bills

During your first month on a new job, your daughter is involved in a serious auto accident requiring emergency treatment, surgery, and rehabilitation. Since you hadn't yet qualified for your employer's health insurance coverage, you're responsible for the total cost of her care. Or you suffer a heart attack. Your medical care has been top notch and you're on the mend, but you've reached the limit of coverage on your insurance and are responsible for the lion's share of the cost.

When Connie Lafontaine, a 58-year-old widow, learned she had colon cancer she was understandably distraught and frightened. The physicians in her local area, a suburb of a major city, were supportive, but not very optimistic. Her internist, however, thought she should approach a specialist surgeon who worked out of a major cancer hospital in the nearby big city. Connie received an appointment with the surgeon who thought she was an excellent candidate for the special procedure he used. With the help and support of family and friends, Connie decided to have her surgery and be treated by the specialist, even though it was more of a burden. Three weeks later, after successful surgery, it appeared she made the right choice. She never regretted her choice, but she did have to face another problem. Her insurance company refused to cover much of the cost of her surgery, hospitalization, and follow-up chemotherapy since it was more costly than they deemed "reasonable and customary." They were only willing to cover what would have been the cost if Connie had been treated locally.

Accept the Problem and Own the Solution

Until the economics of medical care and treatment in this country are changed, this will be a recurring problem for many Americans. In fact, as costs of care and insurance coverage skyrocket, this problem is becoming more and more a middle- and upper-middle-class concern. You can't go back and undo whatever led to the illness or accident. Nor can you, or should you, decide against receiving medical care because it may not be fully covered by insurance. Just as a doctor's first priority should be to heal the sick regardless of financial resources, so your first priority, for your family and yourself, should be to get the best treatment you can find. First worry about getting well; then worry about paying the bills.

All that being said, you are responsible for the bills. The affluence of a hospital or doctor doesn't preclude them from being paid or their services. You were not refused service. In response, you should not refuse payment. Nor should the outcome of their treatment be a rationalization for nonpayment. You own the solution of coming up with some way to meet your obligations.

Unburden Yourself

Although you are responsible for your bills, you may not need to assume the burden entirely. There are few situations more worthy of help from family and friends than a medical emergency. Think of people who you would try to help out if they were in your situation. Now, ask them for help. Don't let pride stand in the way of your family's health or your own physical well being.

Consider asking your employer for help as well. Many large businesses have funds available to help employees who are facing emergencies. Even smaller companies may be able to lend a helping hand, perhaps through a personal loan or gift from the owner. There are few better ways to show an entire company how much management cares than openly helping an individual employee in trouble.

Finally, speak with the hospital social worker or someone from a local family service charity. There are often charitable grants and loans available for patients or community members in need.

Diagnose the Impact

If a potential benefactor asks how much you need, you want to be able to provide a complete and thorough accounting. Demonstrating you know the details of your situation shows a seriousness and diligence that will inspire confidence in anyone contemplating a loan or gift. This will tell them that you're in this situation due to misfortune, not because you've been irresponsible with your finances. Put together a list of all the money you owe for medical care. Divide it up by provider. In addition, calculate how much you will need to spend going forward on things like prescriptions, postoperative treatment, physical therapy, or rehabilitation. Get a firm prognosis on how long this treatment will be necessary, and then project out the ongoing costs until recovery or stabilization.

Take Your Financial Pulse

After determining what your medical bills are and will be, conduct an analysis of your own finances. Go over your expenses very closely, looking for areas where you can cut back your spending. You don't need to have your child go without a winter coat, but going without a new pair of $200 sneakers is probably a good idea. Once again, you want to be able to demonstrate to any potential rescuer that you are neither expecting a handout nor pretending the problem doesn't exist. Try to limit your spending to areas where you are maintaining yourself and your family, and cut out anything that is an improvement. For instance, keep paying to take care of your current car, but don't set aside money for a new motorcycle. Don't keep your numbers hidden. In fact, encourage anyone who's interested in helping to look at your budget and ask for any suggestions they might have. Advice and counsel might be more valuable in the long run than a small handout.

Start Palliative Measures

The most effective places to turn for help in easing the pain of uncovered medical bills are the medical providers themselves. First, there's the obvious fact that the services have already been provided. It's not like a surgeon is going to reattach an appendix whose previous owner hasn't paid his bill right away. In addition, most hospitals and doctors are not assiduous collectors of accounts receivable. Hospitals tend to be very inefficient organizations and are often so mired in bureaucratic red tape that they can be as slow moving as glaciers. Doctors, while not as tied down by paperwork and procedure, know that they will in fact lose money by taking a patient to court. The time they spend would be better spent caring for a patient. And collection, while not costing them time, is unlikely to earn them enough to even cover their costs. That's why hospitals and doctors are quite open to negotiating terms and payment plans with patients who can't afford to pay their bills immediately.

As soon as you realize you'll have problems with uncovered bills, contact the provider. You'll be referred to either the billing department or to a specific person in a doctor's office who handles accounts receivable. Explain your situation. Be honest and forthright. Indicate you are willing to pay your debt completely—it's just that you aren't able to do so right now. Rather than writing off the debt, most providers will offer terms; in effect they'll act as an after-the-fact lender. If you're asked what you are able to pay now, suggest a monthly amount. Don't over promise. The key to making this arrangement hold will be your sticking to your agreement consistently, month after month. At the same time, don't under promise. Paying $10 a month on a $10,000 bill isn't a serious effort at repayment. Paying $100 a month shows you're making an effort and also holds out the possibility of the debt actually be cleared up. Try to be proactive in your payments, sending them in unprompted on the same date each month. In most cases, as long as you keep paying, the hospital or doctor will refrain from putting the bill in for collection.

Launch Revenue Rehabilitation

The best place to turn for revenue rehabilitation is the insurance provider who has failed to cover the complete bill. All insurers have appeals and grievance procedures. The key is not to ask it to change its minds—that's accusatory and means it has to admit making an error. Instead, you should ask for a reconsideration based on new facts. For instance, if it has been ruled that you've reached the limit of your coverage per incident, it's possible that what happened to you actually involved more than just one incident. Or if you're limited to a certain amount per calendar year, that the bill could be resubmitted successfully at a later date. If you've been denied because a treatment was considered unnecessary, it's possible to have your doctors' become your advocates. Similarly, if you've gone to a provider whose fee is beyond what the insurer considers "reasonable and customary," you might be able to demonstrate there's no other doctor providing that service for the fees the insurer believes are standard.

Unable to work during her recovery, Connie Lafontaine made dealing with her medical bills part of her daily activity. Connie didn't have enough money to pay the uncovered portion of her hospital bills and keep up with the rest of her bills. She'd already cut back to deal with being out of work for an extended period so there was no fat left in her budget. Connie began working the telephones. She contacted the hospital, explained what her insurance company had decided, and described her financial situation. Connie asked if it would be willing to accept a partial payment of $200 a month until she could either get the insurance company to reconsider, or get back to work. The hospital agreed. Connie then got in touch with her insurer. She explained the situation and was told about the company's appeals procedure. She spoke with her internist, who wrote a letter explaining that there were no doctors in Connie's local area who did the type of procedure she'd had done. Connie also spoke with her surgeon's office. It sent a letter from the surgeon saying he believed his unique procedure offered Connie a much better chance for a full recovery. Those two letters, along with Connie's persistence, persuaded the insurer to cover more of the costs than it had originally. That allowed Connie to stick to her negotiated payment plan with the hospital and pay off the entire bill in less than 18 months.

Cultivate Antibodies

The best way to avoid having this happen again is to make sure you have good catastrophic medical coverage. I know: That's like saying the best way to avoid being poor is to get a lot of money. However, if you have an opportunity to put together your own package of medical coverage, give serious thought to expanding the catastrophic coverage at the expense of shorter, more preventative care. It's better to pay for most doctor visits, dental care, and flu shots out of pocket yet have hospitalization fully covered. See if your employer offers a Health Savings Account option. This gives you a chance to put your own money away tax free for medical care while providing an inexpensive catastrophic health care policy.

In addition, in the future, if you suspect there will be a problem with an insurer paying for medical care, try to negotiate the issue beforehand. It's easier to get an insurer to bend their rules and provide preapproval, than it is to get them to change a judgment they've already made. Not only are you dealing with different departments, but you're dealing with different attitudes and philosophies. It's much harder for an insurance company, no matter how heartless they may seem, to keep you from getting medical care, than it is for them to say they won't pay for medical care you've already received.

Your Adult Child Needs Financial Help

Your daughter calls one evening in tears. She explains she has lost her job and doesn't know how she's going to pay the rent next month. Or your son stops by one afternoon to ask for help. He and his wife are earning enough to pay a mortgage, but they don't have money saved for a down payment.

Patrick and Betty Smith weren't surprised when they received a desperate call from their son Roy. Roy had married right after high school and had gotten work as a cable television installer. He and his wife, Diane, had two children right away. Diane stayed home to take care of the boys. As a result, money was always tight for Roy and Diane. Despite that, the two spent freely, taking advantage of credit offers to buy clothing, consumer electronics, a snowmobile, a jet ski, and loads of toys for the boys. Many times Patrick and Betty had Roy, Diane, and the boys over for dinner because they knew there was little or nothing to eat in their apartment. The Smiths had been expecting things to come to a head, and they did. Roy tearfully said he couldn't make the rent this month or pay for repairs to his car, which he needs to get to and from work.

Accept the Problem and Own the Solution

When your adult child comes to you with a serious financial problem, you need to decide not just if you can help, but also if you *should* help. The natural instinct is for parents to do whatever they can to help their children. That instinct doesn't end when the child grows up. Your daughter may be 35 years old, married, and have a child—but she's still your daughter.

The need for children to turn to parents for financial help isn't necessarily a sign of ineptness. Real income (wages when adjusted for inflation) has remained stagnant for decades, while prices have climbed. Thirty years ago, a single person who landed her first job out of college was able to afford an apartment. Today, someone working that same job needs to share the rent with two or three others. The U.S. economy is rapidly dividing into the affluent and the poor, with the middle class vanishing. For many young people, the only way they can stay in the middle class is to borrow or get help.

In this kind of situation I believe you should accept the problem as if it were your own. Do everything that you can for your child, even if it means tapping into funds you intend for her future. It is always better to provide help in the present. Money today means more than money tomorrow. Today the $10,000 you give a child could enable her to buy a home, to go back to college, or to start a business. Years from now, when you're dead, that $10,000 will be a nice vacation, or the difference between a Toyota and a Lexus. Nice, for sure, but not life altering. Besides, if you give money now you're able to see it being enjoyed and receive thanks for your help.

Of course, there are also times when young people bring their financial problems on themselves. It might be as a result of making bad choices; say, getting in over their heads with credit card debt. Or it could be because they have a problem; perhaps they've a drug or alcohol addiction, or have psychological issues that led to poor behavior. In these situations it's often not just one incident, but a series of incidents.

A parent having to decide whether to help out in these kinds of scenarios faces a much tougher choice. Will you be giving her a helping hand in a rare circumstance, or enabling her to continue along a self-destructive path? The decision isn't always clear. There may be a point where she starts to turn things around. How do you know when that is? Is there a limit to how many times you help? Should you help with certain things, perhaps those of which you approve, and not others? Do you pay for a stay in a rehab center but not to clear up her debts? Is your help a reward for good behavior and your withholding of help a punishment for bad behavior?

I wish I could offer answers for all these questions. All I can say is, your decisions should be based on your relationship with your child.

You know her better than anyone else. What does your gut tell you? Do you believe you'd be enabling or helping? How does your spouse feel? Try to reach a joint decision. Couples polarize around issues like this; one playing good cop and the other bad cop. Your child's problem is already your problem in some ways. You don't want it also to become a wedge between you and your spouse.

Unburden Yourself

When you're debating whether financial aid to your adult child would be helpful or harmful in the long term, it makes sense to unburden yourself. Speak with social workers or therapists. Get in touch with support groups for the families of individuals with psychological or behavioral problems.

This also might be a good time to speak with your other children. Ask for their advice and counsel, weighing what they say based on their own relationship with the child who's in trouble. Families communicate differently. It's possible that other children are privy to information that could help you make a decision.

If one of your children is particularly well off financially, you might want to consider asking her to help materially as well. Try to present this indirectly, perhaps by saying you're going to help but don't know if you can provide as much as is necessary. Explain to your other children that you're telling them because you want them to be aware of how you're splitting your assets. If they offer help too, great. If they don't, drop the matter.

Diagnose the Impact

If you decide you're willing to help, ask your child to go over the numbers with you and come up with a final, specific number. You want to provide a gift or a loan, not an expanding line of credit. Don't talk about your affordability yet. Just say you first want to know exactly how much is needed. Then you'll see if you can help and with how much.

Take Your Financial Pulse

Examine your finances to determine if you can afford to help your child out, and if so, with how much. Compile a list of all your assets, including real estate and retirement savings. Then, develop a list of your potential borrowing power, including available home equity, margin borrowing on investments, and credit card cash-advance balances. If you have sufficient liquid assets to make a gift or loan of the money, consider the impact on your unearned income. How would cutting that money from your monthly income affect your lifestyle? What would the impact on your future retirement be of giving or lending some of your savings to your child? If you don't have the cash needed, could you borrow the money? It might makes sense for you to borrow the money, pass it along to your child, and have her repay the loan.

If there's a choice between gifting or lending the money, I'd suggest gifting. Loans between family and friends are often problematic. If, for some reason, your child fails to meet her payments, what could you, or would you, do about it? Since you're willing to borrow to help your kid, it's unlikely you're going to sue her for the money if she doesn't pay. If the only way you can provide the money is through borrowing, and you're confident your child will be a responsible borrower, then by all means make the loan. Just be aware that in that case you really do own the solution, since you're ultimately responsible for repaying the loan.

The best way to explain you're not being able to help your child is that, after taking your financial pulse, you discover you simply don't have the money. No one, not even your child, can ask you to do the impossible.

Patrick and Betty Smith knew in their guts that if they helped Roy and Diane over this crisis, it would likely be the start of a recurring pattern. Betty said she didn't care. She couldn't sit by and watch her grandchildren suffer because of their parents' mistakes. Patrick said that if they bailed out Roy and Diane, it would be rewarding their poor behavior and that they wouldn't change until they hit rock bottom. Things grew heated between them, and so they decided to speak with their minister. The minister suggested a compromise. Patrick and Betty told Roy that he should come up with a list of all the bills he needed to keep a roof over the family's head and food on the table. When he returned with his list, Patrick and Betty told Roy they'd give him enough money to pay those bills for three months, and that he and Diane should use that time to get a handle on their other bills and control their spending. Privately, Patrick promised Betty he'd never let the grandchildren go hungry or homeless, and Betty promised Patrick than she'd back him up in refusing any future gifts to Roy and Diane.

Cultivate Antibodies

Perhaps helping your child out this time will give her a financial step up that ensures such help isn't needed again. But if that doesn't happen, your willingness to help out gives the green light to future requests. Alternatively, your refusing to help, either because you can't afford it or because you don't want to enable self-destructive behavior, will almost guarantee you're not asked for help again.

18

Your Parents Need Financial Help

You call your mother to chat and instead of the call going through, you get a recording that the number has been disconnected. Frightened, you drive over and discover your mother is physically okay; it's just that she hasn't paid her telephone bill in two months. Or you notice your father's gout seems worse than usual. When you ask about it, he admits he's taking half the usual dose of his medication because the pills are so expensive.

Christmas was always a big deal for the Schaefer family. Although the five children are now spread all around the country, every year they, their families, and their parents gather at one of the sibling's homes for an extended celebration. That's why Elizabeth, the oldest child, was surprised when, during a discussion of where to gather this coming year, her mother said she and Elizabeth's father wouldn't be traveling this year. Concerned, Elizabeth asked about her parents' health. Her mother said they were both doing fine, they just didn't want to travel this year. It was only after some persistent probing that Elizabeth got her mother to say that airfare was simply too expensive right now, and that they'd rather spend the money on gifts for the grandchildren. Elizabeth immediately offered to pay for her parents' airfare, but her mother was taken aback and refused.

Accept the Problem and Own the Solution

One of the great advances of the twentieth century was increased longevity. When the Social Security Act first passed Congress, the average person didn't live long enough to collect benefits at age 65.

148

Now people are remaining active and healthy well into their eighties. Better medical care, advances in drug therapy, improved nutrition, and increased exercise have all contributed to extending lifespans. But these added years have the potential to create problems. The conservative savings and investment patterns followed by most people simply haven't kept pace with changing longevity. While fewer people today are retiring into poverty, increasing numbers are outliving their money. Relying on unearned income necessitates prudent investing. However, that same prudent investing can result in lower than needed growth.

Sometimes the signs that your parents are in financial trouble are glaring, such as unpaid bills and cutting back on medical treatment. But most often there are more subtle early indications, such as shifts in lifestyle or spending patterns. Perhaps a mother who always was fastidious about her hair stops going to the salon once a month. Or maybe a father who took great pride in his car chooses not to get damage from a fender bender repaired. These signals are a cue for you to make a decision: do you want to accept your parents' financial problems as your own?

Accepting the problem, in this case, may not mean assuming a financial burden. It could mean offering advice and counsel on money management: say, convincing your parents to use the funds they've been preserving for their heirs, or perhaps to get a reverse mortgage. It might involve bringing the family together and figuring out how everyone could help in their own ways. Perhaps a child who lives nearby could offer help with local transportation while a child who lives further away could offer to take the parents in for an extended visit, with all the siblings contributing to pay for the parents' airfare. Accepting this problem actually means resolving to become involved in your parents' lives to a greater degree than you have.

On the one hand, if your relationship with your parents over the years has been problematic, you might not want to become so entwined with them. It's your decision. You might prefer to offer help to them on an ad hoc basis. That could mean buying them a new television, or even sending them on a trip. The idea is to do something specific and finite. On the other hand, if your relationship with your parents has been good, and you have the time and resources, you might want to extend help of some kind to them on a regular basis.

However, even though you're accepting this problem, you shouldn't take ownership of the solution. Your parents need to remain in charge of their lives as long as they possibly can. You can offer suggestions and advice, and provide resources if needed, but you should let them make their own decisions. They may not always choose to do what you think they should, but that's their right. Your help shouldn't be conditioned on their handing you control. If you can't accept that, then don't get involved.

Unburden Yourself

You shouldn't be the only person involved in helping your parents through their financial crisis. There are specialist professionals who could be of tremendous assistance to your parents. In addition to gerontologists and social workers who can give you some guidance about how best to deal with your parents, there are estate attorneys and financial planners whose practices center around senior citizens and their needs. One important caveat, however: Make sure there is a single professional who is the primary advisor in the each of the areas of your parents' lives. Too often professionals work at cross purposes, unaware of what others are doing. In the financial part of your parents' life there should be one professional, say a certified financial planner, who works with them to set a strategy and who directs them to other professionals—maybe an estate attorney and an insurance broker—as needed. Though its outside the scope of this book, the same holds for your parents' medical care. One doctor, preferably a geriatrician, should be the central hub through which all your parents care passes. That will prevent drug interaction problems.

Professionals aren't the only ones who should be part of the team helping your parents. Do you have siblings? They should be involved to the extent they're able, even if it just means getting involved in conversations and discussions. Are any of your aunts and uncles still alive and part of your parents' lives? They might provide a welcome perspective on issues, and also present suggestions that could be embarrassing coming from you. Do your parents have nieces and nephews who they're particularly close to? Get them involved as well. The more caring people involved, the less a burden falls on any one individual and the more your parents will feel like a member of a supportive family.

Diagnose the Impact

Generally, children realize their parents need financial help when they discover a specific problem. Unfortunately, this is often the tip of the iceberg. If you find out your parents are late paying one bill, there are probably more late notices on the way. If you discover they are cutting back on their medication to save money, they're probably cutting back elsewhere as well. To be able to offer help, either materially or just with advice, you need to first diagnose the full impact of the situation. That will probably require taking your parent's financial pulse.

Take Your Financial Pulse

To the extent both you and they are comfortable, go over your parents' income and spending. Don't be judgmental. Explain that another set of eyes might be helpful in spotting things they've missed. Next, go over their savings and investments. Again, play the impartial, unbiased observer. This is for information gathering only. Talk about how you've done the same exercise yourself, and so you might be able to pass along some of what you've just learned.

Start Palliative Measures

Do not suggest areas where your parents can cut their spending. It's their life and their money. If they chose to eat out every night and yet not have enough money to visit family at the holidays, that's their choice. Playing the budget cutter will only ensure they don't listen to anything else you say. Instead of looking for extravagances, keep an eye out for spending that's no longer necessary. Often ongoing bills and services become habitual and continue far beyond when they're necessary. For instance, are your parents still insuring jewelry they've already given away? Do they belong to an auto club and also have towing coverage on their insurance? Are they paying for memberships they no longer use or need? Point these out but don't belabor the issue. Just highlight them on the list you've all drawn up and leave it to them to take any actions.

Launch Revenue Rehabilitation

There are three ways you can help your parents rehabilitate their revenue: by helping them rearrange their portfolio, by suggesting alternative financial ideas, or by lending them money.

Many people fail to modify their investment strategies during retirement. The retirement portfolio that made sense for someone planning to retire 10 years down the road is different from the best portfolio for someone who has just retired. Instead of concentrating on growth, income generation and principle preservation become important as well. Similarly, the strategy of someone who is 75 should be different than someone who has just turned 65. Long-term growth becomes fairly unimportant, while income production becomes more important. Yet most investors don't make postretirement adjustments. They may fixate on preserving principle in order to leave an inheritance, even if it comes at the expense of their own quality of life. Ironically, you might have to lend them money in the short term because they don't want to touch the money they intend to leave to you in the long term. Rather than offer suggestions yourself, recommend they speak with a financial advisor. If they already have someone they like, simply advise them to go back for a "check up." If they don't have an advisor, give them some suggestions. You needn't get involved in the actual reallocation of investments, other than to give the advisor a heads-up telephone call in advance of his or her meeting with your parents. Explain what led you to believe they needed to make a change, and say that you're available if you can be of any help.

Two things you may want to mention to your parents' financial advisor are annuities and reverse mortgages. By purchasing annuities with some of their savings, your parents would be turning an asset into a stream of income that they cannot outlive. Similarly, by taking out a reverse mortgage on their home your parents will receive tax-free payments to continue living in their home. The stumbling block for most people with both these investments is that the asset in question doesn't remain part of their estate. They might not get back all the money they put into an annuity if they die earlier than anticipated. And if they have a reverse mortgage, proceeds from the sale of their home when they die go to the mortgage holder, not the estate. This is why the discussion of investment strategies is an excellent opportunity for you and your siblings to encourage your parents to use their money to help themselves, rather than hoard it for their heirs.

The third way you can help boost your parents' income is by giving them the money yourself. Obviously this is contingent on your having the money in the first place. As a 78-year-old who has been a devoted spouse, doting father, and dutiful son, I feel qualified to suggest you keep your priorities straight. Up until your children are emancipated and established, I think they have to be your priority.

Once you feel they're secure, you need to focus on the future of you and your spouse, if for no other reason than you don't want to become a burden for your children. Then, with the needs (not necessarily wants) of you and your spouse addressed, you should turn to your parents' needs.

Rather than offering your parents a stipend or a large gift, offer to extend them a loan. Tailor it to something specific, say paying their auto and homeowners insurance premiums for the next two years, or buying airplane tickets so they can visit each of their children once a year. That will enable them to reallocate their own money to other expenses. By framing the money as a loan and setting up a repayment schedule, you allow them to retain more of their self-respect. You're also showing confidence in their continued health. Draft a simple letter explaining the loan and the terms, and have them both

Annuities and Reverse Mortgages

I think there are two potential magic bullets for seniors in financial trouble: annuities and reverse mortgages.

Annuities are contracts between an individual (or couple) and an insurance company. While there are a number of variations I think the most relevant is the single-premium immediate fixed annuity, which requires one lump sum payment and instantly delivers a set income. There are three big advantages to annuities. They provide a life-long income; you'll never run out of money. They provide a guaranteed income; you get the same amount whether the market goes up or down. And the income is partly tax free; part of the money you're receiving back is actually repayment of what you put in. The big disadvantage is they're irrevocable.

A reverse mortgage also provides a guaranteed income for as long as you live. A homeowner signs his home over to a bank in exchange for regular lifelong payments. These are tax free because they are actually loan payments not income. The homeowner gets to live in the home for the rest of his life. When the homeowner dies the bank takes possession of the home, sells it, and keeps the proceeds. The advantage is clear: you're paid to live in your own home. The disadvantage is you may not receive as much money from the bank as your home is worth if you don't live long enough. Of course, you'll be dead so it won't really matter.

sign it. Let your siblings know about the arrangement in as matter a fact manner as possible. Having informed them of it, drop the subject. The goal is full disclosure without guilt inducement.

Elizabeth Schaefer took her parents not wanting to spend the money on airfare to see the family over Christmas as an early warning sign. She spoke with all her siblings and they agreed. She decided to have a heart-to-heart talk with her parents. It turned out that besides forgoing the airfare, they had stopped going out to eat or to the movies as often. When Elizabeth probed further, her mother admitted that it was because the return on a couple of the mutual funds on which they relied for their disposable income had dropped dramatically. Elizabeth said that she recently had the same problem with her investments dropping, and suggested they speak with her financial planner. Once her father was reassured that this was a fee-only planner and that it would just be a strategy session, he agreed. Prior to her parents meeting with the planner, Elizabeth spoke with all her siblings and they agreed to suggest her parents begin tapping into their principle rather than looking to preserve any assets in their estate. She then called the planner and let him know the family's feelings. Three weeks after that planning session Elizabeth's mother told her that they'd changed their minds. They'd be flying to see the family this Christmas after all.

Cultivate Antibodies

The antibodies to cultivate after dealing with this problem are within yourself. Look at what happened to your parents as a cautionary tale. Resolve to do whatever you can so you don't place yourself in the same position as your parents. Your goal should be that your children feel close enough to you to want to help, and are successful enough to be able to help, but that you simply don't need it.

Your New Boss Dislikes You

On your new superior's first day, you decide to stop by her office and introduce yourself, but you're met with a blank stare and are told to make appointments in the future. Or you've noticed that during staff meetings, your new superior barely acknowledges your input, and never seems to address you.

Mercedes Jackson was sad to hear her supervisor at the insurance company would be leaving. Her sadness turned to anxiety after one month of dealing with her new supervisor. Even greetings went unacknowledged. This woman barely acknowledged Mercedes's presence. Suggestions and comments that Mercedes offered were either ignored or belittled. Mercedes found herself being given the least desirable projects. Mercedes didn't understand it. She'd been working at the company for more than 12 years and had always received glowing reviews. Mercedes thought she had a future with the company. Now she wasn't sure. It was obvious her new boss had it in for her.

Accept the Problem and Own the Solution

There's no question having a new unfriendly boss is potentially a looming financial crisis. However, before you accept that you've got a real problem, you need to carefully analyze the environment. Is the problem with you, or with your boss. Does she treat everyone the way she's treating you? Are your peers feeling anxious, too? It's possible your new superior simply treats everyone poorly. In that case, you're in no more danger that you'd be with a friendly boss.

It's also possible she's acting this way in an effort to assert her authority. She may be unsure of herself and feel she needs to come on strong to compensate. That's not unusual.

If you determine the problem is with your boss, don't bother trying to change her; that will either happen naturally over time or not at all. Instead, make sure your career is in play. You don't need to be actively searching for a new job, but you should be networking and responding to any openings you think look promising. Soften the image of you as an icon of the company.

If you determine the problem is with you, then you need to accept you have a real problem. A boss who dislikes you will seize on any excuse to let you go—and these days, she won't need much of an excuse. The way to own the solution is to first, start aggressively looking for another position. Don't wait for better opportunities; look for anything comparable. Earning less might be okay, too, if the job has apparent potential. Second, do whatever you can to improve your current situation.

Unburden Yourself

Resist the urge to go over your new superior's head to discuss the situation with her boss or someone in human resources. If you think your boss doesn't like you now, wait until you see how she treats you after you've done an end run. And believe me, no matter what you're told, she will find out about it. Human resource people are dutybound to be Trojan horses. For the company to investigate or call her on this behavior, they'll have to tell her that someone has complained. Since she already doesn't like you, you'll be the number-one suspect. The only time to do an end run like this is when you already have another job locked up and you want to either take a parting shot or make one last desperate effort so you can stay where you are.

Other than talking about the problem with your family and friends to receive support and advice, the only place you can turn to unburden yourself is to your mentor. This could be the person who first brought you into the company or industry, or someone who has helped guide your professional advancement. Schedule a lunch or dinner meeting with her to emphasize that you want to keep this exchange separate from the workplace. Explain what has happened and ask if she has any insights on this new manager. If your mentor doesn't know your new manager, ask if she can find out anything that could be helpful. You're not looking for blackmail material. You're looking for something that will allow you to make a personal connection.

Diagnose the Impact

Obviously the impact of this situation on your career and life could be dramatic. In the most extreme case you might be fired and put in financial jeopardy. You might become the go-to person for every dirty job and problematic assignment that comes up. If you succeed, you'll just end up getting more. If you fail, you'll reinforce your boss's negative opinion of you. At the very least, you'll find your career stalled, with no potential for either advancement or salary increases. If you're less than five years from retirement, that might be something you can live with. Terminating someone close to retirement is dangerous for the company, since it could be grounds for a lawsuit. But if you're not close to retirement, having a stalled career puts you on the short list to be the next person fired.

Take Your Financial Pulse

Go over your personal finances with an eye toward establishing an emergency fund equal to three to six months of your take-home pay. Now, when you first sense your job might be in jeopardy, is the time to start cutting back on luxury expenses and to stop buying anything you don't absolutely need. Funnel those savings into a money market account rather than your checking account so you don't just spend it on something else. Look to solidify any savings and investments, getting out of high-risk stocks or funds and shifting to more conservative instruments. Live and invest conservatively until your job situation becomes more stable.

Start Palliative Measures

In this situation, your palliative measures involve behavior rather than money. Could your new boss's dislike of you be the result of anything you did? Maybe you made a critical comment about her background when she first arrived. Perhaps you are more knowledgeable than she about some element of the job and you weren't shy about it. As a result she might feel threatened by you. Or it could be you disagreed with an early decision of hers, leading her to believe you're not on the team. If you can't think of anything that might have happened, ask your peers if they can think of anything. Check with your mentor as well; she might have heard something.

If you decide the fault is yours, make a formal appointment to meet with your boss. Act as if you were meeting royalty, showing all the respect and deference you can muster. When you come in, begin by thanking your boss for seeing you. Don't sit down unless prompted. Say that your career is very important to you and that you care a great deal about the company. Explain that sometimes your zeal to do the best job possible gets the better of you, and you sometimes get out of line. Add that if you've done anything like that in the past that might have made your boss concerned, you'd like to apologize. Conclude with the promise that your boss will never have to hear you apologize again.

If there was one particular incident that irked your new boss, now is when you'll hear about it. She'll probably take this opportunity to go over it, just so she can get another apology from you. Don't disappoint her. Apologize again, but this time with even more conviction. This should placate your boss long enough for you to find another job. In fact, she'll probably treat you well now that you've assumed a submissive posture.

If there wasn't any one incident that led to her dislike of you, but instead she has a general complaint about your behavior or attitude, now is when you'll get a lecture. She may go into a litany of complaints, or make some sweeping generalizations. Listen as if she was telling you the secret of life. Thank her effusively for all the guidance she has given you. This probably won't lead to any improvement in her treatment of you. She's waiting for a body of evidence to prove your behavior and attitude has changed. The good news is that while she's accumulating evidence you can be looking for another job.

If your boss responds to your apology with puzzlement, wondering what you're talking about, you've made a mistake. Maybe her treatment of you wasn't actually about you, but was about her. Or it could be she dislikes you, not for something you did, but because of who you are. That can only be addressed through rehabilitation.

Launch Revenue Rehabilitation

Rehabilitation in his situation refers to your image, not your revenue. When someone dislikes you because of who or what you are, she's seeing you as representative of some group, rather than as a human being. The only way you can try to overcome this, is by making her look at you as an individual.

Try to find some way you can make a personal connection with your new boss. What traits do you both share? Are you both married? Do you both have children of similar ages? Maybe you're both dog or cat owners. What books do you see in her office? Have you seen her reading any particular newspapers or magazines? Could you discuss those with her? Look around the walls of her office. Did she hang a diploma? That means she's proud of her degree. Do you have some connection to her alma mater? Has she framed pictures from a trip she took to France? Maybe you could talk about Paris, or travel, or photography with her. How does she get to work? You could commiserate with her about the problems of mass transit, or traffic on the expressway. Maybe you both drive Toyotas, so you could ask her for advice on where to get your car serviced. If you can't get insights first hand, do some digging. Ask people in the office for any insights into your new boss. Google her. Do anything you can to find some personal characteristic you can use to make a connection with this person.

When you find a connection, exploit it shamelessly. Don't just complement her photography, ask her advice on buying a camera. Don't ask if she's read the latest John LeCarre novel, buy it for her, saying you received two as gifts. Such over the top behavior can't backfire. She might grow to see you as a human being, rather than as representative of some group she dislikes, and change her treatment of you. Even if she continues to dislike you, she'll now be less likely to fire you. She'll believe that doing so after such overt efforts at friendliness will lead to uncomfortable questions about her real reasons. Once again, use the time you've gained to find another job.

I'd be remiss if I didn't digress and write a bit about the ethics and morality of creating a personal connection with someone who stereotypes. First, I think everyone is correctable and deserves at least one chance to change their ways. Your making a personal connection with someone who is prejudiced has the potential to turn that person around. Second, I assume because you're reading this book that it would be disastrous if you lost your stream of income. Sometimes we have to compromise our principles to keep a roof over our family and food on the table. If you are independently wealthy and don't care about losing your stream of income, by all means call this person on her stereotypes. If you're relying on your salary to survive, do what you have to last long enough to get another job. Once you've formally landed another job, feel free to tell her off or pray for her.

Mercedes Jackson couldn't figure out why her new boss disliked her. She'd been nothing but welcoming and solicitous. They were both African American women, so it couldn't be racism or sexism. Mercedes set out to make some connection with her new supervisor. The woman decorated her office with pictures of her family. Mercedes saw one picture of a teenage boy in a football uniform. Mercedes mentioned that her son played football as well, and asked if that was a picture of the woman's son and what position he played. With evident pride, the woman said that was indeed her son and that he was now playing quarterback for a college in a nearby state. Mercedes and she chatted for a bit and the ice seemed to crack, if not break open. Mercedes did some further digging and learned from her mentor, who was now manager of a different department, that Mercedes's new boss had only reentered the job market recently when her youngest son had gone away to college. Mercedes sensed that perhaps her new boss had a problem with Mercedes being a working mother. Over the next few weeks, Mercedes subtly dropped hints about how she wished she could be home with her son, but how important it was for her to save enough so he could go to college. Slowly, Mercedes's new boss seemed to warm up. A year later, when Mercedes left for another job, the woman actually said she was sorry to see Mercedes go.

Cultivate Antibodies

There are some limited preventative measures you can take so this doesn't happen again. As soon as you first hear you're getting a new boss, go into self-censoring mode. Say nothing that could in any way be construed as critical of anyone, not your old boss, not the company, and not the new boss. Limit your comments to innocuous statements such as: "These things happen," and "You're sure it's in everyone's best interests." Keep a smile on your face. Don't join in any group conversations about the situation or the individuals involved. When your new boss arrives, walk on egg shells. Be solicitous and open minded. Never let the phrases "we always" or "we never" cross your lips. Your new boss defines the new "we." Using these phrases will separate you from her. Characterize her ideas as interesting, new, and innovative. Take your cues on behavior from her. If she shows up early, do so as well. If she wears a blazer whenever she leaves her office, do the same. You want her to look at you and see her reflection, to listen to you and hear a recording of her voice. Do that, and unless she stereotypes you, your job will be as safe as it was before she came.

LIFELINE
20

You've Been Embezzled

On Friday, your regular office manager was out sick with the flu so, rather than waiting for Monday for him to come back in, you decide to stop into the office over the weekend to pay the bills yourself. You're stunned to find bills for six different credit cards, in the names of your office manager and his family members. Or you get a call from two of your employees complaining their payroll checks had bounced. You go into the office that night to check and find that your bookkeeper has been writing checks out to cash for himself, depleting the accounts.

Danielle Kroner was on vacation in Paris when she received a panicky call from Ramona, who managed her dental office. Ramona was more than an employee. She had worked for Danielle for 10 years and had been a guest at both Danielle's daughters' weddings. Ramona said her personal checking account had been frozen and she didn't have money to buy groceries over the weekend. When Danielle asked why the account was frozen, Ramona said she had put some refund credits through to the account from the office's credit card machine. Danielle asked why she had done that, and Ramona said she'd had to buy some supplies for the office. Danielle told Ramona she'd call her back and then contacted the credit card company. Assuming it was only a hundred dollars or so, Danielle was prepared to get angry. The credit card company explained that it was actually $6,000 this past week and that in the past year there was a total of $35,000 in refund credits that had been issued.

Accept the Problem and Own the Solution

Embezzlement is a particularly painful problem because it involves personal as well as business issues. Individuals are able to embezzle funds because they have been placed in a position of trust. In small businesses, the embezzler is often a long-time trusted employee who is almost a member of the family. So when it's discovered that they've stolen from the business, it's a double betrayal. More than one of my clients who have gone through this spoke of feeling violated.

I hate to say it, but in almost every case, suspicions of embezzlement are eventually proven true. If you suspect someone, say your office manager, is stealing, they almost certainly are. That's an important thing to understand, because accepting the problem and owning the solution will require you to go against your instincts. Almost everyone who suspects they are being embezzled concentrates on the personal betrayal. They confront the person with their suspicions and ask for explanations. Sometimes the embezzler will offer a sob story about his own family crisis. Other times the embezzler will deny it and say it's just the result of an idiosyncratic bookkeeping method. Usually the embezzler will ask you not to call the police and instead give him a chance to pay the money back. In each of these potential responses, the embezzler falls back on the personal relationship that has developed.

To overcome this problem you need to accept that it's not a personal issue, it's a crime. And the solution you need to own is first, getting as much money back as you can, and second, seeing the culprit punished. That will require you to refrain from confronting the suspect and instead, getting some outside help.

Unburden Yourself

You don't want to confront the suspect yourself because, whatever he says, the first thing he'll do is try to destroy evidence. That could mean getting rid of documents but it could also mean spending any money that's left. It's likely there isn't a bank account someplace containing all the money that has been stolen. Most often, embezzlers begin stealing money because they can. Maybe they had a bill they couldn't meet or there was something they wanted to buy but couldn't afford. When they see they can do this and not get caught, they get greedy and just keep on doing it. Rarely is it to accumulate cash. It's usually to fund addictive behavior or luxury purchases. The way you might be able to get some of your money back is to have their assets frozen and then eventually sue them in civil court.

To get the evidence you need and take steps to maximize your chances of getting restitution, you need to enlist professional help. Contact your personal lawyer and explain your suspicions. Ask him for the name of an attorney with criminal law experience and for the name of a certified public accountant with experience in forensic accounting or auditing. Do not ask your regular business accountant for a suggestion. In fact, don't say anything about this to your current accountant. The embezzlement is a sign of a failure on your accountant's part. He should have either prevented it or been able to spot it. That neither took place means your current accountant is either incompetent or in cahoots with the embezzler. In either case, you now want to keep him out of the loop. A forensic accountant can cost anywhere from $300 to $500 per hour. An attorney with a background in criminal law will charge between $250 and $600 per hour.

Diagnose the Impact

The forensic accountant will try to diagnose the impact of the embezzlement: How much has been stolen? He will comb the records looking for signs of theft. In addition to gathering evidence, the audit should be able to reveal how the embezzlement was accomplished and determine how long it was going on. For example, the auditor might find a series of checks made out to cash and endorsed with a forged signature. These might stretch back for three years. If possible, have this audit conducted at a time when the suspect isn't on site—perhaps over the weekend or during the evening.

Take Your Financial Pulse

It's ironic, but there is a silver lining to finding out you've been embezzled. As one client of mine jokingly explained, the result of solving the problem was that he got a raise. At some point in the process, it's important to rerun your business's financial statements, adding in the funds that were being stolen. Ever since the theft started, you've been gauging the health of your business by inaccurate measures. You may discover that you really do have enough money to expand, to buy new equipment, or to give raises to the staff.

Start Palliative Measures

The first thing you and your team of professionals need to do is make sure no further embezzlement can take place. Your and your auditor need to quickly come up with a plan to close whatever holes exist in your financial system.

Next, your attorney should attempt to freeze the suspect's assets so that, if there is still some of the stolen money around, he won't be able to spend it. This will involve the attorney going to a court and providing evidence of the theft itself and evidence the alleged perpetrator's accounts could hold illegal gains. This can be kept secret from the embezzler. Courts are usually very good about quickly scheduling hearings to empower such freezes.

Launch Revenue Rehabilitation

Once your palliative measures are in place, sit down with the suspected embezzler. Don't tell him about your suspicions. Instead, present the suspect with the evidence you've uncovered and ask for an explanation. Be prepared for outright denial or a rationalization that plays on the personal connection you share. Whatever the response to your question, say you need to get the money back right away. Say that it's possible this could be handled internally if all the funds are returned immediately. In the unlikely event that the embezzler is able to return all the money that has been stolen, terminate him and say you will not be providing any references; you will simply acknowledge his employment. Unfortunately, things probably aren't going to end that neatly.

Danielle Kroner called her attorney as soon as she'd finished speaking with the credit card company. He told her not to say anything that might scare off Ramona, but to immediately contact a forensic accountant. Danielle told Ramona she'd wire her $500 for the weekend and they'd figure things out when she got back that coming Monday. Meanwhile, Danielle arranged to fly back early and to have the accountant meet her at the office that weekend. It took the accountant only a few hours to determine that in addition to the $35,000 in fraudulent credit card refunds, there were forged checks of probably another $300,000 stretching back nine years. Danielle immediately froze all her accounts. That Monday, she confronted Ramona, who denied almost everything despite the evidence. Danielle fired her and contacted the police. Eighteen months later, Ramona was sentenced to two years in jail. Danielle has changed all her office's bookkeeping procedures and now keeps a measured distance from all the office staff.

Cultivate Antibodies

There are two things you can do to ensure this doesn't happen again: You can institute new bookkeeping procedures; and you can prosecute the embezzler.

The way to have an embezzlement-proof bookkeeping system is to have a set of checks and balances so two individuals are responsible for finances, and that there is a third person—a certified public accountant—who performs periodic oversight on the work of the other two. For instance, if you have a personal assistant who handles finances, make sure he has the authority to write checks only up to a certain amount. Any check above that amount will either require pre-approval or a second signature. Then, every month your accountant goes over the records to make sure they're accurate and procedures are being followed.

I believe you owe it to society to press charges against the embezzler. Firing him and changing your system protects you, but that doesn't protect the next businessperson who hires the embezzler. First do everything you can to intimidate the culprit into paying back the money. Law enforcement isn't a collection agency. There may be some chance for restitution, but usually the authorities focus on arrest, prosecution, conviction, and punishment. Be as supportive and helpful to the authorities during the legal proceedings as you can be. Don't let your formerly close relationship with the embezzler keep you from pursuing the matter to its just conclusion. Once the charge is disposed of, speak with your attorney about the possibility of filing a civil action against the embezzler to get a claim on existing assets or future earnings.

LIFELINE 21

You Haven't Saved Enough for Retirement

You get a call from your stockbroker asking if you'd like to meet to go over your portfolio. You agree, and over lunch your broker explains that at your current rate of investment and with a historically average market performance you'll have a retirement income of $30,000 if you retire at age 65 and live to about 80. Or you've been retired for two years when you realize you're actually spending more than you earn. If nothing changes you'll run out of money completely in eight years.

Daniel and Beth Garcia have had their heart set on retiring to London ever since they visited on their honeymoon. Over the years, they set aside as much money as they could in tax-deferred retirement plans. Sometimes it was difficult or impossible because they were also setting aside money for their son Sam's college education. With Sam having just graduated college and Daniel about to turn 50, the Garcias decided to sit down with their financial planner to gauge their progress. The planner, using a sophisticated new application, input their investment portfolio, ages, Social Security and anticipated retirement date. The result threw the Garcias into a depression. It looked like they'd only be able to count on about $60,000 a year in income; half what they thought they would need to live in London.

Marylou and Arthur Parker were thrilled when they first arrived in Southeast Florida. Long-time residents of a suburb outside

167

Chicago, they sold their split-level home and used the proceeds to buy a luxurious two-bedroom condominium in an adult community surrounding a golf course. The condo was decorated to their specifications, making it all the more satisfying when they moved in. The Parkers were planning to rely on their Social Security as well as income from their investments. They both jumped into the lifestyle of their community, playing golf daily, going out to dinner nightly, and thoroughly enjoying themselves. It was about eight months into their new life that a hurricane hit. Although their unit didn't suffer any damage, the community itself was hard hit. This resulted in a special assessment and an increase in the maintenance. It also led to their insurance being canceled, forcing them to find another policy that cost twice as much while offering half the coverage. Going over their bills shortly thereafter, Arthur discovered they'd need to pull money out of their principle. At this rate, they'd run out of money in less than eight years.

Accept the Problem and Own the Solution

You are not alone. Don't believe all the newspaper and magazine articles that make it seem common to retire in style. Their profiles of people who built up retirement savings of $500,000 by the time they were 50, or individuals who are living like royalty after retiring early, are not the norm. Most people haven't saved as much for retirement as they believe they should. And most retirees don't feel secure and comfortable financially. Accept that this is a very common problem. And here's more good news: This is an extraordinarily easy problem to solve. Why? Because it's a problem of your own creation.

Your problem really isn't that you don't have enough money for retirement; it's that you don't have enough money to give up work entirely and forever at the age of 65. There is no reason why you need to stop working completely at age 65. I'm writing this at the age of 78 and, while I'm not the workaholic I was when I was 68, I'm still in the office working at least four days a week. And I'm no more an exception in my continuing to work than you are in not feeling like you have enough money for retirement. Most people who stop working entirely at age 65 find themselves back at work in two to three years; some because they need the money, and some because they simply like having a purpose. Your real problem is that you don't have the resources to live out what has become the traditional model of retirement. I'm all in favor of most traditions, but this one deserves to be broken.

This isn't even a very old tradition. Retirement as we now know it didn't exist prior to the 1930s. Social Security was developed and promoted by Franklin Delano Roosevelt as a way to convince older Americans to leave the workforce to free up jobs for young people. The Great Depression had led to massive unemployment, and there is nothing more dangerous to social stability than millions of unemployed young men. Since then, Social Security benefits have been expanded dramatically. From the 1930s to the 1980s, private pension plans also boomed. The financial services industry saw money to be made and began relentlessly promoting retirement. In less than half a century, it evolved from a social experiment to a presumed entitlement.

Retirement made a lot of sense at a time when you weren't going to live much longer than age 65, when your job was back breaking, when you got less productive as you got older, and when society had to make room in the job market for lots of young people. An idyllic retirement was actually possible for the postwar generation, who could take those expanding benefits and pensions and add to them a windfall profit from the sale of their real estate. That gave them a big chunk of cash with which to buy a new home, have some leftover principle to invest, and use that pension income and Social Security to pay for endless early-bird specials.

I believe that today retirement is not only *not* worth striving for, it's impossible for most—and something you should do your best to avoid. The notions that it is based on are simply no longer true.

When age 65 was chosen as the retirement age, most people died at 63. Today, not only are you likely to live into your 80s or 90s, but your older years are going to be active and productive ones. Retiring at age 65 will mean spending two decades doing needlework and gardening.

When retirement was first developed, everyone thought leisure was automatically more fulfilling than work. But if you're like most of my clients, you've tried to find fulfilling work and have made it as integral a part of your life as play.

When retirement took hold in the American mind, most work was physical in nature. That meant older workers were less productive than younger workers. Today, the most physically demanding part of your job probably is manipulating the keys on your Blackberry. Most evidence indicates that today, older workers are *more* productive than younger workers.

When retirement was first being promoted, America had a large generation of unemployed young people that it had to absorb into the work force. Today, there are smaller generations waiting in the wings and unemployment is at historic lows.

Finally, the financial trends that made it possible for your folks to retire fully at age 65 have changed: Social Security is shrinking and under threat, private pensions are gone, and real estate in traditional retirement areas is no longer the bargain it once was.

Owning the solution to your "problem" means redefining it. Rather than model yourself after a lemming and jump off the workplace cliff at age 65, model yourself after the Greek hero Ulysses and look at your life as a lifelong journey with ups and downs and twists and turns. Work as long as you'd like. Perhaps in your current career, but maybe in a different one. Continue full time or go part time. Go back to school during the day and work at night, or the reverse. Sell your possessions and travel. Basically, do what you want, when you want, for as long as you want.

Unburden Yourself

If you're not going to follow a traditional path, you'll need to break out of the traditional planning mode. That means hiring an intelligent, independent-minded financial advisor, rather than relying on advice from a salesperson, magazine columnist, or—I hate to say it—author. Your "retirement" is going to be a custom job, so you don't want a plan that comes off the rack. For years I advocated the use of fee-only planners as the best way to ensure getting good, unbiased advice. But despite the urging of myself and others, fee-only planning hasn't been accepted by the general public. With so many salespeople out there offering "free" advice, consumers haven't been willing to spend money on financial planning. That has led most independent planners to come up with hybrid practices in which they charge lower fees but also receive commission on the sale of some investments. As a result, I now suggest you simply look for an independent financial planner who you feel understands your goals and sensitivities toward risk.

Diagnose the Impact

Since the solution here means redefining retirement, you can't simply go by a diagnosis of where you stand in terms of traditional retirement. Instead, you need to develop your own concept of retirement, establish a personal goal, and then diagnose where you stand.

Would you like to keep working in your current career? What about working part time in the same career when you get older? Have you ever given thought to changing careers? Are you interested in going back to school? Does an entrepreneurial venture interest you? How about working part time and volunteering part time?

Do you want to keep living in the same home you're in now? What about staying in the same community or area, but in a different home? Would you prefer to relocate? Does an adult-centered lifestyle interest you, or would you rather be in a multigenerational community? How about moving from the suburbs into a major city, or out to the country? Does moving to a small town or city intrigue you? What do you think about spending most of your time traveling, or moving overseas?

The idea is to give free reign to your hopes and dreams. Come up with a life plan you find exciting. Then, start to fill in the blanks. If your priority is doing some kind of work, how much income would that yield, if any? If your priority is having a certain type of lifestyle, how much income would you need to support it? That's the impact to measure: What will it take to make your dream come true?

Let's say you'd like to leave your job as marketing director of a housewares company and instead open a home-based pottery business. Contact industry associations, trade magazines, and most importantly, others who are doing this kind of work, and get an idea of how much money you could earn as a potter. Maybe your goal is to leave the suburbs and instead split time between a rural home and a small apartment in a big city. How much would it cost to buy or rent that small apartment in the big city? Then, how much would it cost to buy or rent a rural property far enough away to be affordable, yet near enough so you could travel back and forth inexpensively?

Take Your Financial Pulse

With a personal goal now in mind, it's time to take your financial pulse. Do you currently have, or, based on your current investments will you have, enough money to support the lifestyle you'd like? Alternatively, does the work you'd like to pursue now, or in the future, provide sufficient income to live in your current location, or the location to which you'd planned to move? Can you currently, or are you on track to, meet this new specific goal? If you are, congratulations: You don't have a problem at all. If you aren't where you need to be, or if you're not on the right track, don't worry, there are some simple solutions available.

Start Palliative Measures and Launch Revenue Rehabilitation

In this instance, palliative and rehabilitative measures are so closely entwined that it makes sense to review them together.

I don't mean to be glib, but if you're already retired and find you can't afford the lifestyle you've chosen, the answer is simple: Get a job. If you're already retired and find the work you've chosen doesn't pay enough to cover your bills, the answer is also simple: Move to an area that's less expensive. If you're not yet retired, things are a bit more complex, but still readily achievable.

Do you need to have more in savings to achieve a future lifestyle goal? One simple answer is to invest what you do have more aggressively. That, of course, carries the risk that you'll end up with less rather than more. A better choice might be to make further sacrifices now so that you can save and invest more. You'd be trading short-term luxuries for long-term pleasure. Perhaps the best solution is to extend the time frame for your goal. What will it do to the numbers if, instead of moving to Scotland at age 65, you do it at 70? What if you continue working while pursuing your lifestyle of choice? You could also combine all four solutions: Cut back some so you could set more money aside, invest that money a bit more aggressively, give yourself an additional five years to make the change, and then, work part time for the first five years of the new lifestyle.

Will you need to change your lifestyle in order to achieve the work life you'd prefer? You could delay switching careers in order to build up more savings. Maybe you could do your chosen work part time and something more lucrative part time as well. One of the most common responses is to cut back on spending to meet the lowered income. That's often easily achieved by moving to an area with a lower cost of living. It takes a lot less money to survive as an elementary art teacher if you live on a Native American Reservation in Utah than if you live in New York City.

Remember, this is a self-defined, and as a result, a self-created problem. You are totally in control of all the variables in this situation.

All you need to do is determine what's most important to you, and then figure out how to get it.

Faced with falling short of how much they'd need to have the retirement they wanted, Daniel and Beth Garcia did some soul searching. Neither was comfortable investing more aggressively. Nor was there really much cutting they could do to their current spending. They were already tightening their belt a bit, expecting they'd need to help Sam out until he was able to find a job and get settled. Although they were eager to move to London as soon as they could, they realized working until they were 67 or 68 would give them more time to save and let their investments grow, and would also mean they would collect more in Social Security. Since Daniel was a writer and Beth a photographer, they both felt they could continue to work on a freelance basis after they moved. Finally, they decided they analyzed what it was they liked about living in London and realized they could have much of the same lifestyle living in a less expensive city in the United Kingdom, such as Glasgow or Liverpool.

Marylou and Arthur Parker had fallen in love with their Florida lifestyle. Knowing it would be too risky to invest more aggressively and not wishing to move to a less-expensive community, they decided they'd make some changes. They began to eat at home most nights and go out just once a week. Arthur, a CPA, found part-time work doing bookkeeping for a local medical group and applied for seasonal work with a tax preparation firm. Marylou, a former high school teacher, updated her credentials and applied for work as a substitute teacher at a number of local districts. The Parkers were able to bring in enough to continue living in their condo. They decided that when the time came that they couldn't work anymore they'd sell this unit and buy something smaller and less expensive in the same community.

Cultivate Antibodies

This isn't something you're going to go through again, so no preventative measures apply. However you are indirectly cultivating antibodies in your family and friends. By blazing your own trail through the rest of your life you can be an example to others. You don't have to follow the pack. You can take the road less traveled. Robert Frost was right: It will make all the difference.

Your Spouse or Child Is Permanently Disabled

You just get into work when you receive a garbled call from your child's school. There's been a bus accident and your child has been seriously injured. By the time you arrive at the hospital, your son has been stabilized. You're told he'll live, but he has had a spinal injury and may never be able to walk again. Or you're sitting in the waiting room of the ophthalmologist waiting for your spouse to finish his check up. You're surprised when the doctor comes out to invite you inside. With you and your spouse sitting across from his desk, the doctor explains your spouse is losing his vision and will soon be totally blind.

Roger and Selia Jordan were standing in their driveway laughing at their 15-year-old son Ryan's antics when they heard the screech of brakes and a loud thud. They ran around the corner and saw their 17-year-old daughter, Monica, sprawled in the street next to the bicycle she was riding. Later that night at the hospital, the Jordans were told that not only had Monica broken her collarbone and both legs, but that her head had hit the pavement very hard, resulting in a traumatic brain injury. Six months later, Monica's collarbone and legs had healed and her scars were fading, but the effects of the head injury were becoming clear. It was taking her longer to do simple activities, like tie her shoes. Monica was having trouble with both her short-term and long-term memory and having a hard time reading. She also was often at a loss for the right word to describe something. Roger and Selia met with Monica's neurologist who explained that, while therapy can help, Monica will probably suffer from these problems to some extent for the rest of her life.

Accept the Problem and Own the Solution

You had no control over what has happened to your loved one, but you do have total control over how you deal with it. Your loved one is still alive and you are still together. You can choose to look at what has happened, and perhaps even your disabled loved one, as a burden, or you can look at it as an unexpected journey you're both now taking. Your loved one isn't less than he was before. He's the same person, but with a disability. Yes, this disability may completely alter your lives. But it hasn't altered the essential nature of you as human beings. In fact, I've been told repeatedly by those who care for a disabled spouse or child that they've experienced profound emotional and spiritual growth in the process.

I know this will sound absurdly optimistic to someone who is first coming to terms with this problem. However, it's true. That emotional and spiritual growth has come with a material price, and no one says they would have chosen this path willingly. But each and every person I've spoken with says that they've become a stronger, more compassionate human being because of what has happened. The choice, it seems, is to accept what has happened and go along with the change it has forced upon your lives, or to rage against it. The latter only brings anger, frustration, and bitterness. It doesn't change a thing. The former eventually brings its own unique form of spiritual contentment.

None of those I've spoken with would put it in these words, and I hesitate to do so myself, but I've never found people with more self-esteem than those who are caring for a disabled loved one. The disabled individual often comes to see his disability as a gift, opening him up to experiences, insights, and feelings he never would otherwise have known. He can't run away from his disability, so he's forced to come to the acceptance necessary to heal emotionally and spiritually. The spouse or parent of a disabled person can run away, whether figuratively or literally. He must choose acceptance. I think that knowing you could have run away and didn't helps you realize your worth as a human being. Although I've never met with anyone who ran away, I assume the sense of shame eventually becomes catastrophic.

Unburden Yourself

You are not in this alone. If you are married and your child is disabled, you and your spouse will need to share the load. That doesn't mean you need to come up with an exact 50/50 division of labor and time. One parent might stay home caring for the disabled child while the other works outside the home to bring in an income. The roles might be reversed during the evening or on weekends. Tap into family and friends for additional support. You will need time together, apart from your child. And your child will need time apart from both of you as well. Don't feel guilty about respites: Even God took a day off after creating the universe.

If it's your spouse who is disabled, you'll need to reach out to family and friends to share more of the load. Don't hesitate to tell people exactly what you need from them. If they can't provide it, suggest something else they might do to help. The friend who's uncomfortable watching your disabled spouse for an evening might be eager to do your grocery shopping. In addition, you might need to bring in paid help to provide you with a respite. Take advantage of support groups, social workers, occupational therapy, home aides, assistance animals, and supportive technologies. Investigate all your options for physical and emotional support.

Moreover, don't hesitate to take advantage of government or charitable programs. You and your spouse have paid taxes and donated to charity in the past, so you have contributed to the creation of these resource pools. You are entitled to draw on that largess now if you need it.

Diagnose the Impact

You need to become an expert on the physical condition of your spouse or child. Don't rely on a single physician or expert. Research treatment options, both traditional and alternative. Investigate experimental therapy programs and research trials of new drugs. The Internet has made it possible for anyone with the desire and the bandwidth to become knowledgeable about almost any topic. The more knowledge you can gain about your loved one's current and future abilities and limitations, the better you can plan and eventually deal with them.

How will your loved one's condition change and develop? What can be done to delay deterioration or accelerate improvement?

What will his capabilities be in a year, in 5 years, or in 10 years? Will your spouse ever be able to return to his career? Will he need to do different work? Will he be capable of any work at all? What will your child be able to do? What will he need to attend school? What are his educational and career options in the future?

No one knows what the future brings. You know that better than most. But having a general sense of what is possible can help you create a strategy for the future. That's essential for everyone's mental health. You all must have a course you can travel. It isn't enough to tread water. That's survival, not living.

Take Your Financial Pulse

How will the condition of your spouse or child affect your financial life? Look first at your income. If you relied on your spouse's income and he can no longer bring in as much money, or any money, what will that leave you with as a household income? Will one of you need to stop working, temporarily or permanently, to care for your child at home? What impact will that have on your income? Is it possible to telecommute or set up a flex-time schedule? Next, look at your expenses. What will care of the disabled loved one cost? Will you need to pay for special equipment? Will your home need to be remodeled or modified in any way? Will you need a different vehicle? Will you need aides to come into the home? How much will that cost? Will your loved one need to be cared for in a nursing facility, either short term or long term? How much will that cost? Will it be more expensive to care for your loved one at home than in a facility? Will your daily presence and participation make a difference in your loved one's life and prognosis? These are tough questions, but this isn't the time to bury your head in the sand. The more exhaustive your list of expenses, the more effective your efforts to cut costs and increase revenue will be. Knowledge truly is power.

Start Palliative Measures

The way you approach cutting costs in response to a spouse's or child's disability depends on the degree to which you'll be able to maintain your income. If, on the one hand, you'll be able to continue bringing in the same income—say, you were a single-earner family before the disability and will continue to be so after—you need to simply look at your current spending and figure out areas where you can slow down, cut back, or eliminate outflows. If, on the other hand, your income will be cut—say you were a dual-income family and have now lost one, or worse, the single earner is the one who was disabled—you should take a more radical approach.

If the disability of your spouse or child forces a dramatic change in your income, you need to enact an equally dramatic change in your financial life. Instead of trying to squeeze your old money life into your new, more-constrained circumstances, you need to start from scratch. Determine the expenses you simply cannot cut: medical care and treatment for your loved one. Everything else is now up for grabs. Examine all your spending in light of what your income and expenses will be from now on. Consider selling your home and buying something less expensive, or renting. Sell the luxury SUV and buy a used, more economical minivan. Quit the gym and start walking or using free weights at home. Create an austerity budget and slowly add back in only those things you can afford. Buy a new outfit when you need it, not when you want it.

Launch Revenue Rehabilitation

Leave no stone unturned in a search for new sources of income. Does your spouse have disability insurance that will help compensate for lost earned income? Does the family quality for any short-term or long-term assistance, through Social Security, workers compensation, or any other government programs? Are there any charitable grants you could apply for? Pride is one of the seven deadly sins. Now is the time for you to put your pride aside and reach out for help.

Speak with parents and in-laws about money they might have set aside in their estate for future bequests. If there's a possibility of legal action that could produce a stream of income, pursue it. Hire a personal injury lawyer who will work on a contingency basis. Any investments you don't need to cash in immediately should be shifted to income production rather than growth. That goes for retirement and college savings too. If you need to break into tax deferred retirement plans just do it. Now isn't the time to worry about tax implications. Talk to all your family members, and make sure they understand what you're doing. Siblings of a disabled child should know that the family needs to change its former practices and make sacrifices. If that means they'll need to take out more college loans, so be it.

In all these measures, you need to do the best that you can. You owe that not just to your loved one but to yourself. At the same time, you must always be aware there's a limit. Everyone draws that line in a different place, but there should always be a line. To destroy your life, or the lives of your other children, in an effort to provide for a disabled spouse or child, turns this into a double tragedy. Does it make sense for your other children to now assume more of the burden of paying for their own college educations? Yes, I think it does. Does it make sense for them to not go to college so they can stay home to help? No, I don't think it does. Does it make sense for them to go to a college nearby rather than far away so they can come home more regularly to provide some respite for you? It depends on what they're giving up and how essential their contribution would be. Does it make sense for you to pass up on a promotion that will require a great deal of travel? Probably. Does it make sense for you to give up your weekly two hours at the knitting group? Absolutely not. Does it make sense for you to pass up on a trip taking your aging mother back to her birthplace in Italy? It depends on how much it will cost, how long you'll be gone, and whether your absence can be adequately dealt with.

Knowing that their daughter, Monica, would probably always suffer with some mental disabilities due to the brain trauma, Roger and Selia Jordan realized they needed to take stock. They had assumed Monica would go off to college. That didn't seem likely, at least for the short term. Monica would instead need occupational therapy and help with her problems. Caring for Monica wouldn't be a 24-hour-a-day job, but Roger and Selia agreed one of them should be home to take her to and from therapy and work with her. Roger earned more as an advertising agency account executive than Selia did as a graphic artist, so they decided she'd leave her job. Although

Second to Die Insurance

An excellent financial tool to consider if you're faced with caring for a disabled child is what's called *second to die insurance*. This is an insurance policy that pays off when the second of two named individuals dies. Because it takes two deaths to trigger a benefit, the premiums are less expensive than for comparable coverage of a single individual. Parents of a disabled child can take out this type of policy and arrange for the benefits to be paid into a trust for the care of the child. That will free surviving siblings or other relatives from having to assume responsibility for the financial care of the disabled child.

insurance would cover some of the costs of Monica's rehabilitation and therapy, there would still be considerable new expenses. With the family having one less income, things could get tight. Roger and Selia decided to dedicate their retirement savings to Monica's care. If that wouldn't be sufficient, they'd tap into the money they'd been saving for Monica's and Ryan's college costs. They sat down with Ryan and explained that he might need to take out more loans than planned so the family could help Monica. Monica's grandparents offered to help out however they could, including contributing to the cost of the rehab and therapy.

Cultivate Antibodies

You can't stop this from happening again any more than you could stop it happening the first time. There are times when lightening does indeed strike in the same place twice. What you can bring to a second such catastrophe is the knowledge that you were able to weather the first. You already know you have the courage and fortitude to confront and overcome this challenge. You will survive.

You Suffer an Uncovered Property Loss

Your six-week tour of Europe was the trip of a lifetime, but when you return home, you discover your home had been broken into and trashed beyond habitation. To your shock, your insurance agent says you're not covered because the house was vacant for more than a month. Or after three days of record rainfall, the stream behind your home crests its bank and completely floods your basement. While you were able to move most of what was stored down there, your furnace, hot water heater and electrical panel need replaced. When you call your insurance company the next day, the agent patiently explains that you are not covered for flood damage.

Aaron Gordon and Sandy Connors loved the weekend home they'd built on the Gulf Coast of Mississippi. A modern Victorian-style home with a lawn extending to a beach and dock, they'd spent every weekend they could there. They particularly cherished the two weeks each summer when their families gathered for a reunion. Aaron and Sandy knew from the projected path of Hurricane Katrina that their house was in trouble. When they arrived to inspect the house afterward, they found it was almost entirely destroyed. The roof had blown off, as had most of two walls, and what was left of the interior was spread over two acres of what was now a mud flat. Aaron and Sandy knew the damage wouldn't be completely covered, but they assumed their insurer would pick up a good share of the bill. The estimate to rebuild came in at about $130,000, and the adjuster thought about $50,000 was due to wind damage. But their insurer said it would only pay $1,500. It claimed the rest of the destruction was due to the storm surge, which wasn't covered.[1]

Accept the Problem and Own the Solution

Despite their heart-warming advertising, homeowners insurance companies zealously look to minimize their liability for damage claims. That's particularly true for incidents like hurricanes and other natural disasters in which there's a potential for huge payouts. There are a number of different common exclusions, but those that are the most problematic are for flood and earthquake damage. Insurance companies will cover water damage to your home as long as the water does not originate from the ground. In other words, if your roof is blown off and rain comes in, or a pipe bursts, the insurer will cover the damage. However, if a river overflows its banks or a storm surge washes into your home, you're not covered. To obtain coverage for flood or earthquake damage, you need to take out separate policies.

If you've experienced an uncovered property loss, you can't waste time and energy blaming yourself, your insurance agent, or God. You've got to accept it has happened, you're going to have to fight to get even a small portion of the cost of the repairs, and you're going to foot the bill for the rest. The way you own the solution is to get as much as you can from your insurer and then figure out what repairs to make and how to pay for them.

Unburden Yourself

Don't be surprised if a claims adjuster from your insurer is one of the first people who visit the scene. This isn't simply because your insurer is being neighborly. Insurers know that people in desperate straits will often accept whatever they're offered. The adjuster from your insurer may do a quick tour of the damage and say she can cut you a check right then for what she claims is the company's responsibility. If you've experienced only minor damage, you should just take the check. But if you've experienced catastrophic damage that will dramatically alter your lifestyle for some time to come, it pays to turn down the check.

Instead of relying on the insurer's estimate, you need to add someone to your team: a public claims adjuster. These adjusters work for the policy holder. They are trained in deciphering policy language, working through the bureaucracy, and negotiating for larger payouts. Like an attorney, an adjuster will control the flow of information to the insurer so you don't blurt out something that could potentially damage your case. For instance, if that damaged computer equipment was used for a freelance business, it wouldn't be covered. You'll have to pay the adjuster a percentage of whatever the insurance company pays you. This cut could range from as low as 5 percent of a very large settlement, to as high as 50 percent for a smaller settlement.

Diagnose the Impact

Once you've gotten your settlement, you'll need to obtain an accurate assessment of what repairs will cost. The quick estimates by the insurer and even the more extensive calculations of your public adjuster aren't really an accurate guide to what the work will actually cost. If your home isn't a total loss, my suggestion is that you bring in a good general contractor and pay for the contractor to prepare a set of specifications for exactly what needs to be done. You will then take this set of plans to three general contractors (one can be the drafter of the plans) and get bids. If your home is a total loss, hire an architect to draft plans for reconstruction. Once again, turn to three general contractors for bids.

Take Your Financial Pulse

Once you know what rebuilding or repairing your home will cost, you need to decide how you're going to pay for it. If you have the funds readily available, there's no problem. But few of us have this kind of money just sitting around. If you have a home equity line of credit, you could tap into it to pay for repairs. Alternatively, you could take out a home improvement loan.

If you need to completely rebuild, you can obtain a construction loan. This is really a temporary mortgage that acts like a line of credit where the bank disperses as the project progresses. When the project is completed, the construction loan is converted into a permanent mortgage, or you obtain a permanent mortgage from another bank to pay off the construction loan.

Start Palliative Measures and Launch Revenue Rehabilitation

If you find you're not able to obtain sufficient financing to return your home to its original condition, or you can't afford the loan payments total reconstruction would require, you need to make a decision. Do you have other funds you're willing to reallocate to the reconstruction of your home? Are you willing to invest your retirement savings in this home? What about your child's college fund? Do you have a potential inheritance from a parent you could draw on early? If you don't have or don't want to draw on these other sources, you'll need to rebuild on a smaller scale. Personally, I'd suggest cutting back on size and amenities rather than quality of materials or workmanship.

Rather than accept what they thought was a low-ball offer from their insurer, Aaron and Sandy hired a public adjuster. She was able to negotiate a significant increase in the benefit, but it still fell far short of the total cost of repairing the home. Although Aaron and Sandy loved the beach house they didn't want to devote their retirement savings to bringing it back to its original condition. Instead, they hired the architect who originally designed the house to draw up plans to rebuild a much smaller house. It sat on the same footprint but was a single story rather than two, and had two bedrooms and one bath rather than four bedrooms and three baths.

Cultivate Antibodies

The only way to prevent this from happening again is to make sure you don't trigger any gaps in coverage (such as having your home unoccupied for 30 days or more) and to expand your insurance coverage. Earthquake and flood coverage are available in separate policies that complement rather than replace existing homeowners policies. Insurers in California must offer earthquake policies, and it's offered in other areas as well. The federal government offers flood insurance, which carries premiums based on the perceived risk of your property to flooding. These policies won't cover the entire value of a home, and often carry high deductibles, but they do what you need: provide you protection from catastrophic damage.

Your Company Is Sold

Late one afternoon you and the rest of the management staff are called into the office of your company's founder and owner. He announces he has decided to sell the firm to one of his long-time competitors. Or for the past two weeks you've seen groups of men in suits at the plant, sometimes touring the facilities, other times meeting in the conference room. Early one morning, the boss appears on the shop floor, gets everyone's attention, and announces the company has been sold.

Thomas McGuire had been publisher of a successful professional magazine for almost 10 years. The magazine was one of a dozen owned by a second-generation entrepreneur. Before taking over for his father, the owner had been publisher of one of the other magazines in the company, so he, Thomas, and the other publishers had a very friendly, peer-style relationship. The firm was managed in an almost collaborative manner, with each publisher having a great deal of latitude. Thomas often compared it to a feudal system with each publisher having his own little independent fiefdom. The first time Thomas could recall a major decision not being discussed among the publishers was when the owner decided to sell the company.

Accept the Problem and Own the Solution

Many times, particularly in small- and medium-sized companies, long-term employees develop pride of ownership. You and a small group of others are working together as a team to accomplish goals. Good management encourages this sense of pride and belonging.

Employees are prompted to act as if they were, in fact, an owner of the company. The rationale is that "We are all in this together," and that "When the company does well, we all do well."

When your company is sold, all these claims are shown to be, at best, exaggerations. If you're not an owner of the company—you're not an owner of the company. The sense of camaraderie may have made you feel empowered, but you weren't. Your contribution may have been valued, but it didn't give you control of your own fate. That's really what this comes down to: lack of control. The sale of your company can be a rude awakening. It's a splash of cold water in the face. It demonstrates that, without equity in the company, you are nothing more than hired help. Lower-level employees are more likely to have known that all along. It's the mid- and upper-level employees who are more prone to have bought into the myth of empowerment.

To overcome this problem, you need to accept that you have to be like a free agent athlete: You work hard for your employer, but your first priority is yourself. The way to take ownership of the solution is to—from this point on—start putting yourself first.

Unburden Yourself

By all means, speak to your family and friends about what happened. Express your shock, anger, and disappointment to those close to you. But don't express it to your peers, subordinates, or superiors in the workplace. Say as little as possible about what has happened. Avoid gripe sessions and gossip gatherings. If you're asked, reply with a meaningless platitude such as, "These things happen." The company politicians will be playing politics like never before. The company complainers will be grumbling louder and more often. The whole formal and informal structure of the organization has been thrown into chaos. It's like you've all been thrown overboard from a ship. Everyone is trying to scramble back onboard. You need to paddle clear of the melee and rely on your own lifejacket instead.

If you are a key player in the company, either an upper-level management person or a stellar salesperson, there's one person you might want to add to your team: an employment lawyer. He will be invaluable in helping you take advantage of what could be a golden opportunity.

Diagnose the Impact

You might find it surprising that there's a golden opportunity when your company has been sold. Actually, there are number of them. The sale of a company doesn't necessarily put your position in peril. It may actually strengthen you. That depends on what level of employee you are and who is buying the company.

If you're a lower-level employee and the company has just been bought by another company with similar capabilities, you are in big trouble. One of the reasons one company buys another is to take advantage of economies of scale. Let's say one small newspaper buys another newspaper in the neighboring town. The new company doesn't need two mailrooms, or two receptionists, or two bookkeepers. The new owner will keep his own people and fire the people he has inherited.

If you're a lower-level employee and there's no overlap with the new owner, you're safe. Getting a handle on the qualities of lower-level employees is very low on a new owner's to-do list. He just wants to know that there are bodies in place who can do their jobs. His attention will be directed at the upper-level employees. The old owner's underperforming nephew who worked in the customer-service department will eventually be discovered, but even he has got some time.

If you're a key upper-level employee, this could be advantageous. Most companies are purchased, not for their physical plant or inventory, but for a much more valuable resource: people. New ownership is desperate to keep the key employees in place because if they leave, their new purchase drops in value. In addition, defections of key people would send a terrible message to clients and customers who are apt to be a bit concerned over a change in ownership.

If you're a mid-level employee, your fate may be in the hands of your immediate superior. If he is a supporter of yours, and uses the purchase of the company to solidify his position, your position has improved. If he bolts the company, you could be in position to move up. If he isn't a supporter of yours and instead you relied on the previous owner for support, you could be in big trouble.

Upper-level people who are actually in an improved position should speak with an employment attorney about the possibility of negotiating a contract with the new owner. At the same time they should demonstrate the allegiance to the new regime and their eagerness to be supportive members of the new team. The new owner may not be unfriendly, but it won't hurt you to be ingratiating.

Mid-level people who are in good shape should double their efforts to be supportive of their superior. Lower-level employees who aren't in danger should act as if it's their first day on a new job. Those who may be in trouble should continue reading this chapter.

Take Your Financial Pulse

Your financial goal is to do as much as you can now to prepare for a future termination. Do you have enough money saved to be able to pay your expenses for three to six months? If not, you've got to start building up that emergency fund. Put together a list of places you could turn for money until you've built up your emergency fund. Include credit cards, friends, and family members. Compile a list of all your expenses, with contact information for every creditor. Are there any major expenses coming due in the next six months that you might be able to defer or trim?

Start Palliative Measures

Start working on ways to extend your emergency fund now. Trim spending and bank your savings. See if you can make any illiquid assets more liquid without losing money or income in the process. Apply for a home equity line of credit now, while you're still employed. If you're terminated, you might not be able to get one. Similarly, if you need disability coverage, apply now. Stop using your credit cards and do what you can to reduce outstanding balances. Don't buy anything that isn't absolutely necessary. By all means, fix the brakes on your car. But now isn't the time to get a flat-screen TV.

Launch Revenue Rehabilitation

Start looking for another job with alacrity. Don't search just for better jobs, look for openings for equivalent jobs. In your situation, a lateral move is actually a positive one. Expand your outreach efforts to include people and industries you previously thought weren't perfect matches. Contact head hunters and employment agencies and tell them you'd like to put your career "in play."

My philosophy of job hunting is not to look down the road. Concentrate on getting interviews, rather than on landing the "right" job. I've seen lots of instances when a good interview turned an imperfect opening into the perfect one. At the interview, don't focus on whether you want the job. Your goal should be to get an offer.

A great job candidate is all potential. Even the most skilled employee has made mistakes. You, on the other hand, have never made a mistake. You're a potential messiah for the company. That sometimes leads recruiters to suggest increasing the salary or change the responsibilities of the job for which they're interviewing. If you start out looking to hire a house painter and you discover the next Picasso is sitting across the desk from you, your budget might expand considerably.

Initially stunned and angered by the sale of the company, Thomas McGuire took a couple of days to think things through before reacting. He made some subtle inquiries about the new owner among his friends in the publishing industry. It turned out the new owner was the former chief financial officer of a large magazine publishing company who had the backing of a venture capital firm. With no sales experience or experience in any of the industries covered by the individual magazines, it was clear the new owner needed the publishers. Thomas requested a contract. Once the new owner's counsel prepared a draft, Thomas had his own employment attorney look it over. After a week's intensive negotiations he and the new owner came to terms. Thomas's tenure at the company lasted another three years, at which point the new owner brought in an editorial director. Thomas, protected by his contract, received a sizable severance package which enabled him to retire two years earlier than he'd planned.

Cultivate Antibodies

The only ways to guarantee you won't face this situation again are to go into business for yourself, or insist on stock options as part of your future compensation. You could also negotiate an employment contract that stipulates either that any purchaser of the company would also be bound by the agreement, or that the sale of the company triggers a default by the employer. Otherwise, the best you can do is make sure you never again fall for the myth of the *empowered employee.* Outwardly play the part of the loyal subordinate, but make sure you're really always looking out for your own interests. That means constantly looking for a better job or other opportunities. Make sure you're never again this powerless.

You Lose a Key Employee

Your top salesperson, who is often responsible for more than half your store's sales, announces that she's leaving to take a job with another store. Or your general manager, who for more than a decade has been responsible for everything from managing the support staff to supervising the billing and bookkeeping, dies suddenly of a heart attack.

Darren Campbell's business had grown very successful over the years. Darren was an engineer who had developed a unique solar energy home heating system. Although he'd been successful enough at selling to launch and maintain the company, things really took off when he brought in a number of experienced salespeople. One salesman, a former general contractor, was particularly successful. He was regularly the company's top seller, and for a number of quarters was personally responsible for almost 25 percent of the company's revenues. That's why Darren knew he had a problem when the stellar salesman explained that he was leaving the company to launch his own contracting business.

Accept the Problem and Own the Solution

The loss of a vital employee can be disastrous to a business. Although we tend to think only of upper executives as being essential, it's mid-level staff that are often the critical cogs in a company: from the office manager who keeps operations flowing smoothly while the professionals generate revenue, to the field salesperson who's out there selling the products others are designing and marketing. It's these people who usually carry the institutional memory of an organization and put into practice the abstract ideas of upper-level staff.

It's common to have succession plans in place for the loss of upper-level executives, probably because such plans are drafted by other upper-level executives. But because the essential nature of mid-level employees' contributions is easy for executives to overlook, there's rarely a succession plan in place in case the company loses them. In addition, entrepreneurs tend to think of themselves as the only person essential to the success of their company, so they rarely provide for any succession plans. All this explains why you're not the only businessperson who has been caught short by the loss of a key employee. You need to accept that this person's role was indeed essential, and you need to take ownership of the solution by replacing her with alacrity, even if it means taking on more yourself.

Unburden Yourself

Although the selection of a successor may be entirely your responsibility, it makes sense to reach out to others for input. That's especially true if you're somewhat removed from the former employee's area of operations. Rather than reaching out to underlings who might be maneuvering for a promotion, or to managers who might be as out of touch as you, speak with peers of the individual you've lost, if that's possible. For instance, if you need to replace a regional sales manager, ask the sales manager of other regions for their ideas. You should also consider enlisting the help of head hunters and employment agencies. You'll pay a premium for these services, but they'll let you concentrate on stabilizing the company rather than sorting through and checking résumés. Most will present you with a small, prescreened pool of candidates from which to choose.

Diagnose the Impact

If you've overlooked the importance of this person in the past, it's time to compensate. Conduct a comprehensive analysis of exactly what this person did for the company. Part of this will be the formal role she played; say, managing the back office. Another part of this analysis should spell out the informal role she played in the organization. Was she the person who helped you keep your finger on the pulse of the staff's morale, or the feelings of customers? Did she mediate between two antagonistic executives or provide feedback on how marketing programs were working? To truly replace this individual you'll need to find someone to fill both her formal and informal roles. This may take more than one person. For instance, you might need to ask another long-term employee to step up and fill the informal role of a departed office manager. Or you may need to fill it yourself.

Take Your Financial Pulse

The most important calculation facing you is how much will it cost for you to replace this person Start with the costs of recruitment, if you need to look outside the company. Will you need to bring in temporary help of some kind until a replacement is in place or up to speed? If tasks will be temporarily divided up among other employees, how much will you be paying in overtime?

Next, consider compensation. How much will you need to pay a replacement? Don't automatically assume you'll pay the same salary. In some cases, you might be able to pay lower compensation to a less-experienced individual, or to someone you promote from within. In other instances, you might have to pay more. Perhaps the employee earned less than the market rate, either because she wasn't aggressive in asking for raises or because she didn't want to shift to another job.

Think about outsourcing the task rather than hiring a full-time employee. It's possible you could spend less and get equal-quality work. An accounting or business services firm might be able to take over the role of head bookkeeper or financial manager. Hiring an independent sales rep might be the best option for replacing a stellar field salesperson.

This is an opportunity to change the structure and operations of your business in such a way that you're never again so dependent on one person.

Start Palliative Measures

If you're replacing an inside employee—someone who didn't have regular contact with clients or customers—it makes sense to first look inside for a candidate. Office and plant staffs are like families: they are a web of unique and complex relationships. Bringing an outsider into this web can be problematic. For example, hiring an office manager from outside the company could be the equivalent of a widow with children bringing a new spouse into the household. It could turn out great or it could turn into a nightmare. For stability's sake, look to whoever is next in line inside the company. Who filled in for the departed individual when she went on vacation? Don't jump someone up the ladder of promotion over others unless you don't mind losing those employees who've been jumped. A logical promotion from within could go a long way toward easing tensions and fears raised by the key person's departure. If there is no obvious internal successor, or if the heir apparent fails to rise to the new job, an outside candidate will be less problematic for the other employees.

Launch Revenue Rehabilitation

If you're replacing an outside employee—someone who had regular contact with clients and customers—you must step into the breach. When a client learns that her regular contact person with a company is leaving, it may call into question the entire relationship with the company. Rightly or wrongly, the client sees the contact person as the personification of the company.

If the client receives good service, it's due to the efforts of the contact person. If products show up on time, it's because the client person focused on the issue. If the client is able to negotiate a good financial arrangement, it's because the contact person was able to intervene. The client may fear that the loss of the contact person could also mean the loss of all the good things she has come to expect from the company. That's a big problem.

An even bigger problem arises if your former key employee has now become a competitor's key employee. Your client might feel a primary allegiance to her contact, not to your company. When the contact person comes back as the representative of another company, the customer might shift to that new company. That's largely the reason company's poach each others salespeople.

The way to prevent this from happening is for you to reestablish yourself as the face of the company. This needs to be an entirely positive effort. You don't want to denigrate the past efforts or accomplishments of the former employee. That will only alienate. Instead, you want to resell each of these existing customers. Explain that until a replacement is in position, you will personally be handling the account. Stress that you are looking at this as an opportunity to demonstrate why your company is her best choice. In effect, seduce her like a potential customer you're looking to win over. Wine her and dine her; treat her special. Your goal is to show that her allegiance should be to your company, not to any one individual.

Darren Campbell realized the loss of his star salesman could be disastrous for his solar energy company. There was no logical replacement, since the salespeople all worked independently. And transferring a salesperson from another region would be like robbing Peter to pay Paul. The company's products were unique, so there wasn't a pool of experienced candidates from which he could draw. Darren knew he'd need to train someone from scratch. He also knew he'd need to make a personal connection to all the customers of the departed salesman. The first thing Darren did was sign the departing salesperson to a handsome two-month contract to select and train his replacement. Simultaneously, Darren personally touched base with each affected customer. Darren had the departing salesman set up the meetings and explain to each customer that he was leaving to go back into the contracting business. At each of the meetings, Darren sold the merits of the company and its products. He also invited each of the customers to an all-expenses-paid weekend seminar at a resort near the company's headquarters.

Cultivate Antibodies

Refocusing customers' allegiance from an individual to the company is a big part of making sure you're not in this position again. Consider marketing programs that support your efforts. For instance, why not invite customers to a company-sponsored event? Having quality salespeople is a big plus, so don't do anything to get in the way of their creating personal relationships with their customers. Just make sure that the relationship isn't the only reason your customers choose your company.

When it comes to inside staff, make sure you have a succession plan in place for your key staffers. One way to do that is arrange for the "next in line" for vital spots to assume the role for brief periods of time during the year—say, when the key person goes on vacation. You can't rely on someone being selfless enough to willingly help train a potential replacement. That's why I'd suggest you train

Key Man Insurance

One way to help ease the financial strain of losing a key employee due to death is to take out what is called *key man insurance*. This works just like a life insurance policy, except the company is the beneficiary. These can be whole life policies, but smaller businesses tend to purchase term instead, paying the premiums only as long as the individual is employed by the company. Coverage can range dramatically, but most smaller businesses opt for a benefit equal to two to three times the key employee's salary. These benefits can be used for any purpose, from paying down company debt to buying out the deceased's shares in the company. One other thing to consider: Since your business could suffer just as much from the disability of a key man as from his death, it makes sense to take out key man disability insurance as well.

yourself downward, learning essential operational skills you've always delegated. If you know the job you'll be able to bring someone else up to speed in an emergency. Consider signing key employees to employment contracts with secrecy clauses and restrictive covenants to keep them from defecting to competitors. Think about instituting rewards for departing employees who provide extended—for example, six months—notice.

26

You're Falsely Accused of a Crime

You're driving to a party one night when you get into a car accident. The two bottles of wine that were sitting on the passenger seat broke due to the collision. When a police officer arrives, he smells the alcohol and arrests you for DUI. Or you're in your office one day when two policemen arrive and place you under arrest. A disgruntled former employee has been arrested for drug possession and has fingered you as his financial backer.

Jerry Pryor was having a great time at the stadium. He and his 12-year-old son hadn't been to a baseball game for a couple of years, and they were really enjoying it. The only sour note was the four drunks in the row behind them. In the bottom of the eighth inning, a fan of the visiting team rose to his feet to cheer a home run. The four drunks taunted him. He responded in kind. When things started to calm down and the visiting-team fan turned around, one of the drunks tossed a bottle in his direction, hitting him in the head. Security guards and police arrived, and fans sitting around the injured fan pointed up to the drunken fans behind Jerry. But as the police started rushing over, the four drunks began pointing to Jerry, fingering him as the culprit who threw the bottle. Before he could even explain, the cops grabbed him, and pulled him out of his seat. Downstairs in a small police station, he was arrested for assault.

Accept the Problem and Own the Solution

People are falsely accused of crimes more often that we'd like to think. Police aren't in the business of judging guilt or innocence. They're in the business of making arrests. Newspapers aren't in the business of judging guilt or innocence, either. They're in the business of providing information and selling newspapers—and arrests are the kind of information that sells newspapers.

You need to accept that while the law says you are innocent until proven guilty, in the court of public opinion an arrest is as good as a conviction. Your reputation is damaged. There's nothing you can do to turn back the clock. The police won't be apologizing, and the press won't report dropped charges. You need to look forward and own the solution, which is making sure you're not convicted of a crime you didn't commit.

Unburden Yourself

This is not a solve-it-yourself problem. You need professional help. Don't use your family lawyer. Instead, ask her to give you the name of the best criminal lawyer she knows. Call that lawyer, interview her, and hire her if the fee is fair. You can tell your family the truth, but do not speak to anyone else about the situation. If you're asked, simply say you've been falsely accused but your attorney has advised you not to speak about it with anyone. Add that once this is all over, you'll be happy to discuss it at length. Say that to friends and extended family. Say that to employers and employees. Say that to coworkers and clients. Say that to the press and the police. The more you sound like a broken record, the better. Cut off your communications with the outside world to the extent possible. Go to work. Do your job. And keep your mouth shut.

Diagnose the Impact

You are not going to be able to determine the effect of this false accusation on your career or business until after it's all over. There's nothing you can do about it other than work to get this taken care of as quickly as possible. Financially, the impact will be that you have to pay a criminal attorney between $300 and $500 an hour to clear your name.

Launch Revenue Rehabilitation

Don't try to cut corners on your legal defense. Beg, borrow, but don't steal, to raise the money you need to pay your legal bills. Take out a second mortgage if you must. Use your retirement funds. Max out your credit cards. Ask your family and friends for loans. Do everything you need to in order to raise enough money to pay your legal bills.

Jerry Pryor was stunned when he learned that not only was he arrested, but that his arrest had been shown on television during the telecast of the game. He was released with an appearance ticket. Jerry knew he needed to hire a good lawyer and do what he could to clear his name. His family lawyer recommended an experienced criminal lawyer who charged $500 an hour. The lawyer was able to get the charges dropped at the next hearing. Jerry took out a home equity line of credit to pay his legal bills, and spent the next six months explaining what happened to his family, friends, and clients.

Cultivate Antibodies

There's no way you could prevent this from happening to you, and there's no way you can prevent it from happening again. The best thing to come out of all this would be that the next time you hear about someone being accused of a crime or some heinous act, you don't automatically assume guilt.

Your Bank Calls Your Line of Credit

Your banker calls to warn you that, rather than simply having to clean up your line of credit for a month as you'd done in the past, the new management of the bank is going to want it cleaned up permanently. Or your banker calls to tell you that the latest analysis of your financial statements shows you're no longer eligible for your existing line of credit and that it will have to be cleaned up in 60 days.

Jon Abrams had always cleaned up his cabinet making business's line of credit at his local bank over the summer, when business was very slow and most of his staff wasn't working. He'd pay of the balance at the end of June, keep it clean through July, and then tap it again in August, when he'd start ordering material for the fall season. That's why Jon wasn't surprised when his banker called in April to tell him he'd need to clean up the line. But he was stunned when he was told it wouldn't be reopened.

Accept the Problem and Own the Solution

In the past, commercial banks were very accommodating about business lines of credit. Typically, they would simply require the business to clean up—completely pay off—the line of credit for 30 days during the year, so they could characterize the line as a short- rather than long-term loan. But in recent years, banks have become more vigilant. Mergers and takeovers are leading to increased scrutiny by

bank examiners, and a stricter enforcement of lending rules. That
has led to more lines being called.

There's no point in berating yourself or your banker for the situation. Think of the situation as if you were pulled over by a friendly
local police officer for driving one mile an hour over the speed
limit during a week of intense enforcement, forced on the police
by political pressure. Both you and your banker are subject to forces
beyond your control, placed in a situation neither wanted. The way
to own the solution is to work on parallel tracks: trying to get your
existing bank to reconsider, and lining up an alternative lender.

Unburden Yourself

Although you may need to become more personally involved to solve
this problem, don't immediately jump to that conclusion. Instead,
speak with your investors. It's possible they could take over the loans.
Do you have any family or friends who might be able to make a short-
term loan to your business? You might also be able to obtain a bridge
loan from a vendor or supplier you're very important to. It's also
possible to arrange for the bank to change the line of credit into an
installment loan without allowing you to pay it back over a period of
years without providing additional collateral.

Diagnose the Impact

How much will you need to raise to clean up the line of credit? How
long do you have to raise it? Banks who push for a permanent clean
up tend to provide advance warning so you shouldn't be under
terrible time constraints. That said, if this problem comes at a time
when your business is short of cash it could be painful. The good
news is that there are some simple and effective methods to deal with
the situation.

Take Your Financial Pulse

All those methods will require that your business and personal
finances be in as pristine shape as possible. Sit down with your
accountant and go over the books. Have you been carrying accounts
receivable for too long? Offer a discount on outstanding balances
if they're paid off immediately. Is your inventory too large? Have
a sale and convert some of those boxes back into cash. Speak with
your banker and find out why your line of credit has been called.

Is there a specific number that bothered the examiners? Was there a financial ratio that was troubling to new management?

Start Palliative Measures

Knowing the reason for your line of credit being called is the key to launching your palliative measures. It's next to impossible to get a bank to change its mind. True or not, it will claim it was a completely objective decision. Suggesting there was a mistake or an error will only lead bankers to dig their heels in deeper. Instead, you need to say you understand and accept the decision, but ask for a reconsideration based on new facts you'll be providing. For example, you might be able to show that the sudden jump in the age of your accounts receivable which the bank found so troubling was due to a temporary glitch in your industry, not a permanent substantive change in your business. Revenue might have dropped precipitously due to a large payment being held back by one customer for tax purposes. The drop would therefore be balanced by a soon-to-come jump. Offer to reduce the bank's risk by putting more of your own money in the business, or by a cash infusion from one of your investors. Do whatever you can to get the bank to reopen your line of credit. Perhaps you can offer additional collateral. That may mean closing out your existing line and opening an entirely new one 30 days later so the bank can present it as a completely new transaction.

Launch Revenue Rehabilitation

Revenue rehabilitation in this situation comes through finding a *take-out bank*. Many businesses create borrowing relationships with two banks, not to double their borrowing power, but to be able to tap one to pay off the other. Ask your professionals for recommendations of candidate banks. Commercial lending has become a competitive business, so there should be institutions in your area eager to sign on new clients.

Jon Abrams asked his banker why his line of credit was being permanently called. It turned out that the bank's new ownership used different criteria and thought Jon wasn't collecting his accounts receivable quick enough. They were afraid the accounts that were more than 90 days overdue were actually uncollectible. Jon sat down with his accountant and put together a memo. He asked for a reconsideration based on a more detailed description of the nature of the outstanding money. It turned out, the accounts receivable the new examiners had found troubling were from a major university located in Jon's town. The university was notoriously bureaucratic and slow to pay, but the bills were certainly not uncollectible. At the same time, Jon approached another commercial bank in his community and negotiated a second line of credit, based on his personal credit. He used this to pay off the existing line, which was reactivated as a new loan 30 days later.

Cultivate Antibodies

Lining up that second line of credit is the best insurance you can have to protect yourself against this happening in the future. Another preventative measure would be to pay much more attention to your banking relationships. Keep in regular contact with your banker so you can learn about changes in bank policies ahead of time. If there are any changes in your business finances that could be of concern to your banker, let him know ahead of time as well. It's always easier to get prior approval than it is to get a reconsideration.

Someone Is Promoted Over You

Y ou're the senior regional sales manager in the company, yet the job of national sales manager went to the owner's son. Or you've been the top performing account executive for six years, yet the big new account was given to someone who'd only been with the agency for two years.

Paul Duffy had spent more than a decade heading up marketing for a privately held chain of high-end grocery stores. His actual responsibilities expanded to include far more than marketing. Eventually, he became a close confidant and colleague of the president of the company. When the long-time executive vice president of the company retired, Paul thought he was the logical successor. After all, he had been performing many of the executive vice president's functions the past two years as the man with the title eased himself into retirement. Paul was stunned when he was called into the president's office and found the man's nephew already there. The president announced that he was naming his nephew executive vice president and hoped that Paul would continue providing the great support he had in the past. Paul of course agreed and congratulated his new superior. But on the drive home from the office that evening he let loose a torrent of profanities.

Accept the Problem and Own the Solution

For some reason, many people still expect fairness in the workplace. They think promotions should go to those with seniority or who've been the top performer. The deserving should be rewarded; that's justice. Well, it is time for you to accept there's no justice in the workplace. The only reward the hardest working person usually gets is more work. The top performer is often compared to himself rather than everyone else, so excellence becomes the expectation. Many times the most skilled is passed over because superiors are frightened of her. You need to accept there is no justice in the workplace. The solution to being passed over is to find another job. The only question is how quickly you should act.

Unburden Yourself

It's best to share this information with your family and friends. They're apt to give you a needed boost of self-confidence and to reaffirm the unfairness of what's happened. This is also an opportunity to activate your professional and personal network. Explain what has happened and indicate that you're now actively looking for another position. If you have an in-company mentor, have a heart-to-heart conversation off premises to get her take on what has happened and why. Then, ask for her confidential help in your job search.

The people you don't want to open up to are your new superior and those who chose to skip over you. Instead, have a meeting with the newly promoted individual as soon as possible. Put on your most charming smile and say you're happy for her and are really eager to work for her. Say you're sure she's going to do a great job. Don't worry about this coming off as disingenuous. It never does. This person believes she deserved the promotion, not you, so your comments simply reinforce her own feelings.

Diagnose the Impact

The impact is clear: You have no future with this company. What you need to determine is how quickly you should get out of there. That depends on the reason why you were passed over.

If you were passed over because you lacked a particular skill that the other candidate possessed, your current position isn't in immediate danger. This wasn't an indictment of you or your performance. It was simply an indication you didn't meet the job requirements. However, it's also an indication you're probably not going to meet the requirements for any other promotions that come along, so you have no chance to move up. You have time to take palliative action and look for a better, not simply equivalent job elsewhere.

If you were passed over due to nepotism, your job might not be in immediate danger, but it's likely to get very difficult. It's obvious you'll never be promoted further unless you marry into the family. Your new superior may be in over her head, but she is also untouchable. That means she'll need someone to lean on to do her job, and someone to blame when things go wrong. Odds are, you're going to fill both jobs. She won't push you out the door, but she'll make your life miserable. You have some time, but not a lot. Start looking for an equivalent job. If that starts taking too long and the job starts getting intolerable, lower your sights.

If you were passed over for political or personal reasons—say, the person who got the job is a brown-noser—your job is in immediate danger and you need to get out of there as soon as possible. You area double danger to the newly promoted individual. First, you're living evidence of her scheming. She'd rather that be forgotten. Second, you could take revenge. There's an old adage: If you're going to overthrow the king, you'd better kill him. Well, you've been overthrown, and your usurper is going to now try to "kill" you. Find another job.

Take Your Financial Pulse

Prepare for a possible termination now so you won't have to start from scratch if you are fired. How much money do you have in your emergency fund? Are there any major expenses coming due in three months? How about in six months? Could you defer or trim them if you had to? Put together a list of all the places you could get additional money, including credit cards and family members. Compile a monthly budget with contact information for every expense.

Start Palliative Measures

Your goal should be to maximize the length of time you can live off of whatever is in your emergency fund. Cut your expenses to the degree possible and put the savings into your emergency account. See if you can make your illiquid assets liquid. For instance, apply for a home equity line of credit. Pay down your credit card balances. That will save you money and free up borrowing power. Stop making luxury purchases.

Launch Revenue Rehabilitation

If you're in immediate danger look for any acceptable job. If you have some time, start out looking for a better job but be prepared to make a lateral move if an opportunity presents itself. Expand the types of jobs for which you're applying. Network more broadly, including people and industries you used to think were too much of a stretch. Reach out to head hunters and employment agencies.

Apply for any and every possible opportunity with the goal of getting an interview. At those interviews, don't spend time deciding whether you want the job, focus on getting an offer. Once you have an offer, you can decide whether the job is right for you.

There are lots of times when attractive offers make candidates rethink their reluctance to take a job. Great job candidates are often perceived as workplace messiahs, leading interviewers increase the salary they're willing to pay, offer to change job titles, and maybe even rewrite the job description. Open yourself up to more potential offers and you open yourself up to more potential jobs and dramatically increase the speed with which you'll land a new position. Speed is vital if you believe you're in danger. You want to land a new job before you lose this one, because someone who's still employed is likely to get a much better offer.

Paul Duffy believed his job wasn't in any immediate danger. The new executive vice president was in over his head and would need Paul's help. The president, Paul believed, knew his nephew would be in over his head, but figured Paul would stick around to clean up any messes. Paul realized that no matter how close he was to the president, he wasn't family, and as a result, he'd never move any higher in the company. He started looking for another job. After six months of searching Paul found a position similar to the one he currently held, but with a regional supermarket chain. It paid more and offered stock options as well. Paul enjoyed the desperate look on the face of the executive vice president when he heard Paul was leaving.

Cultivate Antibodies

Other than going into business for yourself, there is nothing you can do to completely avoid being passed over for a promotion in the future. Don't count on fairness or justice. There will always be nepotism and politics involved in promotions. However, if you were passed over because you lacked a particular skill—say, you didn't speak a foreign language—acquiring that skill could prevent it from happening again. Most importantly, don't ever again fall for the myth that there's justice in the workplace.

29

Your Employer Has Declared Bankruptcy

You show up for work at your normal time, find your coworkers gathered outside, and see a sign posted on the door that says the company has filed for bankruptcy. Or the owner of your company calls everyone in your department into the conference room and says the company is undergoing a Chapter 11 reorganization but encourages everyone not to worry and just get back to work.

Marilyn Stamps had been a production manager at a mid-sized printing company for nearly 20 years. She'd often thought of leaving since she worked the high-pressure swing shift when most of the prepress work was done. But the benefits were far better than she could receive anywhere else, so she stayed. In retrospect, the extended meetings and long absences of the senior executives should have been a tip-off. Still, Marilyn and everyone else were shocked when the doors were locked at a change in shifts, leaving her and her coworkers out of work. A handful of uniformed security guards posted signs saying the company had declared bankruptcy, and telling everyone they needed to leave the grounds.

Accept the Problem and Own the Solution

When a business files for bankruptcy it means it's unable to pay its debts to its creditors. If your employer believes its business is still viable, but in need of relief, it will file a Chapter 11 bankruptcy. This means the court will protect the company and let it continue operating while it attempts to reorganize its finances by negotiating with creditors. If your employer believes the business is no longer viable, it will file a Chapter 7 bankruptcy. This is a liquidation in which the business sells off all its assets and the court directs the proceeds to the creditors.

Whatever form of bankruptcy your employer is going through, you need to accept that this is the end of the line for your job. Although management will likely encourage continued loyalty during a Chapter 11 reorganization and hold out hope for eventual growth, it's a smoke screen. One of the most common ways companies restructure is to cut employee salaries and benefits. A skeleton staff may survive the reorganization, but they will be underpaid and overworked and have no security. In a Chapter 7 bankruptcy, your job has just ceased to exist. The solution is to make sure you get as much of your pay and benefits as you can from your employer, while looking for another job.

Unburden Yourself

Figuring out whether you qualify for unemployment insurance, what will happen to your health coverage, and how you might be able to salvage pensions or retirement plans, will be a complex process.[1] This isn't a do-it-yourself situation. But that doesn't mean you need to hire professional help. Instead, turn to the counselors at your State's Department of Labor and the local office of the Employee Benefits Security Administration. In addition, you'll be able to get information and guidance from the administrators of your health plan. If you're a union member your shop steward should also be able to direct you to sources of assistance.

Diagnose the Impact

The long-term impact is that your job is over, whatever you're being told. Diagnosing the short-term impact is a bit more complex. In a Chapter 11 filing, your wages will still be paid as long as you're employed, although you might be asked to take a pay cut. Your pension and health plans may or many not be affected. In a Chapter 7 filing, your wages have ended, and since the company is using all its resources to pay off creditors, your pension and health plans are probably terminated.

In a liquidation, you can kiss goodbye any wages, bonuses, or reimbursements you're owed but haven't yet received. Any company stock or stock options you may have are now worthless. Bankruptcy laws prioritize creditors by category, determining who should get paid off first. Secured creditors, usually banks, are first in line. They often represent most of what a business owes, leaving little for the next class of creditors: employees who are owed wages, salaries, or commissions; and trade creditors. If your employer declared Chapter 7 bankruptcy while still owing you money, you'll probably only be able to collect a fraction of every dollar.

If your employer filed for Chapter 11 and you lose your job, but it continues to offer health insurance coverage to remaining employees, you will be able to obtain coverage through COBRA[2] protection. If the company drops its health benefits entirely in an effort to save costs, you won't qualify for COBRA protection. If your employer files for Chapter 7 bankruptcy, you won't qualify for COBRA protection.

[Special note: You'll now need to pursue two parallel tracks in solving this problem. On the first track, which I'll explain here, you'll need to gauge the status of your health coverage and pension benefits and seek to address any issues. On the second track you'll need to address your personal finances. For advice on that track, turn to Lifeline #2: You've lost your job.]

Take Your Financial Pulse

To get a handle on your rights to continued health insurance coverage and the status of your retirement funds and pension monies, you'll need to gather some documents. Look for the *summary plan descriptions* of both your health plan and your pension plan. These were among the documents you were given when you first signed up. If you can't find them, ask the plan's administrator for a copy. See if you can obtain a *summary annual report* for each plan. These will outline the plans' finances as well as provide names and addresses that could be helpful later on. Put together a file of all your pay stubs. These will help document your dates of employment, compensation, and regular contributions to the plans. Ask the administrator of the health plan for a Certificate of Creditable Coverage. This is a statement showing that you indeed had health coverage, and stating the general nature of the plan. Finally, gather together all the *individual benefit statements* you've received describing how much money is in your retirement account or the value of your pension benefit.

Contact the administrators of the benefit plans, preferably by telephone. Get the name of the person you're speaking with and ask for a direct telephone line or personal extension. If you can have all your conversations with this one individual, you'll save time by not having to go over the same information endlessly, and you'll also have a chance to establish a personal connection, which could be helpful. A friendly contact might be able to give you tips on how best to navigate a complex bureaucracy, or make sure your file doesn't get lost in the shuffle. Ask your contact whether the plan will be continued or terminated. Find out who will be acting as the plan administrator during and after the bankruptcy filing, and who will serve as trustee of the pension plan. If your pension plan is going to be terminated, ask how accrued benefits will be paid. Find out if terminated employees will qualify for COBRA protection. If the health plan is going to be terminated, ask how outstanding health claims will be paid. Get a date for when *certificates of credible coverage* will be issued—you'll need one to get new coverage.

Start Palliative Measures

Address your health insurance situation first, since that's your most pressing need. As I wrote earlier, if your employer is continuing to offer some form of health insurance coverage to remaining employees, you are entitled to COBRA protection. Be aware, however, that it might not be the same coverage you were receiving. For example, the company might eliminate coverage for most of its remaining employees and only continue a separate, more expensive plan for the executive staff. To qualify for COBRA protection you might need to purchase this more expensive package.

An alternative to COBRA protection is that you might qualify for special enrollment rights in your spouse's group health plan. Generally, this requires that you request enrollment within 30 days of losing your previous coverage. If you chose COBRA protection, you'll need to exhaust that coverage before you'll have another special enrollment opportunity to get onto your spouse's plan.

If you run out or don't qualify for COBRA protection, and you can't sign onto another person's plan, you'll need to get individual coverage. The Health Insurance Portability and Accountability Act (HIPAA) guarantees, under most circumstances, that you can convert your group plan into individual coverage.

With your health insurance coverage addressed, at least temporarily, you can focus on your pension and retirement plans. There are two important issues: safety and access. Bankruptcy usually doesn't put pension assets at risk. The Employee Retirement Income Security Act (ERISA) requires pension benefits be adequately funded, that pension money be kept separate from the rest of the business's assets, and that the money be either held in trust or invested in an insurance contract, such as an annuity. This should keep pension assets out of reach of creditors. When pension plans are terminated, your accrued benefit must become 100 percent vested. That means that even the benefits you would have lost had you left the company are now owed to you.

Defined contribution plans, such as 401(k)s have no further protection. You will receive all the contributions due you, however the continued health and growth of the money will then be up to you. If most of your savings were in the form of now worthless company stock. you're out of luck. Defined benefit plans are insured by the Federal Government through the Pension Benefit Guaranty Corporation (PBGC). This corporation guarantees that, if the plan doesn't have sufficient funds to pay the promised benefits, the federal government will make up the difference.

Your employer's bankruptcy will have no impact on when you can collect your retirement money. If the plan required you to turn 65 to collect benefits, you still won't be able to collect until then. Of course, whatever provisions may have been in place for early withdrawal will also remain in effect. Before you pull any money out, check with a your tax advisor, because the tax impact could be significant.

Marilyn was worried about how long it would take for her to find another job and what would happen to her 401(k). But most of all, she was concerned about her health insurance. Her husband's job didn't offer medical benefits, so the family's coverage came from Marilyn. When she returned home from the plant, Marilyn dug all her benefit information out from the file box they kept on the floor of the bedroom closet. She found contact numbers for the administrator of the health plan and gave them a call. After wending her way through a long series of automated messages, Marilyn finally got through to a human being. When Marilyn explained what had happened, the woman on the other end of the line told her she had only a couple of options. Since the company was being liquidated Marilyn couldn't continue the plan using COBRA protection. She was told she had a month-long window during which she could shift the whole family over to her husband's health plan. When Marilyn explained that her husband's employer didn't offer health coverage, the woman from the plan administrator suggested Marilyn convert her existing group coverage into individual coverage. It would be more money than she was currently paying, but it could tide the family over until Marilyn and her family qualified for benefits at another job.

Cultivate Antibodies

Other than working hard to make your employer profitable, there's nothing you can do to prevent another employer declaring bankruptcy. What you might be able to do, though, is get more advanced warning. If you work for a public company, obtain every quarterly financial filing and the annual report. Bring them with you to your accountant or financial advisor and ask for a quick informal assessment of the company's health. Once a month, check the business press and local newspapers for any mentions of the company. If you work for a private company, pay careful attention to any changes in behavior among the owners and top executives. Have they stopped providing free coffee to employees? Are they working late into the night or coming in on the weekend? Have they cut back on travel? Are there more closed-door meetings than usual, perhaps with groups of people you've never seen before? Alternatively, are they splurging on personal items using company money? If your boss replaces his company Ford Explorer with a Range Rover it could be a sign he's looking to pull as much money as he can out of the business before it goes belly up. If you're noticing unusual things going on, there are other unusual things going on that you're not able to see. Where there's smoke, there's fire. And if your workplace threatens to ignite, it's time to find another job.

You're Transferred Against Your Will

Your boss calls you into his office and tells you the company has decided to transfer you from New York to California to become the new manager of the Los Angeles office. Or your department is called into a conference room and told the company has decided to centralize operations and your functions are being transferred to Chicago. You are welcome to transfer along with them.

Susan Washington had seen her career steadily improve for the past 12 years. A journalist, she'd started out as a reporter on a small-town newspaper owned by a large national publishing chain. One year later, she'd been moved to become a reporter at the daily newspaper in a larger town. After two years she'd become a reporter at a paper in another location, this time a mid-sized city. Three years later, she'd been offered the spot as managing editor of the paper in a small city. She held that spot for six years, at which point she was offered one of the company's plumb assignments: an editing job on its national publication. It was what she'd been working toward all these years. However, her life had changed during that time. Susan's husband, Charles, was always supportive of her career. A carpenter and cabinet maker, he'd been able to find work wherever they moved. When they had children, Charles stayed home with each of the girls until they went off to school. They had put down roots, and the girls were particularly upset over the prospect of moving again. Charles said he would do whatever Susan wanted, but she could tell he was no more eager than the girls to uproot their lives yet again.

Accept the Problem and Own the Solution

There are times when a company decides to relocate operations. It may be due to economic factors. Perhaps the company has realized it can save money by consolidating two facilities into one. Or it could be for organizational purposes. The company may have decided it makes more sense to centrally locate a function rather than have it spread among different regional offices. There are also careers and industries in which advancement requires moving from location to location, pursuing opportunities no matter their geography.

Forced transfers can come at inopportune times. Maybe your spouse is happy at work, or your child has just made the high school basketball team. Perhaps you've found a house you love and have made close friends in the community. There may be some financial sacrifice as well: You could be asked to move from an area with a low cost of living to somewhere more expensive, or your partner may need to give up his job to come with you.

If you work for a company that has decided to relocate your function, you need to accept that your choice is between your job and your current location. If you're in a profession or industry that requires frequent moves, you need to accept that to climb the ladder you will need to be peripatetic, at least until you reach a high level. Owning the solution to this problem means focusing on the true choice: job versus location, or career versus location.

Unburden Yourself

This isn't simply a personal decision. If you are in a committed relationship, this will have profound impact on your partner. And if you have children, this could be traumatic for them. Even if you are not part of a couple, other people will need to be brought into the discussion: You have family and friends, and your moving will impact those relationships.

For couples, this situation usually requires one partner to become what is called a *trailing spouse*. He puts his career on the back burner, sacrificing opportunities and advancements so his partner can pursue her career. The same is often true of children who, if taught early on that this will be the pattern of their lives, learn to adjust to frequent moves. The key is that everyone in the family is in agreement and that a conscious choice is made to follow this lifestyle. If there is no agreement, or perhaps just a grudging acquiescence, resentments and guilt are sure to develop.

Even singles need to bring family into the discussion, particularly if there are aging parents involved. Moving far away from the rest of the family could mean not being able to provide emotional and physical support. This could end up alienating not only parents but also siblings who might have to pick up the slack caused by the move.

Diagnose the Impact

What will be the impact on your job or career if you *don't* accept the transfer? If you are in a career or industry that requires moves for advancement and you stop being willing to move, you're going to stop advancing. If you're within five years of retirement age, not accepting the transfer probably won't have any perceptible impact on your job. Your influence will be diminished, but you're unlikely to lose your job. You'll be viewed as a "dead man walking," just putting in your time until you leave. If you're more than five years from retirement from a peripatetic industry or company, not accepting the transfer puts your job in long-term danger. Careers aren't stagnant unless you're close to retirement, especially in companies that value flexibility. Since you've chosen not to move forward, you're now actually moving backward. You'll find yourself on the short list of possible termination candidates. When something goes wrong or finances plunge, you'll be out the door. If your company isn't normally mobile, but has shifted operations, turning down the transfer is the equivalent of quitting. No move, no job.

What will be the impact on your relationships and family if you *do* accept the transfer? How will your partner feel about, in effect, giving up his job so you can pursue your career? If he isn't career driven, it might not be problematic. This could actually be a great opportunity for him to change careers, or go into business for himself. But if he's even a slight bit concerned with his career, this could be a real issue between you. How old are your children? Moving is never easy for children, but it's particularly difficult for those in their middle school and high school years, when student bodies become very cliquish. However, if your child has been having a hard time in his current school, this can be an opportunity to start over.

Do you have aging parents? How will their care be affected by your move? Can your siblings help out more? If they're forced to take on more responsibility, how will that affect their relationship with you? They might feel as if you're "escaping" and leaving them to carry the burden of future elder care.

Take Your Financial Pulse

Do a thorough analysis of your current financial life, focusing primarily on your income and expenses. How will a transfer affect the numbers? Go over each expense line in your budget and try to estimate what it will be in a new location. You can get good information by contacting real estate brokers, tourism bureaus, and chambers of commerce in the area to which you'd be moving. Don't forget to explore the impact on your income as well. Although your income might go up, your partner's will likely drop, or perhaps even vanish for a time. Would your financial life improve, stay the same, or be hurt, by moving? Weigh that against the long-term impact on your career. Is it worth taking one step back in the short term to take two steps forward long term?

Conduct the same kind of analysis except now gauging the impact of not accepting the transfer. Your expenses will pretty much stay the same, but your income will end if you lose your job. How will your income be affected if you change careers, switching to a job that doesn't require frequent moves? How much money do you have in your emergency fund? Will that and your partner's income be sufficient to carry you until you find another job? If not, what assets and credit could you use to help bridge the gap?

Start Palliative Measures

Employers who require employees to move frequently usually provide some financial assistance. In most cases, this takes the form of covering moving expenses. Some employers assume responsibility for the sale of an employee's home and provide a housing loan or grant to help pay for a new home. A few provide counseling for trailing spouses to help them find a new job, and assistance in getting children acclimated to a new school. There are even a few enlightened firms that provide outplacement counseling for employees unable to make an enforced move. However, if you're in a business that expects frequent moves and you choose to opt out of the pattern, don't expect any assistance from the company.

Launch Revenue Rehabilitation

You likely won't get a severance package if you choose not to accept a transfer. However, you probably qualify for unemployment insurance benefits. That's because most states equate a forced transfer beyond a reasonable distance with termination. Check with the local office of the Department of Labor for an estimate of the benefits you're likely to receive. If you won't be going and you don't have a home equity line of credit already, get one now while you're still employed. Similarly, see if you can increase the limits on your credit cards while you still have a job. Speak with your partner about increasing his income to compensate for what you've given up. Reach out to family and friends for any kind of material support. They, after all, are some of the reasons you've stayed.

The longer she thought about it, the more Susan Washington realized she wasn't thrilled about the possibility of transferring again. She knew, however, that if she didn't accept it, she'd eventually be forced out of the company. The job she held was considered a stepping stone, not a sinecure. She and Charles had a series of long talks, trying to decide what to do. They agreed she'd refuse the transfer. The Washingtons cut back dramatically on their spending to build up an emergency fund in case Susan was fired before she could find another job. Luckily, after nine months of active searching, she found a new position doing public relations for a local hospital. It didn't pay as much as her newspaper job, but Charles also found a new spot, managing the shop of a custom cabinetry business, to help ease the financial strain.

Cultivate Antibodies

The way you and your family respond to this problem sets the stage for how you'll deal with similar issues in the future. If, after lots of thought and discussion, you and your partner decide to pull up stakes and hitch your personal lives to the trajectory of your career, you're setting a life pattern for years to come. You all will continue to move where the opportunities are. Of course, if after analysis and debate you all decided to turn down the transfer, you're also setting a precedent. You will have chosen to place geography and personal stability over career advancement. Your chances for advancement will now automatically diminish, since you're pulling in your sights. What makes these decisions right or wrong isn't which you choose, it's how you choose them. You and your family will be able to live with whatever you choose, as long as the decision came after everyone was consulted and all the ramifications were discussed. This isn't just about you. Show you realize that, and things will turn out okay.

You're Asked to Change Your Job Function

Your superior calls you into her office and asks that you hand over your sales responsibilities and instead manage the regional office. Or after presenting a plan for streamlining the company's product development process, you're asked to shift over to marketing and see if you can shake up that division.

Leah Freeman was the top field salesperson for an office furniture manufacturer. She was told that was the primary reason the company wanted her to come in from the field and manage a new division that would be designing and selling furniture specifically designed for schools and libraries. Leah had never viewed herself as a manager. She loved the challenge and freedom that came with being a salesperson.

Accept the Problem and Own the Solution

It's only the largest and most hidebound businesses that still view the three core disciplines of management, marketing, and finance as being separated by impenetrable walls. Today, executives are expected to be conversant with all the disciplines, and are prized if they show the ability to move back and forth between assignments in two or even all three. Unless you're the child of the owner who has to be found a spot, being "asked" to assume a new function is a compliment rather than an insult. The company has a need and believes you'll be able to fill it.

Of course, this is a compliment that may come with problems. First, it's the proverbial offer you can't refuse. Your image in the company will do a 180-degree turn if you refuse this assignment. You're viewed as an effective problem solver right now, and you've been directed to address a perceived need. Turn that task down and you'll be viewed at worst as disloyal and at best as a prima donna. You'll be placed on the short list of people to be let go when an opportunity presents itself. Second, changing your function, while good for the company, may not be good for your future either inside or outside the company.

Unburden Yourself

You cannot share your trepidations with anyone inside the company. No matter how friendly and loyal they might be, it's possible that news of your concerns will leak out. That will only make matters worse since you'll have taken on an objectionable or problematic role and yet you won't receive credit because news of your qualms will have stained your reputation. Open up to family and friends, and seek out ideas and counsel from peers and mentors outside your company. You're interested in whether they think this shift in function is good or bad for your future.

Diagnose the Impact

Diagnosis is the crux of this problem. A change in job function is taking you off one career track and placing you on another. Are you moving from a track that offers more room for advancement inside the company to one that offers less, if any? How about outside the company? Does this new track expand or contract your external opportunities? Will this new track add skill and expertise to your repertoire making you a more attractive candidate for higher level positions? Or will this new track lead you to a dead end, limiting your chance for growth and advancement?

Think about how this impacts you inside your current company, within the specific industry, and also in the general job market. For instance, in some industries upper-level executives all come from one discipline, say marketing. A shift out of marketing into management might severely limit your chance to move further in your company or your current industry. However, it might position you better for opportunities in other industries. Part of your analysis will therefore need to focus on your employer and your industry. Is this a sound company that would offer you financial growth in the future? What's the health of your industry? Is it a mature and stable business, a declining one, or a new, exciting industry?

There are a couple of other things to keep in mind. The largest short-term salary increases come when you move from one company to another *within* the same industry. That's because not only is the new employer gaining your services, but it's taking them away from a competitor. The largest long-term salary increases come when you move from a mature or declining industry to a young, expanding industry. Short term it might be a wash, but over time your compensation will grow at a faster pace. That's because a rising tide lifts all boats.

Take Your Financial Pulse

How does your current salary compare to what those filling this new function at other companies earn? While you're almost certainly being asked to shift because the company believes you can help address a need, economics may play a role. A frugal supervisor may believe he can underpay you to fill a new function, and also underpay the replacement filling your old function. He'll rationalize it by saying he's providing you and your replacement with growth opportunities. Do a thorough analysis of what the compensation for your new function should be. Check employment ads, industry associations, and any compensation surveys you can find in the business media. If you have relationships with headhunters and employment agencies, ask for their opinions. In addition, see if you can chart the long-term compensation patterns for those filling your former function and your new function. Would you earn more continuing on your previous path or moving along the new path?

Start Palliative Measures

If all your analysis convinces you this shift in functions is a bad thing for your career, you'll need to start some palliative measures. First, accept the new task with enthusiasm and express gratitude for the confidence the company is showing in you. Don't let your superior even suspect you're taking on the assignment grudgingly. Second, do what you can to keep yourself qualified in your prior discipline. That could mean taking some professional courses or attending seminars. It might involve becoming active in a trade association or professional group. Consider volunteering to provide your former function for charitable, philanthropic, or service organizations. The idea is to have material for your résumé to demonstrate continued activity in the business area you've been forced to abandon. And third, start looking for another job in your preferred discipline. As long as you've not disclosed your true feelings about the shift your job search can start off somewhat deliberate. Look for a position that gets you back on the track you want. For the first six months, look for one which is a step up from where you've been. After that, start looking with alacrity for a move that takes you back to where you were prior to having your function changed. The longer you stay on the wrong track the harder it will be for you to shift back.

Launch Revenue Rehabilitation

If you've decided the shift in functions may actually be a good thing for your career, launch revenue rehabilitation efforts by asking for an increase. The fact that you've been asked to make this switch and have accepted, throws your old compensation schedule out the window. It doesn't matter if you'd just gotten an increase three months ago: Circumstances have changed, and you're now owed at least consideration for another raise.

The most effective argument you can make is that your compensation doesn't meet the going market rate for your new function. Use the research you compiled in analyzing whether this was a good move to make. Summarize your findings in a memo and present it to your superior. If you meet a great deal of resistance you'll need to reconsider your assessment that this was a good move; the company might be looking to perpetually underpay for the function. If you need to, negotiate for an increase that will take effect in the future. If you can make it retroactive, all the better.

If your research shows that you're actually being paid fairly for your new function, you should still ask for an increase. You have leverage at the time you first accept the shift. If you don't use it you'll lose it. Instead of citing the marketplace, point out how your contribution to the company has increased and outpaced your compensation. It's inarguable that you've become more valuable to the organization, because you're now qualified in two disciplines and have confirmed your loyalty and dedication.

Leah Freeman knew she couldn't turn down the request to shift from field salesperson to division manager. If she did she'd be signing her own pink slip; maybe not today, but as soon as her numbers took a dip. Leah did an analysis of the shift and found that it was a mixed blessing. Her total compensation would actually go down, since as a salesperson she received commission and bonuses as well as a base salary. However, as a manager she wouldn't have to travel as much. Although she liked some travel, being on the road constantly was beginning to wear on her. It had certainly put constraints on her personal life, which she laughingly described as "nonexistent." In addition, moving into management would give her more opportunities to advance both inside and outside her current company and industry. Leah drafted a memo requesting a dramatic increase in her base compensation, to compensate for the commissions and bonuses she'd be giving up. She also requested to continue to keep her company car, cell phone, laptop, and expense account, explaining that she'd still be making some calls in support of the sales staff, particularly in the division's launch stage. Leah got everything she asked for.

Cultivate Antibodies

There's no way you can prevent this from happening to you again in the future. Ironically, you may even have increased the chances of it happening again by handling it well. However, having handled it well and perhaps using it to improve your short- or long-term position, you shouldn't look on future occurrences as problems; they'll actually just be opportunities to further increase your compensation.

32

Your Business Is Forced to Close Temporarily

You're watching the news late one night and are shocked to see there's a fire raging in the building that contains your office. Or after being evacuated from the area, you return to your store after the hurricane and discover your windows are smashed and much of your inventory has been damaged by rain.

Bill Strauss's first stop when he returned after being evacuated from his community was to his condominium. He and his wife were grateful there was only minimal damage. Their building had lost a few shingles and trees, but their windows had held and there was no water damage inside the apartment. As his wife got to work checking the apartment more closely, Bill drove over to the office of his career consulting and outplacement firm. He was stunned to find that the windows of the building had all broken and that his office, as well as those of the doctor and law firm who shared the building, were damaged extensively.

Accept the Problem and Own the Solution

Studies show that one-quarter of all businesses forced to close by some kind of disaster never reopen. Small businesses fare even worse: Nearly 40 percent of them are forced out of business permanently by a temporary closing. The problem isn't that the costs of repair are insurmountable. Business insurance usually covers most of the expense, and if the disaster is widespread enough for the location to be named an official disaster area, you may qualify for low-interest government loans to help your recovery. The real problem is that you'll have no stream of income for as long as your business is closed. The solution is to do everything in your power to reestablish a revenue stream as quickly as possible.

Unburden Yourself

Though you're facing the losses, you're not in this alone. Obviously family and friends can provide moral support and, to the extent they're able, labor and financial help. Employees could actually be the key to your business surviving this disaster. Some may need to deal with disruptions in their personal life, brought on by the same disaster that struck your business. But others left personally unscathed can provide you with a motivated and energetic pool of labor. It's in their interest to get the business up and running again, since their livelihood depends on it. Suppliers and vendors might also be willing to lend a helping hand: If you go out of business they lose a customer. Most surprisingly, you might find direct competitors willing to come to your aid. Even though you and, let's say, another accounting firm in town have historically competed for clients, they may be willing to help, knowing you'll be there for them if the roles are ever reversed.

Diagnose the Impact

The first step is to assess the actual physical damage to your business. What's the condition of your premises? Are your fixtures operational? Does your equipment still work? How clean is your inventory: Can some of it still be sold, or is it a total loss? What about your files and records? How much is recoverable from other sources or digitized back-ups? All this will help with your insurance claim. For the purposes of this chapter, I'll be focusing on your rebuilding your income, not your business. You, however, will need to manage both processes simultaneously.

Let's turn to your revenue stream. How much did the business normally bring in daily, weekly, and monthly? What are your expenses for those same lengths of time? Do the math and come up with daily, weekly, and monthly profit figures. Based on your conversations with the insurance company, your landlord, contractors, and local authorities, how long do you think you'll be unable to operate? The short-term impact of this disaster is the amount of profit you'll lose being closed for that length of time. The longer-term impact of the disaster is that you could lose this business forever.

Take Your Financial Pulse

Your revenue is easy to calculate: You have none. Actually, that's overstating the situation. If you are owed accounts receivable, they could represent income going forward. Be forewarned, however, that some clients or customers may stall paying their bills in the assumption that if they wait and you go out of business, they'll never need to pay up. Go through your regular expenses and determine which will be ongoing and which will stop during the time you're closed. Understand that if you don't continue to pay employees, they will, justifiably, look for other work. Start by including your own income and benefits package in the calculations. Don't automatically cut your marketing expenses. You're going to need to continue outreach efforts to your customers during your closure to ensure they'll still be there when you reopen. In some cases, you may actually spend more on advertising while closed than you did when open. My suggestion would be assume that marketing costs will be ongoing, even if they take a different form.

This total of ongoing costs you've come up with should be your goal for how much you'll need to cover to be able to stay in business until you reopen. Does your business have enough existing financial reserves or credit to meet these obligations? If it does, you're in good shape. Cutting costs to the degree possible and boosting revenue will provide you with a cushion in case reopening takes longer than anticipated. If your business doesn't have sufficient financial reserves to get you through this closing you'll need to work both on trimming your spending and boosting your revenues.

Start Palliative Measures

Go through your list of ongoing expenses line by line and determine whether there is any way to reduce each item. Contact suppliers and vendors and put an immediate stop to any orders of unsold materials that are due to arrive. Ask if they can provide extended terms on your payables. See if there is any way you can defer existing loan payments. Consider cutting your salary, either partially or totally. Do you have enough personal resources to weather an extended period without pay? If you do, consider it an investment in your future. If you don't, can you borrow funds from family or friends, or tap into personal credit such as home equity? In this situation, you may find it easier to borrow for yourself than for your business. Cutting your own salary gives you an opening to speak with employees about reducing their salaries. Suggest temporary pay cuts that can be recouped when the business reopens. Discuss the option of trimming benefits instead of salary, or the reverse. Employees with a working spouse whose employer offers medical coverage could shift to their plan, freeing up some money for your business. Employees who have no other source of benefits might be willing to take a temporary pay cut in order to keep their benefits in place.

Launch Revenue Rehabilitation

Aggressively pursue accounts receivable. Consider offering special terms such as a fair discount for immediate payment. Push for speedy delivery of any outsourced work or products so you can potentially collect that revenue. Ask them to drop ship if necessary. If you have sufficient personal resources, consider investing more of your own money in the business. This is also a good time to approach friendly investors with attractive deals on becoming financial partners in the business.

If your area is categorized a state or federal disaster area, you may qualify for subsidized loans to help your rebuild and reopen. To qualify for a disaster loan from the Small Business Administration, for example, you'll need to document your damage and loss of business, and then also demonstrate your ability to pay the loan back. There is often a great deal of paperwork and red tape involved in obtaining these loans, but they could be the difference between reopening and permanent closure. Most of these programs want to be the lender of last resort, so you'll need to have tapped out any existing credit resources before applying. In addition, loans of more than $10,000 generally need to be collateralized in some way. Don't hesitate to use the office of your state legislator or your congressional representative as an advocate with these subsidized lenders.

Could you continue operations, fully or partly, from another location? Perhaps you could transfer your inventory to your garage and run the business from a home office. Maybe you could expand your online presence to bring in more revenue. Do you have a friend in a similar business who might be willing to let you share facilities on a temporary basis? Maybe you and your staff could use a friend's law offices when her firm is closed for the day. Investigate services from disaster-relief companies. Some rent fully equipped office trailers, which could be parked outside your existing site, allowing some operations to continue. Think outside of the box to come up with any combination of ways you can keep bringing revenue into the business.

Try to be just as creative in coming up with ways to stay in touch with your clients and customers. You want to make it clear it's not a question of *if* you're reopening, but *when* and perhaps *where* you're reopening. Have signage up at your former site announcing your plans. Make sure to update that signage constantly, so there are obvious signs of progress. Stay in touch via e-mail, fax, or regular mail. Make the customers feel like they're part of the recovery effort. Let them know where and how to get in touch with you and your employees. Explain your efforts to run the business from temporary locations or online. Establish a specific date for your reopening and build up to it. Just make sure you can actually open on that day. Plan and publicize a grand reopening celebration that will not only reaffirm the customer's personal connection to the business—say, by offering refreshments—but also provide an economic incentive to return—perhaps a special one-day discount. Do absolutely anything and everything to ensure you do indeed reopen on that day. Having to postpone a grand reopening will shatter internal morale and destroy any remaining credibility you have with customers.

Bill Strauss was glad he'd remembered to back up his files to an Internet storage site before he closed up the office in preparation for the storm. However, it looked like his computer, telephone, and office equipment were all waterlogged and probably useless. The facilities themselves were certainly unusable. Bill called the two counselors who worked for him and the administrative assistant who ran the office and invited them all to a strategy dinner that night at a local restaurant. Meanwhile, Bill contacted his insurance agent, who sent an adjuster to examine the office. Bill called his accountant, and over lunch they went through the books. It looked like Bill had enough business and personal credit that he could weather three weeks of no revenue. The insurance adjuster told Bill to plan for the office to be closed for at least six weeks, since local contractors would be overstretched. Bill realized he'd need to bridge that gap. That night over dinner, Bill presented each of his three employees with a laptop computer and a cell phone. He told them all that he believed he had enough resources to pay their salaries and get the business through this adjustment, as long as everyone hit the ground running the next day. Bill explained that he'd rented a suite at a local hotel from which they could run the business. He'd arranged for a printer and high-speed Internet service to be available in the suite. The hotel had conference facilities they could use for their larger sessions. He'd also downloaded a client list that afternoon. The next morning, he and his two counselors would spend the day contacting clients and telling them of the new location and that there would be no break in business. His administrative assistant would develop an e-mail newsletter to send out to their entire mailing list.

Cultivate Antibodies

Obviously, you can't prevent another disaster from striking. But you can prevent it from becoming as disastrous to your business by taking out business interruption or added expense insurance. These are both additions to the standard business property insurance policy, which covers damage due to fire, wind, rain, and other hazards. Business interruption protection provides a benefit based on the income an owner normally earns, as well as the cost of ongoing expenses. Think of it as disability insurance for your business. Rather than a deductible, these policies usually have a waiting period of 48 hours. Added expense protection provides a benefit that covers the costs of reestablishing operations elsewhere, while your facilities are being repaired. For instance, it might pay for the rental of an office trailer so you can work in your parking lot while reconstruction is taking place.

Your Spouse or Life Partner Dies

You're lying in bed late one night when your spouse wakes you to say he's feeling chest pains. On the way to the bathroom, he collapses to the floor and dies. Or you're on your way home from work and see a police car parked in front of your house. The officer tells you there's been a bad accident and your wife has died.

Wendy French and her husband, Archie, had retired to Arizona as soon as he turned 65. Wendy had been a stay-at-home mom for most of her married life, despite having a master's in art history. Archie was a successful attorney who worked as in-house counsel for a large corporation. They had two sons, both of whom had married and now had children. Wendy and Archie bought a condominium in an adult community and spent most of their days golfing, playing tennis, or socializing around the pool. Their travel consisted of visiting their children and grandchildren since, as Archie liked to joke, they were living a vacation. That changed when Archie suffered a massive coronary on the golf course. He appeared to stabilize, but a week later took a turn for the worse and died.

Accept the Problem and Own the Solution

Trying to describe your pain can only serve to minimize it, so I won't even try. Perhaps you can take some comfort knowing that, for perhaps the first time since you came together, your loved one isn't sharing your pain. Whatever physical, spiritual, emotional, or psychological pain he'd been experiencing has ended. Your pain, I'm afraid, will last a while longer. The absence of someone so integral to your life creates a powerful ache. There is a vacuum in your soul that nothing can fill. There's an overwhelming hunger for a touch, a word, a scent, that cannot be satisfied. That vacuum will never completely be filled. That hunger will never fully be sated. But you will endure. Imperceptibly, pain begins to abate. Those who've been hovering close by tending your pain begin to edge back into their own lives, leading you to assume more responsibility for the stuff of daily life. Slowly, the empty hours of grief grow shorter. Life—your life—moves in to fill some of your emptiness.

Whether you believe it's human nature or divine providence, you'll naturally come to the solution at some point: You must take charge of your life. It may be tempting to look for someone to keep leaning on. It could be a friend, a sibling, or a child. You must accept that you cannot replace what you've lost. Lean on someone too long and you'll compound this tragedy. Resentment and guilt will infect both of you, threatening one of your remaining pillars of strength. There will have to come a time when you take ownership of your new life.

Unburden Yourself

During the grieving process lean on all who offer support. Do your best to minimize feelings of expectation. I can tell you that there will be some whose efforts you'll find underwhelming, perhaps even disappointing. But I can also tell you there will be some who surprise you with the extent of their generosity and compassion. Don't try to analyze why someone is doing something: Are they doing it for me? Are they doing it for my dead loved one? Are they doing it for themselves? Try to accept all words, gestures, and deeds offered with gratitude.

Once you've begun to take charge of your life, assemble a team of professionals to help. You'll need an attorney to help you navigate the will and probate process. If you're a surviving spouse, this won't be complex. Still, it makes sense to have someone knowledgeable handle it for you. This will also give you a chance to see if you want to use this same attorney to address your own estate issues going forward, since your will may now need to be changed. Besides an attorney, you'll need a tax preparer. Once again, start with the individual who has been preparing your joint returns. If you and your spouse had done this yourself, or had used a tax service or software package, I'd suggest shifting to a qualified CPA at this point, since your return will now be more complex. Ask your attorney for suggestions. You're also apt to need a financial planner. Your financial situation has changed dramatically with the death of your life partner. It needs examination by a seasoned eye. If you're happy with someone you've used before, by all means keep him. If you need someone new, ask your attorney and accountant for recommendations. Finally, you'll need an insurance broker to help you calculate the new risks you face, investigate ways to deal with those risks, and help you select and purchase protection.

Diagnose the Impact

The emotional, spiritual, and psychological impact of the death of your spouse or life partner is immeasurable. Your life has changed dramatically forever in ways I can't begin to comprehend. What I can help you with is measuring the ways your financial life has changed.

How much income did your spouse earn? Obviously, you'll no longer have that income coming in. Did your spouse receive a pension? What is the difference, if any, between what he received and what you as a survivor will receive? Was your spouse collecting Social Security? You cannot collect Social Security unless you're old enough to qualify, and you also cannot collect two benefits. When you do qualify, you'll receive the larger of your benefit or your spouse's benefit.

Your spouse also spent money. Go through your monthly budget and estimate how your spouse's death will affect each item. Some expenses will be reduced. For example, one person will spend less than two on things like food, entertainment, clothing, medical bills, and memberships. If you had two cars, your auto expenses will be cut in half. However, some expenses will be unchanged. Your rent or mortgage bill, utilities, and telephone bill will probably remain the same. Spending on your dependents will be unchanged as well. Insurance bills may increase if you need to replace medical coverage you were receiving as part of your spouse's compensation.

Turn next to your assets. Odds are, your current assets will remain unaffected by your spouse's death. If your loved one had life insurance and you are the beneficiary, you'll be receiving a lump sum, which will increase your total assets.

Finally, examine your liabilities. You remain responsible for liabilities for which you were a cosigner. If both names are on your mortgage or home equity line of credit, you remain liable for the loan. The same holds for auto loans or jointly held credit cards. If your spouse had debts for which he solely was responsible, the issue is a bit less clear.

You cannot be held liable for a debt for which you didn't sign. However, your spouse's estate remains liable for debts he incurred alone. If these were secured by property, say a car in the case of an auto loan, the creditor can repossess the asset in payment of the debt. But unsecured lenders, such as credit card companies have no assets they can repossess. What they have is a partial interest in the estate. In the real world, however, a partial interest in an estate isn't worth anything. That's why most unsecured creditors will simply write off the debts of people who die owing them money. Of course, they'll try to collect by contacting you, saying you're responsible, and asking you to fulfill your spouse's obligations. This is a moral and ethical, not legal decision for you. Note that most unsecured creditors in this situation will eventually give up, however. You can simply mark bills that arrive "DECEASED" and include a copy of the death certificate. If you receive any calls, you can just say the person is dead and you've sent a death certificate. You don't even have to listen to their pleas for repayment.

Take Your Financial Pulse

Compare your income, both earned and unearned, to your expenses. If your new income is sufficient to meet your new expenses you can maintain your current lifestyle until you choose to make changes. If your new income isn't sufficient to meet your new expenses, you'll need to address the gap relatively quickly. I'd suggest using insurance benefits to provide you with some time to make changes thoughtfully.

Start Palliative Measures and Launch Revenue Rehabilitation

I believe it's a mistake to try to cut your expenses and boost your income solely in an effort to maintain the same lifestyle you had when your spouse was alive. It isn't a tribute to your deceased loved one to seal your life in amber as if he were still alive. If anything, it's detrimental to your long-term health. You don't owe it to him to stay in the same house and to drive the same car. Nor do you owe it to your dependents to maintain them in the same standard of living as they had before. What you owe everyone, including yourself, is to do your best in the way you think is best.

I'll suggest to you what I suggest to my clients in this situation: If possible, make no changes for six months. Instead, spend that time thinking about your needs and wants and discuss things with friends and family. Meet with an attorney, accountant, financial advisor, and insurance broker and go over the details of your legal and financial life. If you're already working, do you want to continue doing the same thing? Would you like to change careers? If you're not working now, do you need to? Do you want to? Try to imagine a new life for yourself and your family. I know it's not the life of your dreams— that would be to have your loved one back. But try to picture a life you want.

Do you want to move to a different location? There's something to be said for stability, particularly if you have school-age children. But there's also something to be said for starting over in a new place. I've learned that geography can make a significant difference in the quality of your life. The culture and excitement of an urban environment can be exhilarating. The peace and quiet of a rural area can be soothing. The family orientation of a suburb can make it easier to raise children. It also can do wonders for your soul to be in a place that brings you contentment or joy. Of course, it may be that you're already in such a place. In that case, by all means do what you need to in order to stay there.

Remember, as well, that you're a human being, not a human doing or a human consuming. Material possessions can provide pleasure. I like watching television on a big screen, for example. And my collection of classical music CDs brings me enjoyment. But they don't bring me happiness. Happiness only comes from inside. Maintaining the material trappings of your prior life will not make you happy. Having a new X-Box or a Mini Cooper will not make your child happy. And they certainly won't fill the void created by the loss of your loved one. I encourage you to start over and create a new life for yourself—a life that you want; a life that gives you another chance at happiness.

Wendy was distraught after Archie's death. She was lucky enough to have Archie's pension and would qualify for his Social Security in another two years. They had a healthy portfolio that generated some income, and had been able to use the proceeds from the sale of their home in Chicago to pay cash for their condo in Arizona. She knew she could stay in Arizona if she wished. Wendy received a great deal of support from her friends in the community, all of whom wanted her to stay. One of her sons suggested that if Wendy didn't want to stay in Arizona, she could move up to St. Louis, where he lived. Wendy decided to think things through rather than act rashly. She went through grief counseling and spent time at a widow's support group. But actually, it was an old friend of hers from Chicago who made the suggestion that struck home. The friend had suggested Wendy now do what she'd always wanted to do but hadn't. Wendy thought about that for a long time. Six months after Archie's death, Wendy announced to her family and friends that she was selling the place in Arizona to move back to Chicago. She was going to buy a small apartment downtown and see if she could find work at a gallery or museum. If she couldn't get a job, she'd volunteer. She said she'd always wanted to be involved in the art world, and this was her chance. She also said that Archie would have loved the idea—as long as he didn't have to live in the city.

Cultivate Antibodies

Because we are all mortal, love always ends in the pain of death. So the only way to ensure you'll never feel this pain again is to never love again. But I believe we're designed to love; it's part of our wiring. You can no more not love again that you can not eat or breathe again. You probably still have love in your life, with a child, with family, with friends, even with a pet. If you don't, seek it out. The way to cultivate antibodies against the death of another loved one is to love even more openly. Make sure the people you love know you love them, not just through your actions, but through your words as well. Expressing your love in this way won't make the pain of death any less. But it will speed the recovery, minimize any guilt, and perpetuate positive memories. Always remember: Love is a verb not a noun.

Notes

Chapter 2

1. Not his real name. The names of the clients whose stories I recount throughout this book have been changed to protect their privacy. Some of the details of their stories may also have been altered in cases when a more accurate retelling could make them identifiable.

Chapter 4

1. Viaticals are the sales of death benefits, in advance. These entered the financial mainstream during the peak years of the AIDs crisis when individuals dying of AIDs, desperately in need of cash, sold the death benefits to life insurance policies at a discount to investors.

Lifeline 1

1. There are some nonneed scholarships available, but they are quite rare and very competitive.

Lifeline 10

1. The only possible exception is if the superior who made this negative judgment is fired before you've been pushed out the door. In that situation, you could effectively make the case to your new superior that you were being made the scapegoat or were being unfairly blamed. The odds still aren't in your favor, but at least there's a chance.

Lifeline 11

1. The exception to this rule is if you are being wrongfully accused of something that could lead to your being fired for cause. In that case, you need

to fight tooth and nail to clear your name since such a termination could result in your receiving no severance and there being a blot on your reputation that could extend beyond your current workplace. If termination for cause is a possibility, pull out all the stops—up to and including the threat to sue. In most cases, the threat of legal action will deter an employer from pursuing a questionable termination for cause. At worst, they'll offer a compromise of termination without cause, allowing you to get severance and to retain your reputation.

Lifeline 13

1. This doesn't stop when you reach adulthood. My feelings toward my own father changed dramatically for the better when I was in my sixties and he was in his eighties.

Lifeline 23

1. A recent court ruling in response to claims stemming from Hurricane Katrina's storm surge backed up insurance-company claims that they are not liable for wind-driven water damage.

Lifeline 29

1. I've included unemployment insurance here as an area to investigate because in the case of a Chapter 11 bankruptcy, your eligibility might not be so clear-cut. Obviously, if your employer goes into liquidation or you lose your job outright in a Chapter 11 reorganization, you qualify for unemployment insurance. However, you might also qualify if you quit after being asked to take a significant reduction in salary, after having your job descriptions changed dramatically, or after being asked to transfer beyond a reasonable distance.

2. The acronym COBRA actually has nothing to do with health care. It stands for Consolidated Omnibus Budget Reconciliation Act. That was the name of the legislation to which the law was attached.

Index